Existence and Heritage

Hermeneutic Explorations in African and Continental Philosophy

TSENAY SEREQUEBERHAN

SUNY PRESS

Published by
STATE UNIVERSITY OF NEW YORK PRESS
Albany

Printed in the United States of America

For information, contact
State University of New York Press
www.sunypress.edu

Production, Laurie D. Searl
Marketing, Anne M. Valentine

Library of Congress Cataloging-in-Publication Data

Serequeberhan, Tsenay, 1952–
Existence and heritage : hermeneutic explorations in African and continental philosophy / Tsenay Serequeberhan.
pages cm. — (SUNY series, philosophy and race)
Includes bibliographical references and index.
ISBN 978-1-4384-5789-5 (hardcover : alk. paper)
ISBN 978-1-4384-5790-1 (paperback : alk. paper)
ISBN 978-1-4384-5791-8 (e-book)
1. Philosophy, African. 2. Hermeneutics. 3. Africa—Colonization—Philosophy. I. Title.
B5315.H36S468 2015
199'.6—dc23 2014042148

10 9 8 7 6 5 4 3 2 1

Existence and Heritage

SUNY series, Philosophy and Race

Robert Bernasconi and T. Denean Sharpley-Whiting, editors

In memory of Petros Yohannes

and the ideal that inspired his commitment

Those who made our heroic virtues triumph
Long buried will not return today
Will not return today

White, Black, distinction of color
You who exposed the deeds of the Italians
Forever your name will endure

Federation, a time of confusion
You who rejected the foreign flag
Forever your name will be honored

The time of the Dergue, most horrid
He who declared for his country, inexplicably
Strangulated, utterly desiccated

—Lyrics from an Eritrean ballad
(Original in Tigrinya)

Contents

Acknowledgments

I would like to acknowledge my wife and friend, Nuhad Jamal, for sharing her critical insights and Barry Hallen for reading an early version of the preface and chapter 2. I thank my sons, Nesim and Awate, for their forbearance in tolerating my many mood swings occasioned by the difficulty of working on most of this book while carrying a full load of teaching. I am grateful to my home institution, Morgan State University, for a sabbatical leave that allowed me to finish and make the book ready for publication with a minimum amount of stress and tribulation.

Preface

The Possible in Philosophy

> Then Polemarcus said: Socrates . . . you must either be stronger than we are, or you must stay . . . Is there not another alternative, said I, namely that we may persuade you to let us go? Could you, said he, persuade men who do not listen?
>
> —Plato, *Politeia* (327c)

> It is a terrible, an inexorable, law that one cannot deny the humanity of another without diminishing one's own: in the face of one's victim, one sees oneself.
>
> —James Baldwin[1]

I

Philosophy, unlike other disciplines, does not have a specified and preordained field of discourse. This lack of ordination, however, does not mean that it functions in and is sited on a chaotic, nebulous terrain. It only means that philosophic reflection has the totality of what *is* as the object of its endeavors. These endeavors, furthermore, are always undertaken from within a plurality of bounded intellectual parameters whose varied and noncommensurable discursive norms can never be, once and for all, universally established and/or accepted as such.[2]

In pursuing their concerns, philosophers present to each other—and whoever else is willing to listen—persuasive, or what they take to be convincing, arguments. This they do from within the accepted parameters of given philosophic perspectives focused on an interpretative exploration of a situation, in keeping with accepted and established assumptions and "shared presuppositions."[3] Those engaged in such endeavors try to persuade each other by citing acceptable authors and by articulating arguments they deem convincing. In this, the truths argued for, and upheld, are focused on persuading our partners in dialogue of the veracity of what follows in view of what we both accept to be, or not to be, the case.

Indeed, as Parmenides noted long ago, "Persuasion . . . attends upon truth."[4] In other words, in light of the thinkers you appreciate and in view of what you accept, shouldn't you assess and/or revise, modify, alter, reject, or confirm the attitude(s) that you have maintained thus far? The intent is to persuasively explore "shared presuppositions" in terms of issues and concerns situated in our lived existence. To *persuasively explore* here means to interpretatively query and render the sense of what is being explored in view of "shared presuppositions," or *prejudices*,[5] which are themselves not static but revisable—and indeed constantly revised—effects of this circular interplay, an ongoing interpretative process, assessed in terms of what is in question.[6]

It is in this manner, then, that in the second decade of the twenty-first century, long after the end of colonialism and the Cold War—in the era of imperious[7] United States unilateralism, most blatantly manifested in the open-ended war on terror, which is itself a euphemism for the war on the Arab/Islamic world[8]—that we must engage our philosophic reflections. Much has happened in the second half of the twentieth century, and to be relevant, a vital necessity for philosophy, it has to engage its reflections against the backdrop of these "happenings." For, these "happenings" are the totality of differing and/or contradictory effects that, as a whole, constitute our hybrid and variegated heritage: the effective-past which—in its staying power—effectively structures and actuates the lived historicalness of the present.

This is what Hans-Georg Gadamer refers to as "effective-history,"[9] from whose effects, in and on the present—which is itself the actuality of these *effects*—arise the issues, concerns, understandings, and so on that animate and provoke our persuasive engagements, in and out of which we consider, and reconsider, how and what we are and have been. It is that about which we agree and/or disagree, and it is also that which we invoke, or make use of, to back up our efforts at swaying each other's minds. For, in philosophy, as in much else in life, "there isn't an objective conducting line of tradition" that binds us, permanently, to past choices or situations because "it is always possible to rethink history."[10]

The past shows itself in the acuity of the lived present, by giving us differing vistas of our history "through our scientific discoveries,"[11] situated in our ongoing engagements. In this way, it makes possible, for us, novel understandings of ourselves, by giving us a "better grasp of our identity,"[12] of what we have been and what we possibly can become. It is this circular and circuitous interplay—of the effective-past in the exigencies of the lived present—which makes possible the concerns in and out of which we interpretatively face *our* future. And it is in terms of these always changing concerns that our interpretative involvements sift, sieve, and query the enduring effects that constitute our historical heritage, out of which we spin the actuality of our existence by *projecting* (i.e., throwing ahead) into and as the future the possibilities we hope for and struggle to attain. In the non-vicious circularity of this " 'circle' "[13]—our human situation—this study locates and explores the thematic that concerns it.

II

The title *Existence and Heritage* is thus focused on the actuality of our world-historical situation—that which has endured—since the end of colonialism and the reinsertion of Africa, and the non-European world, into history. This mid-twentieth-century event has marked and oriented all subsequent historical-political developments. For, after the mid-twentieth century our world could no longer be the exclusive domain or "playground" of Europe,[14] given that *we*, the formerly colonized, had terminated our "plaything" status. Concretely, Dien Bien Phu (1954) and Algeria (1954–1962) saw to this by decisively reaffirming the actuality of human historical existence, beyond the limits of the colonizing West. Reaffirming, that is, the suppressed heritage of the formerly colonized by tangibly reclaiming the lived actuality of human existence exterior to European (i.e., colonial) confines.[15]

This "effective-history," that of the anti-colonial struggles of the last century, is today an integral component of the generic/general inheritance of humanity. Unlike the horrific memories of its antagonist—the colonial depredations of imperious Europe—it does not occasion shame and/or disgust. To give but one example: No *sane* Italian, today, can recall what the Fascists did in Ethiopia—the use of mustard gas—or Eritrea without feeling shame, disgust, and/or guilt and disassociating himself/herself, as best she/he can, from this barbaric period of his/her country's history which is, itself, internal to the history of European colonial imperialism.

The heroism of Ethiopia's patriots—as distinct from the cowardice of Emperor Haile Selassie—on the other hand, and the heroism of the Eritrean *ascari* who deserted en masse[16] the Fascist colonial army, and the deeds of people like Abrha Deboch, Moges Asgedom, and Zerai Deress, along with the heroism of all those who resisted Fascism and Nazism—the fighters of the Warsaw Ghetto and the Italian, French, and Greek Partisans, for example—all of this (and more, along similar lines) comprises the core actuality of the "effective-history" that constitutes the varied political patrimony of our shared humanity. Our present is the concrete actuality of this *pasticcio* that has sedimented, or has arisen, out of our mutually hybridized past. It is *this* past, as it has been actualized—and is being actuated—in the lived reality of the present.

In this interpretation of our shared history, the struggles against Fascism-Nazism and the African anticolonial struggle are organic antecedents of our present. This, then, is the lived "effective-history," the enduring core of the community-of-experience,[17] which constitutes *us*, present day humanity, as who and what we are. It is in terms of this "effective-history," this concrete effective-past that we critically calibrate, evaluate, and when possible try to ameliorate our present.[18] This is the measure of our humanity, the standard of our existence, even when we are critical of it. The values vested in it and nurtured by it, constitute our heritage and are the cutting edge of our critical reflections, aimed at the sustenance of our shared existence. Indeed, as Amilcar Cabral affirmed in 1962, addressing the United Nations General Assembly,

> In fighting . . . for the liberation of our countries we are giving our lives, in the present context of international legality, for the ideal which the UN itself has defined in its Charter, in its resolutions, and in particular in its resolution on decolonialisation [sic].[19]

To the extent that the United Nations is the closest thing in existence to Kant's idea of a *civitas gentium*,[20] this concurrence of ideals, which Cabral points to, effectively makes the hopes and aspirations of the African anti-colonial struggle an organic and essential component of the "effective-history" which constitutes the community-of-experience of our shared world. For, indeed, it is the norms and standards of legality among states, incarnated in the UN and its various institutions and pronouncements, which Cabral invokes in articulating the hopes and aspirations of his people. In like manner as Frantz Fanon noted, a few years earlier, in 1958,

> The XXth century, on the scale of the world, will not only be the era of atomic discoveries and interplanetary explorations. The second upheaval of this epoch and incontestably, is the conquest by the peoples of lands that belong to them.[21]

It should be emphasized that, "the conquest by the peoples of lands that belong to them" unfolds within the context and the legality of "the right of nations to self-determination," a Wilsonian principle enshrined in the Charter of the United Nations. Thus, for Cabral as for Fanon, it is "the scale of the world," the Charter of the UN—our present community-of-experience—which is the reference point in terms of which the possibilities and/or achievements of the struggles that they are involved with are assessed. Indeed, the persuasive power of their rhetoric, of the perspectives they articulate, derives from the salient use they make of this effective-history—even as they are critical of it—in articulating their anti-colonialism.

And yet, when we look back, as inheritors of their legacy, we see not only great achievements but equally great and grave disappointments. When we look at our recent history, since the days of Fanon and Cabral, we see that the formerly colonized are presently, under various guises and new modalities, being, in effect, re-colonized. I say *under various guises and new modalities* because, up to the end of the Second World War, colonies were a "legitimate endeavor" presently, however, "colonies are constructed in the face of their denial. It is morally and politically embarrassing to own and to found 'colonies,' so the same institutions are created without being *named as such*."[22] The United States, for example, is building in Baghdad, Iraq, an embassy "the size of Vatican City" which has its own "defense force" and comprises "21 buildings on 104 acres."[23] The question then is: Will Iraq's sovereignty survive the weight of all this cement? This is one of the many ways in which, in our postcolonial world, colonies are established "in the face of their denial." It is in this context then that we must explore our concerns and articulate our philosophic undertakings.

The relevance, coherence, and the persuasiveness of our reflective endeavors derive from the lived exigencies of our world: the community-of-experience that concretely constitutes the actuality of the present. Otherwise, the arguments of philosophy—persuasive or not—will be superfluous and not hinged onto the tangible concerns of lived-life; interesting intellectual aerobics perhaps, but nothing more. For, indeed, the previously colonized have reclaimed the "lands that belong to them" but the "shared presuppositions"—the *prejudices*—which sanctioned the colonial past are still with us and constrict, from within, the lived actuality of the present.

The challenge for our efforts is to seek the possible beyond these strictures; for, in this constricted space, "in the face of one's victim, one sees oneself." To appreciate the boomerang effect of this "see[ing]" is to explore that which is possible beyond the mutually inter-implicative and debilitating sight of victims and victimizers. It is to *hearken* to that which, out of our shared heritage, *calls* us to a conceivable future. To be open to the possible—in our effective-history[24]—beyond the incapacitating residues of a dead-past[25] encrusted as our present.

III

What I am proposing is not new to the heritage of philosophy that traces its roots to the Greeks. In its inception this tradition was not an endorsement of what is but a critical exploring of what could be. In the oracular sayings of the pre-Socratic thinkers and in the dialogical meanderings of Socratic questioning, what we have is an explorative seeking focused on the possible, in being, beyond the limits of the present.[26] This, too, is central to the discourse of contemporary African philosophy and to my efforts documented in this study, as specified by the subtitle "hermeneutic explorations in African and Continental philosophy."

To explore is to seek. Seeking, as indicated in all of the above, is necessarily oriented by the community-of-experience, the effective-history, in and out of which it seeks.[27] As I have argued elsewhere: "African philosophy as the hermeneutics of the postcolonial situation" is concretely engaged in exploring "the future embedded . . . in the possibilities of the heritage of its own enduring horizon."[28] To explore what is possible for our shared existence in and out of our postcolonial hybrid heritage: this, then, is the thematic that will concern us in this study.

Introduction

Reflections and Encounters

Up from Earth's Centre through the Seventh Gate
I rose, and on the Throne of Saturn sate,
And many Knots unravel'd by the Road;
But not the Knot of Human Death and Fate.

—Omar Khayyám[1]

I

Writing in philosophy is the effort of putting words on paper in a sequence of significations focused on a theme that constitutes itself in this very process. In this way and in these words are expressed, or pressed out, the reflectively appropriated experiences of lived life[2] that compel she or he who writes to explore and concretely engage the sense of this lived world philosophically. From the outset it should be noted that, in the persuasive endeavors of philosophy, that which is expressed and the manner in which it is expressed are integral moments, each of the other, in a process of self-articulation. In this regard, as Quentin Lauer has noted, "As our thinking becomes more authentically rational, we become more [and more, in an ongoing manner] authentically human."[3] The catch, of course, is the meaning of "authentically rational." Or, the question is, What does it mean to be "authentically human"?

Reflections are contemporaneous with this process of expressing that is impregnated by existence. As Martin Heidegger has emphatically noted, the root meaning of the word *existence*—or, as he puts it, *ek-sistence*[4]—is a process of standing out. It is in an ambient—an expanse cleared, as in a forest clearing, by a concrete historical standing out—that encounters occur.

Encounters thus always happen in a space, or a clearing, already established by the standing out of a concrete historical ek-sistence in which Otherness has been nullified or its encounter has been made possible.[5] In this sense, true Otherness—the radically Other—is that actuality (or actualities) which does not originate in the shared standing out that makes possible the space of our existence. The radically Other does not partake of our sociopolitical space of existence, our *Sittlichkeit* or ethical life.[6] This is an Otherness that has not been leveled off, or not completely, into the sameness of what could otherwise possibly be a risky affront to our lived ek-sistence, our Otherness. Thus, being open to encounters, or to an encounter of Otherness, is risky, but could it also be the true, or root,[7] sense of the "authentically human"? Could it be that this openness to what is dicey is a core aspect of what it means to exist, that is, to *stand out*—to be human?[8]

II

Here, it is imperative to start with the actuality of our lived world-historical situation. At present, the earth is *not* constituted by differing "polarities of radical Otherness."[9] In fact, we inhabit a commingled globe hybridized to the core by European colonial expansion, which started, in full force, in the fifteenth century.[10] By the early 1960s, most of the European colonial empires had been terminated by the historic struggles of peoples who had been deemed to be without history. These differing peoples, in forcefully and conclusively affirming their freedom, articulated the possibility of a shared world by establishing the context within which Europe was compelled to recognize their hybridized Otherness.[11] It could not any more simply impose, and force on them, its own particular perspective, which it took to be universal.[12]

For example, at a crucial point in these developments—the Bandung Conference of 1955—one of those formerly colonized, President Sukarno of Indonesia, in his welcoming speech as the host of this historic conference had, among other things, the following to say to the twenty-nine representatives of the Asian and African countries in attendance:

> No task is more urgent than that of preserving peace. Without peace our independence means little. The rehabilitation and upbuilding of our countries will have little meaning. Our revolutions will not be allowed to run their course.
>
> What can we do? The peoples of Asia and Africa wield little physical power. Even their economic strength is dispersed and slight. We cannot indulge in power politics. Diplomacy for

> us is not a matter of the big stick. Our statesmen, by and large, are not backed up with serried ranks of jet bombers.
>
> What can we do? We can do much! We can inject the voice of reason into world affairs.[13]

In reclaiming their freedom, those who were subjected by the West are concerned with "preserving peace" and with "injecting the voice of reason" into global relations. Otherwise, argues Sukarno, all the trouble we went through to secure independence and our efforts to rehabilitate our countries will come to naught. Reason, then, historically saturated and culturally hybridized, seems to be directly and profoundly linked to the "justice and . . . justness"[14] of the struggles of the formerly colonized. This is a situation in which differing hybridized incarnations of human existence/experience (i.e., Otherness) can possibly encounter each other, without nullification or violence and with a minimum sum total of mutual estrangement. For we are not anymore—we the differing peoples of the world—complete strangers to each other.[15]

III

The basic concern of this study is to explore this hopeful possibility in the actuality of the present. It will do so by reading/interpreting the promise embedded in the entwined fibers of our shared human existence. Part I, chapter 1, looks at Africa's postcolonial condition and reflects on the responsibility, on the level of ideas and thinking, which this situation imposes on the contemporary discourse of African philosophy. Chapter 2 explores what I see as a convergence in the contemporary concerns of Continental and African philosophy. In this chapter, we will query and look into the source of this thematic confluence in these two areas of contemporary research and, in doing so, point the way toward the encounters of Part II.

Part II unfolds, in three chapters, aspects of the European tradition in terms of concerns that are germane to our postcolonial present. Chapter 3 presents a reading of Immanuel Kant's *Perpetual Peace*, originally published in 1795, in the context of our contemporary, hazardous post-9/11 international situation. Chapter 4 examines Hans-Georg Gadamer's conception of the "effective-historical consciousness" as a way of thinking about relations among differing self-standing traditions. Chapter 5 explores Martin Heidegger's analysis of existence in modern society as it converges with Karl Marx's critique of alienation. It then shows how these converging assessments express concerns parallel to those Aimé Césaire articulates in conceptualizing colonization as a process of *chosification*.[16]

In all of this the aim is to see what the European tradition has to offer when encountered, or glimpsed, from an "outsider perspective."[17] What I hope to achieve is the philosophic exploration of our postcolonial present without regard for pre-established theoretic positions and/or formulations. To engage the present with an open and focused sense of itself, disclosed out of itself. What I intend to do is to explore the possible in the "effective-history"[18] that has endured—beyond the demise of Europe's colonial empires—as the actuality of the present.

At this point one might ask, Why these thinkers and not others? My response can only be that it is these thinkers, and the indicated themes that they elaborate, that I have found helpful in thinking about the situation of postcolonial Africa. I am offering what, in my view, can be gainfully employed to think about the situation of our shared present; in effect, I am presenting the results of my ongoing research.[19] This, however, is not merely an indication of my research interests but an expression of developments in Continental philosophy, as I see them, that are favorable inclined toward the claim to humanity—on an equal footing—of the formerly colonized world.[20]

As indicated earlier, chapter 2 will explore this encouraging development in some detail. And in the three chapters, which constitute the encounters of Part II, we will see how the above-named philosophers, and the indicated themes they focus on, can be of service in thinking about the promising possibilities of our shared hybrid postcolonial present.[21] Part of a larger ongoing reflective project, the present study is focused on laying out a way, a perspective, that seeks beyond our truncated present the possible in our shared existence. For the rest, I leave to the reader the critical judgment regarding the merit and/or worth of my sustained efforts.

IV

In the conclusion, taking my cue from Frantz Fanon, I propose a conception of thought as openness to the possible in that which is.[22] I will do so by retroactively suggesting that the chapters that compose this book are exercises in this kind of thinking. For keeping within the bounds of finitude (i.e., "the knot of Human Death and Fate"), "'demythologization' inevitably calls for 'remythologization,'"[23] or as Gianni Vattimo has noted, faced with intractable problems, a dry rationalism leads to the revival of faith.[24] But, beyond the duplicity of faith and reason, one can also explore the view that human ek-sistence—the concrete actuality of what is[25]—always, and of necessity, has need of the assuaging service of "beneficent fiction."[26]

This is the sense of Fanon's insightful remarks on truth and falsehood: "To the falsehood of the colonial situation, the colonized responds with an equal falsehood."[27] It is imperative to keep in mind that philosophic reflection invents around "the facts" (i.e., the accepted interpretation of things/events/situations[28]) an understanding of what is in question. This it does in view of the possibilities of life, of human ek-sistence, and what it calls for.[29]

This, then, is a rendering of the sense of life and its living, which makes for an openness focused on appropriating life's this-worldly, fragile, and contingent possibilities: a sensitive disposition to the here-and-now concrete happenings of life. "What is your aim in philosophy?" asks Ludwig Wittgenstein and answers, "To shew the fly the way out of the fly-bottle."[30] But maybe there is no "way out of the fly-bottle" or, in Plato's image, the "cave-like dwelling"[31] we all call home—perhaps/possibly, the beyond is here and now.

In this awareness, the lived exigencies of our ek-sistence call for a focus attuned to the transient and contingent possibilities of life. Not to exit but to teach us to live, with a minimal amount of stumbling and of violence, in the chiaroscuro netting of existence: this may be the proper task of philosophy. Like Penelope's web, a never-ending task, vigilantly devoted to and sustained by its chosen fate: the concrete, and yet contingent, possibilities of our ek-sistence.

Human beings are thus like "acrobats," not cave dwellers or flies, precariously navigating, traversing, and re-traversing the netting of existence.[32] It is this network and the balancing acts, in various roles—as father/mother, worker, customer, intellectual, and so on—it calls us to, that is and constitutes our lived life. This also is how we deploy our political concerns out of this network of involvements and entanglements and become protagonists, active and/or passive, of history.[33] The openness of thinking accordingly focuses on being attuned to, or in sync with, the intricacies of the ways and byways—the chiaroscuro netting of existence—traversed and actuated in our lived ek-sistence, the sum total of our effective heritage, our "effective-history." In this regard, it ought to be noted in passing that acrobats, in due time, in the pursuit of their vocation, no matter how talented, alert, and/or diligent they may be, die: this, too, is our fated end.

This end, however, which is not in any way or manner a fulfillment, does not call for going beyond the "bottle" or the "cave." All it calls for is for us "to ponder matters in the light of death."[34] To resolutely face up to the possibilities in and through which we can minimize stumbling and gratuitous violence in our lived mortality. And this, always and necessarily, happens within the netting of a heritage. Like acrobats on the high wire without a safety net, on the web of existence, our finite ek-sistence (i.e., our standing out), unstable at best, (shaky, fickle, uncertain, faltering, contingent, precarious, anxious, etc.) calls for a sober and engaged awareness of and an open disposition to the possible in that which is: the transient and fluid temporalness of our existence as the heritage of its own self-actuation.[35]

Part I

Reflections

I

Decolonization and Philosophy

> Not so long ago, Nazism transformed the whole of Europe into a veritable colony. The governments of the different European nations insisted on reparations and demanded the restitution in cash and in kind of the wealth that had been stolen from them: cultural works, paintings, sculptures, stained glass, have been returned to their owners. In the mouths of Europeans on the morrow of V-day 1945 only one phrase: "Germany will pay."
>
> —Frantz Fanon[1]

> When the axe came into the forest, the trees said: the handle is one of us.
>
> —Turkish proverb[2]

I

What has been, to date, the character of African decolonization, and how is it related to the practice of philosophy? In engaging this double question, what I hope to do is to look at the actuality of decolonization—our postcolonial condition—and the way in which the obdurate residue of the colonial past still controls our present. Concurrently, I will also look at how the contemporary practice of African philosophy can contribute toward changing this situation.[3] In this double task, my efforts will be focused on exploring the reality of our postcolonial condition and the responsibility this imposes on those of us engaged in the practice of African philosophy. But first let us begin by looking at philosophy's own lived self-understanding.

II

In *Vocazione e responsabilità del filosofo*, Gianni Vattimo points out that arguments in philosophy are discourses aimed at "persuasion" and situated in the shared views of "a collectivity."[4] And so, he observes, "It becomes clear that it [philosophy] essentially concerns proposals for interpreting our common situation according to a certain line and starting from shared presuppositions."[5] In such "proposals" and deliberations we try to persuade each other by presenting arguments and citing authors we value and our counterparts in dialogue also value and appreciate. The authors we cite, furthermore, are not concerned with demonstrating that such-and-so is or is not the case based on indisputable facts,[6] but are themselves engaged in persuading each other and searching for shared interpretations of a "common situation,"[7] which has become—in view of lived exigencies—problematic and worthy of questioning. Our persuasiveness is, therefore, not merely a rhetorical ploy directed at others, but a self-reflexive and self-reflective critical exploration of our situation—the situation at hand—directed not only, or primarily, at others but more importantly at ourselves.[8]

Thus, to validate our respective interpretations of the "common situation," we cite to each other interpreters and interpretations with whose esteem or appreciation we agree. From this it follows that the truth we try to maintain, and the way in which we maintain it, is along the lines of arguing for a stance, or a perspective, in view of certain accepted reference points in terms of which we can then pose the critical question, "how can you still say this?"[9] In other words, asks Vattimo, "Is it not perhaps true that the experience procured for you by a reading of Nietzsche (or of Kant, or of Hegel) impedes you from saying things that perhaps at one time you might have said and sustained?"[10] That is, don't the insights secured in reading such and similar authors compel us to rethink the presuppositions, or prejudices,[11] that ground our outlook?

The affirmative response to this rhetorical question takes for granted accord in our words and deeds and assumes rigor and consistency as indispensable for the practice of philosophy; a kind of reflection that incessantly assesses and re-assesses itself in light of "all that which happens in human reality."[12] Otherwise, the "how can you still say this?" of philosophy, as Socrates patiently explains to Crito, would be "in truth play and nonsense."[13] In all of this, our efforts aim at validating and/or discarding our lived prejudices, our "shared presuppositions," by calibrating and synchronizing, accordingly, the line of sight that they make possible.

Philosophy is, therefore, focused on sifting our presuppositions or prejudgments—the prejudice we live by—in view of the shared possibilities of our lived present. Consequently, it stands in very close proximity to history; it is the reflexive and reflective critical self-validation of its time, its historicity.[14] Conversely, the historicity in which a philosophic discourse finds itself furnishes the problems of concern and the context-background within which a philosophic discourse foregrounds its interpretations.[15] As Hans-Georg Gadamer tells us, the function of "temporal distance," the role of history, is to allow "those prejudices that are of a particular and limited nature [to] die away" while making possible "those that bring about genuine understanding."[16] Philosophy is thus a historically situated and saturated interpretative querying, sifting, and sieving of lived existence focused on, and open to, the possible in that which is.

This conception of philosophy, furthermore, is not a view that is idiosyncratic to Vattimo. It is the basic self-understanding of the practice of philosophy. In other words, as Hegel points out, "philosophy . . . is its own time apprehended in thoughts."[17] It is the critical-reflective and persuasive exploration of the viable conceptions and ideas (prejudices?) of its lived moment in time. Kant, referring to his own era as "the age of criticism," notes that, "everything must submit" to critical scrutiny and be "able to sustain the test of a free and open examination,"[18] which is, properly speaking, the practice of philosophy. This too, *grosso modo*, is what Nietzsche means when he states that "this art of transfiguration *is* philosophy."[19]

In sum, philosophy is the practice of reflectively exploring grounding concerns that originate in specific cultures/regions.[20] To speak of "European" or "African" philosophy is to indicate the particular culture/region in and out of which "a specific type of intellectual activity (the critical examination [interpretative exploring] of fundamental problems)" is being actuated.[21] In like manner, the qualifiers "contemporary," "modern," "ancient," and so on, indicate the time period or history (i.e., the historicity) in which this "specific type of intellectual activity" is being undertaken, in confronting and/or exploring the exigencies or concerns of its time.

With this understanding in mind, let us now turn to the historicity in which European philosophy served colonialism and indicate how it did so.[22] We will then examine the way the central and underlying assumptions and justifications of the colonial project were directly and indirectly or tacitly—and thus, that much more effectively—imparted to Westernized Africa. In this, colonial rule is seen and presented as a benevolent process of molding, or forming, which "justifies" itself retroactively, that is, by the civilizing effect it has on the colonized. In conclusion, given the character of this intellectual-historical context and horizon, I will articulate what I take to be the critical task of the contemporary practice of African philosophy. I will specify, in other words, what has been abstractly stated in the preceding paragraph.

III

Philosophy, in premodern Europe, as the handmaid of theology was focused on otherworldly concerns. With the coming of modernity, having secured employment with science, it became the attendant of conquest. In keeping with Europe's progressive and scientific understanding of itself, in contrast to the medieval past and the "backwardness" of the rest of the globe, philosophy mapped out the metaphysical (i.e., the grounding) presuppositions of this stance. The practice of philosophy, the most sublime realm of European culture, thus served as the theoretic buttress of colonial expansion. As Anne Hugon points out,

> In 1788 [i.e., the heyday of the Enlightenment] a booklet was issued in London by the newly formed Association for Promoting the Discovery of the Interior parts of Africa (or the African Association). It stated [at its founding] that at least one third of the inhabited surface of the earth was unknown, notably Africa, virtually in its entirety. For the first time this ignorance was seen as a shameful gap in human knowledge that must immediately be filled.[23]

"But," as Hugon further points out, "geographic curiosity was not the only motive"[24] that inspired the efforts of the ascending intellectual-political classes of European Modernity.

> The European elite—stirred by the discoveries of Sir Isaac Newton, the writings of René Descartes and Francis Bacon, and Denis Diderot's publication in 1751 of the first encyclopedia—was becoming increasingly fascinated by science and in particular by ethnography . . . Interest in the facts of the natural world was not, however, an end in itself. Toward the end of the 18th century, it was believed to be *the mission of human reason to achieve perfect mastery of the world by discovering the laws of the universe*. Thus the African Association, resolutely up-to-date in its optimism, proclaimed its conviction in the usefulness . . . of enlarging human knowledge through the exploration of Africa.[25]

It was in light of this newly noticed "shameful gap" and to remedy this shortfall in "human knowledge" that the Association advocated for "the exploration of Africa." There is here, it should be noted, a seamless confluence in the pursuit of knowledge and the conquest of Africa. Internal to this pursuit, furthermore, there is a *vicious* circular self-validating interplay between the way the "Interior parts of Africa" show themselves to be and that which the enlightened "European elite" projects, expects, and *finds* in these supposed remote regions.[26]

This gratuitous self-validation was anchored in the view that Europe or, more accurately, its intellectual-political elite had of itself: the view that "the mission of human reason," which it saw as synonymous with its own historical calling, was to "achieve perfect mastery of the world by discovering the laws of the universe." This mindset, as Sir Isaiah Berlin tells us, arose out of the belief that "human omniscience was . . . an attainable goal."[27] The hubris of this stance encouraged a rather aggressive demeanor. Inebriated by the majesty of this grandiose undertaking, Europe objectified the globe as the terrain—the virgin soil—on which to inseminate and actualize true human existence. It saw itself as the incarnation of this truth and its worldwide escapades as the propitious process of spreading out, globally, this same truth.

In this manner, cocksure of itself and spurred on, enveloped, and encouraged by the grandeur of "the mission of human reason," as Romano Guardini tells us,

> For the new man of the modern age the unexplored regions of his world were a challenge to meet and conquer. Within himself he heard the call to venture over what seemed an endless earth, to make himself its master.[28]

Europe's expansion, fueled by the economic dynamism of an ascendant capitalism, found scientific authorization in the enlightened effort to "master" "the unexplored regions of his world." It mattered little that these regions were already inhabited by diverse populations slightly different, in physical features and complexion, than modern Europeans. Indeed, this very difference fueled "interest in knowing other men and other societies."[29] It aggressively prodded and encouraged the development of new sciences and fields of study.

It has to be emphasized that "mastery" and "knowledge" were elements of an incessant, self-propelling, and self-augmenting discourse of and on learning. Within this frame, the more one knows, the more one knows how little one knows, and this calls for further mastery and, in turn, this calls for more knowledge. Each inter-implicative cycle—of knowledge and mastery—authorizes further expansion by reference to the need to keep on striving toward *the truth*. Not, any more, the truth of revelation but that of science and "human reason," focused on this-worldly concerns (i.e., mastery), encyclopedic in scope, and answerable only to itself.

"Enlightenment" after all, as Kant reminds us, "is man's release from his self-incurred tutelage."[30] And this "tutelage" is the lack of courage in using and following the guidance of human reason independently. The contrast here is between an incipient rationality (scientific reason) self-assured by the boldness of novel developments and discoveries, and the lethargic inherited prejudices of a religious past, now felt as oppressive, being discarded if not completely surpassed. In conjunction with this audacity, Enlightenment thinkers, in contrast to classical authors, had also a progressive/optimistic historical orientation. From their critique of the mediaeval past, they had appropriated a noncyclical notion of history as the progressive improvement of humankind. This concept, a secularized version of the Christian narrative of "fall" and "redemption,"[31] bestowed, on those who wielded it, a felt sense of superiority and concretely encouraged expansion. As Heinz Kimmerle puts it,

> In the period of the Enlightenment Western culture began to regard itself as the climax of all histories which have happened on earth from the beginning of mankind up to the 18th century. The different lines of what had happened in the various parts of the world led to Western history and finally ended in the presence of Western Europe in the 18th century. In fact philosophers [such] as Voltaire and Turgot, Lessing and Kant spoke of *one* history only, and that was the history and prehistory of Western culture. The main idea of the conception of one world history was the idea of progress. History was conceptualized as [a totalizing unilinear] progress from an early beginning on a primitive stage to the climax of culture and humanism in the period of the Enlightenment.

In this linear hierarchal frame of things, as Kimmerle further points out,

> Other cultures did not exist . . . other cultures just formed stages on the way to the presence of this period. For the conception of world history, which thus became possible, the price had to be paid [which was] that the different histories and cultures [i.e., other peoples] were reduced to the prehistory of one culture.[32]

In this way, the Enlightenment masterfully masked the mastery of humankind under the exacting mantel of the progressive advancement of a *singular* humanity.

Unlike the otherworldly orientation of the medieval past, the Enlightenment's stance of learning and progress was a motivating factor of conquest, in seeking knowledge. Within this frame, "what seemed an endless earth" called for endless undertakings. And the dark natives that inhabited this "endless earth" were depicted and seen as residues of a surpassed humanity to be conquered and studied, relics of earlier forms of *anthrōpos*—"native societies" to be utilized "for imperial purposes."[33] Thus, the "new man of the modern age" obliquely prompted by the economic energies and enticements of an ascendant—and thus vigorous—capitalism and snugly cloaked by gratifying and learned ethnic-political myths,[34] embraced his superior destiny.

All of this, to be sure, occurred as if it was meant to be.[35] For Europe, or its dominant intellectual-political elite, was mesmerized by the majesty of the *idea* of the "mission of human reason." In this context, oriented by this "mission," the philosophers of the modern West articulated differing perspectives with one core point in common: the absolute preeminence of Europe and the legitimacy of its globalization. Thus they laid out the metaphysical scaffolding on which the primitive past was to be dispatched. Their metaphysical pronouncements—in keeping with the ideological aroma of their day—were seen, and presented, as the most advanced thinking of the time, alert to the atemporal transcendent truth of humanity.

And so Hume, the great skeptic, was of the opinion that "white" was the only color of civilization and that humanity was constituted by differing types, or gradations, with the white race at the top.[36] Locke, who had direct economic interests in plantations and slaves, held the view that the divinely sanctioned improvement of the earth necessitated its conquest by those heedful of this authorization.[37] Kant affirmed that the "unsocial sociability" of human nature was such that progress occurred only through conflict and Europe was destined to establish "the law" for humanity as a whole.[38] In this regard, as Thomas McCarthy points out,

> [I]n trying to make moral sense of history, he [Kant] ironically constructed an early version of the very rationale—biological and cultural—that would serve as the dominant proslavery ideology later in the following century.[39]

In keeping with the above, Hegel saw slavery as needed to civilize the African, and colonization was, for him, the globalization of *Weltgeist*.[40] Along similar lines, Marx's *Communist Manifesto* welcomes the colonial globalization of Europe. In various places in the first volume of *Capital*, he affirms the immature and/or underdeveloped nature of premodern humanity. In sync with this, in his numerous, detailed, and meticulously written articles on India—a placeholder for the non-European world as a whole—Marx endorses British colonialism as a necessary civilizing project, in view of the anticipated communist future of humankind.[41]

It is imperative to keep in mind that the great minds of the West, in formulating their differing metaphysical views, relied heavily on the dubious literature of travelogues. To be sure, there was awareness at the time—as Kant tells us, for example—that based on such literature one could argue the equal validity of contrary positions.[42] And yet, the great minds of the West, Kant included, formulated their views in categorical terms and circuitously validated these same questionable narratives—the very narratives they utilized to confirm their speculations.

In this regard, Jean-Jacques Rousseau's outlook is a bit more circumspect, in contrast to Kant or the other great thinkers mentioned above. On the rather myopic information to be found in travelogues, at the end of a long note on those who report on their travels, Rousseau writes,

> I say that when such Observers assert about a given animal that it is a man and about another that it is a beast, they will have to be believed; but it would be most simple-minded to rely in this matter on coarse travelers about whom one might sometimes be tempted to ask the same question they pretend to answer about other animals.[43]

With all his sarcasm, even for Rousseau, the champion of the "noble savage," it is in the state of society—European society, properly speaking—that the humanity of the human is rightly established, by the acquisition of "moral liberty,"[44] which is superior to the "natural" condition of human beings in the non-European world. This felt sense of superiority, shared even by Rousseau, is thus the benchmark of Europe's colonial stance. It is the linchpin of the *social imaginary*[45] in and through which European modernity violently globalized itself.

Now, as Cornelius Castoriadis has observed, "there is . . . no superiority, nor inferiority to the West. There is simply a fact: namely that the Earth has been unified by means of Western violence."[46] To themselves and—more important—to the age engaged in implementing it, the great minds of the West embellished this violent unification and made it appear as a necessity inscribed in the inherent "superiority . . . [of] the West" and sanctioned by the very nature of things human, historical, and/or divine. They thus served the function, or played the role, of intellectual—moral and metaphysical—sanctifiers of violence (i.e., normalizers of brutality).[47]

Explorers, missionaries, adventurers, and the "scientific expectation[s] of an educated public"[48] were all under the spell of this mindset. What captivated equally ordinary Europeans, missionaries, philosophers, adventurers, and so on was the *idea* that their civilization was destined to rule, just as darker peoples were destined to be ruled. Their God was the true God, the God of Israel, just as everybody else worshiped idols and falsehoods. In this regard, it ought to be noted, at least in passing, that starting with "Gregory VII (Pope from 1073 to 1085),"[49] key internal changes in Catholic theology and the later and more radical transmutations that led to the establishment of Protestantism made it possible for Western Christianity to bypass Augustinian otherworldliness and focus on "Human work" as an "expression and revelation of the divine ideal directing it"[50] toward preparing the world for the second coming, "so that it would be worthy of Christ's return."[51] As Philippe Nemo further points out,

> In the eyes of the Eastern Christian, the enterprising effort to organize the world is proof that God has been forgotten; for the Western Christian, it is the most sincere expression of our [i.e., the Western Christian's] adoration of God.[52]

This restructuring in the thinking of Western Christianity was an opportune mutation that was interior to and, with the advent of modernity, nicely fit Europe's colonialist proclivity. It concretely manifested itself in the fervor and zeal of missionary work, focused on converting heathens—a crucial aspect of Europe's self-imposed task of civilizing the world[53]—in view of "Christ's return." All of this, it has to be noted, must have been felt as a heavy burden, but also as very gratifying. How could it not be? It is gratifying indeed—heavy as the burden may be—to think and to believe and to be confirmed in this belief, by science and religion, that the actuality of one's cultural-historical existence is the proper measure of all that is truly human.

In this regard, the sharp cutting edge of Hume's skepticism, or Kant's or Marx's critical bent of mind, for example, did not avail these great thinkers a detachment from the conventional prejudices of their day. Indeed, and ironically, it made it possible for them to see themselves as the "objective" enunciators of the grounding truth that made sense of the tumultuous "surface" political eventuations of their age. To give but one example, Marx, writing on India, states that "England . . . in causing a social revolution in Hindustan, was actuated . . . by the vilest interests, and was stupid"[54] in its manner of enforcement. But, all of this surface tumultuousness is of little consequence. What matters is the question, "can mankind fulfill its destiny without a fundamental revolution in the social state of Asia?"[55] In other words, vile and "stupid" as they may be, these actions are justified by the *telos* of a higher purpose (i.e., mankind's "destiny"). Violent conquest—and all that goes with it—is thus made palatable by the workings of the dialectic internal to the self-actuation of "mankind fulfill[ing] its destiny." It should be noted in this regard that "mankind," be it in Marx as in all the other great thinkers of the West, is an abstraction that is always thought of (i.e., specified/concretized) by reference to the West.

In all of this, to be sure, there was also at work a cynical and demonic orientation keenly focused on wealth and plunder. As J. H. Parry points out, for example, "Bernal Díaz, frankest of *conquistadores,* wrote that he and his like went to the Indies 'to serve God and His Majesty, to give light to those who were in darkness, and to grow rich, as all men desire to do.' "[56] But, even in the blunt words of Diaz, "grow[ing] rich" is placed within the larger, more generous and pious context of serving God and giving "light to those . . . in darkness." Indeed, plunder always takes place under wraps! As James Baldwin has pointedly remarked,

> So that . . . when I talk about colonialism—which is also a word that can be defined—it refers to European domination of what we now call underdeveloped countries. It also refers, no matter what the previous colonial powers may say, to the fact that these people entered those continents not to save them, not, no not, to bring the Cross of Christ or the Bible—though they did; that was a detail. And still less to inculcate into them a notion of political democracy. The truth is that they walked in and they stayed in, and they recklessly destroyed whatever was in their way, in order to make money. And this is what we call the rise of capitalism, which is a *pre-phase* covering an eternity of crimes.[57]

Or, as A. J. Baker tells us, "The young conscript soldiers who sailed from [Fascist] Italy [to invade Ethiopia] in 1935 sincerely believed" in part that "they were going on a civilizing mission to a country oppressed by a feudal regime."[58] To be sure, land for poor peasants, profits for industrialists, and the greater glory of Italy, its "place in the sun," were all important motivating factors in Fascist war propaganda, but always cloaked by lofty and disinterested ideals.[59] As Father Placide Tempels, a missionary priest, put it in 1945, "It has been said that our civilizing mission alone can justify our occupation of the lands of uncivilized peoples."[60] It is to this cover, and all that it conceals, that the great minds of the West render effective metaphysical-moral service. It should be noted, in passing, that there is here at work the obliquely self-deceiving mechanism of "bad faith," a duplicitous fraudulence, in "good faith" about itself.[61]

This duplicitous frame of mind, furthermore, is not merely a relic from the remote past. In textbooks, novels, movies (*Out of Africa,* 1985), and in the commonsensical understanding of ordinary Westerners, the colonial project—on balance—is viewed as having benefited the colonized. The exploitation of colonies, as D. K. Fieldhouse maintains, for example, in a textbook published in 1966, is a myth.[62] And "although 'pacifying' armies were often barbarous in their methods . . . conquest was quickly followed by civilized methods of government."[63] The effect of these remarks—intended or not—is to suggest that only ingrates, when all is said and done, could possibly fail to notice the beneficial effects of colonial rule. Indeed, as Chinua Achebe tells us, he was chided as "an ungrateful upstart of a native"[64] by an English reviewer when *Things Fall Apart* was published in 1958. Achebe is, without a doubt, an ingrate. We shall soon meet others who in gratitude perpetuate—as our postcolonial condition—the odious colonial past.

IV

Thus far, we have been looking at how Europe, in actuating its modernity, enthralled by its own self-image, subjected the globe. This it did in "good faith," that is, in the ardent belief that its conquest of the world was a vital service to humankind. As Edward W. Said puts it,

> [W]hat distinguishes earlier empires, like the Roman or the Spanish or the Arabs, from the modern [colonial] empires, of which the British and French were the great ones in the nineteenth century, is the fact that the latter ones are systematic enterprises, constantly reinvested. They're not simply arriving in a country, looting it and then leaving when the loot is exhausted . . . modern empire requires, as Conrad said, an *idea of service*, an *idea of sacrifice*, an *idea of redemption*. Out of this you get these great, massively reinforced notions of, for example, in the case of France, the "*mission civilisatrice*." That we're not there to benefit ourselves, we're there for the sake of the natives.[65]

Mantled by the *idea*, the end of the nineteenth century witnessed Europe's global ascendancy and the balkanized subjection of Africa.[66] In shouldering its "heavy" responsibility to the rest of us, "The White Man's Burden,"[67] in Rudyard Kipling's memorable words, Europe generously used force "but much more important . . . than force," as Said further points out, "was the *idea* inculcated in the minds of the people being colonized that it was their *destiny* to be ruled by the West."[68] Colonial rule utilizing a violent pedagogy—the strenuous hard work of missionaries and benevolent educators[69]—firmly ingrained in the colonized this *destiny*. It chiseled into their heads the *idea* of Western supremacy. In doing so it molded/originated a stratum, or layer of people, Westernized Africans[70] who—having been formed by Europe's imperious gaze—see themselves and their place in the world in these terms. Europe converted those sections of the subjugated it Westernized to the view that their subjection was a necessity if their territories were to progress and develop and become places of civilized human habitation.

It hammered into their heads the providential and beneficial nature of their subjection. It firmly inscribed in their consciousness—subliminally and explicitly—the civilized/uncivilized dichotomy and persuaded them of their appalling default within the scope of this all-engulfing distinction. And so, in this circuitous manner, violent de facto dominance secured de jure hegemonic acceptability and legitimation.[71] As Basil Davidson points out,

> [M]ost Africans in Western-educated groups . . . held to the liberal Victorian vision of civilization kindling its light from one new nation to the next, drawing each within its blessed fold, long after the local facts depicted a very different prospect.[72]

Having accepted the self-proclaimed European civilizing idea, in 1901 for example, Angolans living in Lisbon published a protest against Portuguese misrule of their country. They noted that "Portugal had conquered Angola centuries earlier . . . but [had] done nothing for the people's welfare." To this day "'the people remain brutalized, as in their former state,' and such neglect was an 'outrage against civilization.'"[73] What we have here, ironically enough, is an immanent critique, by Westernized Africans, of the colonial idea in its failure to implement the destiny it, itself, prescribes. The categories of this internal critique are the desirability of civilization—in the singular—and the necessity of surpassing African backwardness.[74] In this, it is implicitly understood and explicitly conceded that precolonial Africa was immersed in "darkness."

It should be obvious, by now, that the effectiveness of this critique depends on the internalization—as an "objective fact"—of the colonial perspective. As we saw in section III above, this originates in modern Europe's social imaginary, grounded in the impossible claim of the Enlightenment that it is possible to "achieve perfect mastery of the world" (note 25). The Westernized African reared and educated in mission schools—and even more, the African who lives in urban centers, domestic servants, chauffeurs, conscript soldiers, shoeshine boys, the African "schooled" by his/her close proximity to white settlers, "learned" by proxy, by "osmosis"—is in awe of this conceited *image*. S/he takes it to be the unvarnished truth.

Colonial or mission school rearing and, even more, the "education" of the white urban centers (i.e., the education of the "streets") inculcates, cultivates, and nurtures in the taste, common sense, and the quotidian practical judgment of the subjected an appreciation for all things Western, in tandem with weeding out any sense of the value of things African and/or local. Such education positively directs the subjugated toward all things foreign while aptly reinforcing its "lessons" by the violence at its command. As Tempels tells us,

> The technological skill of the white man impressed the Bantu [i.e., the African]. The white man *seemed* to be the master of great natural forces. It had, therefore, to be admitted that the white man was an elder, a superior human force, surpassing the *vital force* of all Africans.[75]

Colonial education mystifies. It nurtures this *seeming*. It presents the workings and achievements of science as effects of the superiority of "the white man." It presents—implicitly and explicitly, directly and indirectly, and thus tacitly and more effectively—science, European religions and languages, European ways, and so on as occult qualities that emanate from "whiteness": indicators of the intrinsic superiority of the West. It convinces its pupils that "whiteness rubs off," that they can become—if not white—like the whites. And "the vital force"—the effectiveness—of the colonizer's military hardware (e.g., the Maxim gun) concretely ensures that this mystified acclaim does not waver in its deference. In this way, the normative claims of colonial rule—the imposed order of life—are firmly ingrained in and through the ordinary interactions of daily life, in the subjected psyche and imagination of the "native." As Ngugi wa Thiong'o points out,

> The coming of Christianity . . . set in motion a process of social change, involving the rapid disintegration of the . . . frame-work of social norms and values by which people formerly ordered their lives . . . The evidence that you were saved was not whether you were a believer in and follower of Christ, and accepted all men as equal: the measure of your Christian love and charity was in preserving the outer signs and symbols of a European way of life; whether you dressed as Europeans did, whether you had acquired European good manners, liked European hymns and tunes, and of course whether you had refused to have your daughter circumcised.[76]

The Westernized African is indeed an extrovert. His/her categories of thought are controlled, from within, by that which is exterior and foreign to the local setting. S/he enacts and lives the life of a "half-caste" who intuitively/tacitly and incessantly regrets the half of his/her "caste" that is the indigent-indigenous society and is grateful for the Other, which forms and indeed validates—in his/her own eyes—her/his own proper humanity. Such a person is a being formed by incessant and ongoing self-scorn, that is, an interiorized servile deferential awe of the Other—the true template of what it means to be human. Such a person is a *replicant.*[77]

This, then, is what constitutes the operative internalized "pretext"[78] (i.e., the disappointed expectation of beneficial effects to be secured from European rule by the rightly conquered primitive society) that explicitly condones and excuses conquest. This consenting to, or accepting of the "pretext" of the *idea,* is the "ideological pacification"[79] of the colonized. It is the concrete intellectual-cultural subjection, correlate to the violent-military pacification,[80] which inaugurates the presence of Europe in Africa. It is, in plain language, as we shall soon see, the creation of grateful natives, replicants, who unlike the ingrate Achebe, affirm—as an "objective truth"—the colonial formation/molding that constitutes their insalubrious being.[81]

As Fanon points out, "In the colonial context, the colonist's work of breaking-in the colonized is not finished until the latter recognizes in a loud and intelligible voice the supremacy of white values."[82] The colonial project fulfills itself by breaking the indigenous allegiance to aboriginal values and by enforcing a willing acceptance of its claimed superiority.[83] What is broken is the internal cohesion of a culture-history, the adherence of the subjective incarnations of a culture (i.e., human beings) to the objectified-institutional forms of said culture. From the objectified forms of Spirit, to use Hegelian language, is divorced the living substance (i.e., human beings) in whose flesh and bones a culture-history (i.e., Spirit) institutes and sustains itself. Once broken, this culture-history is reduced to a deracinated existence: to being nothing more than the discarded relic—the empty husk—of a defeated heritage.

This is what is achieved by the forming or molding effect of colonial rule—the enduring psychic/cultural damaging of the subjected: actuated by undermining their sense of self and history; undermining the ethos of the indigenous culture-history; stagnating and tangibly mummifying[84] its once living forms of ek-sistence.[85] Long after the end of formal colonial rule, this "breaking-in" goes on paying handsome dividends to the West. As if ordained by nature, it institutes the ongoing and self-effacing perpetual replication of the *periphery;* that segment of the world referenced—always—in view of the *center.* In other words, that segment concretely constituted, in its lived self-awareness, by the heritage of its defeats.

V

To date, the most enduring legacy of colonialism has been this broken replicant segment of African society, which has internalized the colonial *idea* of human existence and history. This is the segment that rules postcolonial Africa. Not grounded in local histories but in the residue of colonial Europe, it has as the touchstone of its existence what lies beyond its shores. This is what Fanon refers to as the defense of the "Greco-Latin pedestal."[86] But what exactly does this mean? Let us, by way of an example, look at a prominent case of such a defense.

Léopold Sédar Senghor, writing in 1960—the year of Africa—ardently affirms, "Let us stop denouncing colonialism and Europe. . . . To be sure, conquerors sow ruin in their wake, but they also sow ideas and techniques that germinate and blossom into new harvests."[87] But what exactly does this mean? Senghor explains at length and in detail:

> When placed again in context, colonization will appear to us as a necessary evil, a historical necessity whence good will emerge, but on the sole condition that we, the colonized of yesterday, become conscious and that we will it. Slavery, feudalism, capitalism, and colonialism are the successive parturitions of History, painful like all parturitions. With the difference that here the child suffers more than the mother. That does not matter. If we are fully conscious of the scope of the *Advent*, we shall cease to inveigh against it; we shall be more attentive to contributions than defects, to possibilities of rebirth rather than to death and destruction. Without the deaths, without the Arab and European depredations, no doubt the Negro Africans and Berbers would by now have created more ripe and more succulent fruits. I doubt that they would have caught up so soon with the advances caused in Europe by the Renaissance. The evil of colonization is less these ruptures than that we were deprived of the freedom to choose those European contributions most appropriate to our spirit.[88]

Having colonized Africa, Europe dislocates the symmetry of its existence and re-forms it in and through the hegemony of the *idea*. What speaks in and through Senghor is thus the educational cultural formation (i.e., Bildung) of the colonial period (i.e., modern Europe's global projection). To borrow Said's words, "we're not there to benefit ourselves, we're there for the sake of the natives." This is the view that is here presented, by a grateful évolué—a replicant—as the condition of the possibility for future favorable advances, "whence good will emerge." Provided that "we, the colonized of yesterday, become conscious and that we will it," that *we accept*, in other words, the *truth* that in order to secure "the advances caused in Europe by the Renaissance" such "death and destruction" was necessary. Indeed! To the contrary, as the founding father of Tanzania, President Julius K. Nyerere, informs us,

> At independence, Tanzania or as it was then called, Tanganyika (a country four times the size of Great Britain) had approximately 200 miles of tarmac road, and its 'industrial sector' consisted of six factories—including one which employed 50 persons. The countries which had sizeable Settler or mineral extraction communities (such as Kenya, Zimbabwe, Zambia or Congo) had strong links with the world economy, but their own development was entirely concentrated on servicing the needs of the settlers or the miners in one way or another. Again, despite the Education and Health services provided by some Christian Missionaries and later begun by colonial governments, at independence less than 50% of Tanzanian children went to school—and then for only four years or less; [and] 85% of its adults were illiterate in any language. The country had only two African engineers, 12 Doctors, and perhaps 30 Arts graduates, I was one of them.[89]

This can hardly be considered as catching up with "the advances caused in Europe by the Renaissance." Besides, in view of the massiveness of the devastation precipitated by colonial conquest, one could respond to Senghor by repeating Albert Memmi's rhetorical question:

> How can one dare compare the advantages and disadvantages of colonization? What advantages, even if a thousand times more important, could make such internal and external catastrophes acceptable?[90]

But beyond Memmi's rhetorical question, and Nyerere's marshaling of evidence, it is necessary to emphasize that Senghor's way of "seeing" falls squarely within the confines of the idea which informs and directs colonial subjection. He is, in effect, the evidence of the proof.

In his use of the childhood metaphor, in his endorsement of suffering in order to secure future benefits, in his view that colonialism is "a historical necessity whence good will emerge," in advising attentiveness to colonial contributions without ever decrying all that Africa lost in being enslaved and colonized, in his singular and totalizing conception of history implicit in the notion of catching up "with the . . . Renaissance," in his eagerness to "choose" from "European contributions," in all of this, Senghor faithfully replicates the language of "the idea," he defends the "Greco-Latin pedestal." He dotingly parrots, as his own, the self-image of the idea. This is what makes him a replicant—in contradistinction to Achebe, Nyerere, or Cabral, for example.

His thinking is inscribed within the confines of "la mission civilisatrice," the conceited self-image of modern Europe—globally projected—that it is the destiny of non-Europeans "to be ruled by the West" (note 68). He is focused on "European contributions" and not the devastations Baldwin refers to as, "a pre-phase covering an eternity of crimes" (note 57). Nor is Senghor concerned with "reparations," as Europe was, soon after its own experience of being colonized.[91] His sole concern is with choosing "those European contributions most appropriate to our spirit." But "our spirit," does it not have its own contributions to make?

With most of the founding fathers of independent Africa—memorialized by Afework Tekle's mural in Africa Hall, Addis Ababa (Ethiopia)—Senghor is an excellent example of what Fanon means when he says that colonialism completes its "work of breaking-in" the colonized only when the latter extols "white values." Senghor is not sparing in his praise, so long as "colonization" is "placed . . . in context." But, isn't this the logic of the idea? Isn't this "la mission civilisatrice"? The idea and the destiny it prescribes structure—from within—the mindset of replicant Africa. In Senghor, our prime example, it directs the logic of his thinking. This, then, is what Said refers to as "the epistemology of imperialism."[92]

Western philosophy, in its service to colonialism (section III), establishes the grounding core of this epistemology. In conjunction with colorful travelogues—both on the level of common sense and learned opinion—it institutes the centrality of Europe. It constitutes, verifies, and fabricates a "knowledge" of Africa that confirms the socioeconomic and political setup of its framing. In the guise of describing and narrating it authorizes and validates. This it does with a "clear and clean conscience" for it is, itself, beguiled by its own self-deluding image of itself.

As Achebe has noted, there is "a four-hundred-year period from the sixteenth century to the twentieth" of abusive writing on Africa which has "developed into a tradition with a vast storehouse of lurid images to which writers went again and again through the centuries to draw 'material' for their books."[93] The contents of this "storehouse" sedimented in the Bildung of Westernized Africa, and reinforced by ongoing metaphysical backing, is at the core of the "alienated discourse and self-identity"[94] of this broken/replicant segment of African society. This "storehouse of lurid images," which finds its ultimate anchorage and/or justification in the metaphysical fabrications of the great minds of the West, institutes the "normal discourse,"[95] the presuppositions and grounding prejudices, of the "epistemology of imperialism."

In Senghor and the Westernized stratum of African society he belongs to, we have a sector of society that thinks of Africa, and itself, in colonial terms. Indeed, as Kwasi Wiredu has noted, we are in dire need of "conceptual decolonization." But this cannot mean that we merely revert to thinking in our "own African languages."[96] The present reality of Africa is hybrid. It is, therefore, the content and composition of this hybridity that we must challenge, explore, and concretely sift through. This we can do by critically engaging and de-structuring on the level of ideas the colonial project, "the epistemology of imperialism," that controls us from within.

As we saw earlier with Vattimo (section II), philosophy is a critically focused exploring of ideas (i.e., of prejudices and presuppositions) in light of the exigencies of our lived "common situation." In this, as Gadamer tells us, "philosophical thinking . . . consists in making what we already know another step more conscious."[97] In what remains of this chapter, we will do just that: explore further what we "know" to be the obdurate residual source of the debilitating predicament of our postcolonial condition.

VI

By 1960, most of Africa had attained independence. The 1970s witnessed the end of Portuguese-NATO colonialism.[98] And the early 1990s—with the demise of apartheid South Africa and the victorious consummation of the Eritrean Independence Struggle[99]—finally saw the fulfillment of Africa's age-old struggle for political sovereignty. It is imperative to remember that, at the time, as it was occurring, this was not something that was given universal acclaim.

> In 1960, a resolution at the United Nations General Assembly calling for the independence of all colonies was opposed by every European colonial power—Britain, France, Portugal, Belgium and Spain—plus the U.S. and South Africa.[100]

It was, therefore, against tremendous odds that independence was secured. This, however, should not be understood to mean that, at independence, radical agendas were established at the constituting centers of the newly independent states. Quite to the contrary, in more cases than not, this was a process through which—directly and/or indirectly—the substantive core of independence was effectively eroded. Formal sovereignty was secured and concurrently diluted (i.e., emptied of anything beyond form). As Claude Ake accurately points out,

> With a few exceptions, the gaining of independence was not a matter of the nationalists' marshaling forces to defeat colonial regimes. More often than not, it was a matter of the colonizers'

> accepting the inevitable and orchestrating a handover of government to their chosen African [replicant] successors, successors who could be trusted to share their values and be attentive to their interests. This approach did not succeed in all places where decolonization was peaceful, much less where it was occasioned by revolutionary struggle. But on the whole . . . independence in Africa was rarely the heroic achievement it was made out to be; it was often a convenience of deradicalization [sic] by accommodation, a mere racial integration of the [replicant] political elite.[101]

In this manner, Africa, along with the rest of the formerly colonized world, that up to then had been expunged from history, reinserted itself into the actuality of human historical existence. And the formerly colonizing world, the West, best it could, relinquished to the newly independent states, the absolute bare minimum in all aspects of international economics and politics which, to this day, it firmly controls. Grudgingly under duress the West assented, while simultaneously maneuvering to maintain its claimed cultural-spiritual dominance. Its hegemony, to this day, is held in place by those it "trusted to share" its "values" and guard its "interests": the Westernized segments of African society and their replicant political elites.

In this way, *grosso modo*, the stage was set and the odious colonial past reinstated as our postcolonial condition, the actuality of independence. As Said has noted, "the history of post-colonial states in Africa . . . is a very sad history," which begins in a "period of independence and liberation with a lot of hopes"[102] and which—in more cases than not—has ended in neocolonial marginalized despair. For, indeed, Africa has reclaimed sovereignty over its territory. In large measure however, it has failed to reclaim *itself*. It has not extricated itself from the forming or molding (i.e., deforming) effects of the colonial past. More than in Asia or Latin America, this is the case in postcolonial Africa. As one of Ousmane Sembène's tragicomic characters confesses, in a rather lucid moment of angst,

> We are nothing better than *crabs in a basket*. We want the ex-occupiers place? We have it. . . . Yet what change is there really in general or in particular? The colonialist is stronger, more powerful than ever before, hidden *inside us*, here in this very place.[103]

This is our postcolonial condition: How, then, do we purge the colonial residue that controls, from within, the actuality of the present? As we noted earlier, using Senghor as an example, this is the internalized echo of colonial

Europe's sense of history and human existence. But what exactly does this mean? In this regard, as Castoriadis explains, what the West asserts is

> not that it had discovered the trick of producing more cheaply and more quickly . . . but that it had discovered *the* way of life appropriate to all human society. Fortunately for the Western ideologues, the unease they could have felt on this score was allayed by the haste with which the "developing" nations [or, more accurately, the replicant ruling strata of these nations] try to adopt the Western "model" of society.[104]

Again, as Castoriadis further points out,

> Factually speaking, the West has been and remains victorious—and not only through the force of its weapons: it remains so through its ideas, through its "models" of growth and development, through the statist and other structures which, having been created by it, are today adopted [or more accurately, aped, mimicked, etc.] everywhere.[105]

Within the symmetry of these "'models' of growth and development," within this framework of concepts, ideas, in short, interpretations (i.e., prejudices and presuppositions) that constitute the paradigms of knowledge and of common sense that sustain Western global hegemony, Africa plays the part of a willing victim. In servile mimicry its ruling strata perpetuates its subjection. And so, beyond direct colonialism, the project of domination—which effectively constitutes its practice—endures in the imitative rule of Westernized Africa (i.e., the replicant segment of contemporary African society), bereft of imagination.[106]

Indeed, at the dawn of independence, Fanon had prophetically observed that, without eradicating the debilitating effects of colonialism and restructuring the actuality of independence to the measure of what it names, "independence," in and of itself, could be nothing more than

> A minimum of readaptation, some reforms at the summit [of power], a flag and, all down below, the undivided mass always [la mass indivise toujours] "medievalized" [moyenâgeuse], which continues its perpetual [restless-nervous] movement.[107]

In this context, to the "vast storehouse of lurid images" (note 93) has been added the picture of an innately incapacitated continent. Within this debilitating setup, and constantly nurtured by it, the myth of an inherently impaired "darker" sector of humanity, incapable of doing for itself, continuous unabated. The daily news (i.e., man-made famine, corruption, blood diamonds, genocide) in an ongoing manner confirms and thus "normalizes" this image. Frozen in this frame the continent presents itself as a perennial problem, perpetually testifying against itself.[108] Indeed, it is a "fact"—isn't it?—Africa is a continent wedded to perdition!

While systematically stoking the fires of this inferno and self-servingly managing its effects, the West intervenes—in various humanitarian ways, directly and/or indirectly—to save Africa from "itself." In this way, the hegemonic position of our former colonizers is perpetuated and sustained. Within this frame, our inferior station, by reference to our "innate" incapacities, is affirmed by the intellects of Westernized Africa, trained in Western centers of higher learning. As we saw in Senghor—a prominent member of the Academie Française—and noted with Castoriadis, this replicant segment of African society is both the product and perpetrator of this situation. Another exemplary figure in this regard is Dr. Kamuzu Banda, who holds advanced "degrees from American and Scottish universities." He was known, among other things, for his refusal to "make speeches in African languages" and for having "established a school modeled on Eton in his birthplace Mtunthama, where penniless students were taught Latin, Greek, and African history from the British point of view" and he "hired only white foreigners to teach at the school and to run the ministries and businesses that built his personal fortune."[109] Indeed, "cette caste," as Fanon noted not so long ago, "has done nothing other than to take over unchanged the legacy of the economy, the thought, and the institutions left by the colonialists."[110] And so, the hegemony of the West—the rule of replicant Africa—goes on unabated.

What should never be forgotten is that colonization did not merely destroy the modes of life and thought through which pre-colonial Africa lived its existence. It constituted Africa as a servile appendage of the West. To this day, the residue of this heritage—our postcolonial condition—is held in place by its most tangible colonial legacy, the *colonial-postcolonial state*. This state, formed out of the residual apparatus of violence and coercion that was colonial rule, is nothing more than a "well-developed military bureaucratic superstructure of power over an underdeveloped infrastructure of participation."[111] This is the cultural-intellectual and material "pre-phase" of our lived present. A suffocating overlay on life, the colonial-postcolonial state is "merely an extension of the metropolitan state."[112] It is the concrete embodiment of the heritage of our defeats. Its pro forma exercise of power is the fig-leaf behind which colonial rule continues to this day. As Martin Plaut, a BBC Africa analyst, has observed,

> Driving round many African cities one is constantly struck by the blue and white of the UN flags and logos. Its white 4 × 4 vehicles are to be found in the most remote corners of the rural areas. Frequently one is left with the impression that UN officials know at least as much, if not more, about [African] countries than [African] government ministers, many of whom spend more time nursing their political careers than their constituents. It is hard to escape the conclusion that if Africa is not being re-colonized by the UN, then it is certainly being run at least as much from New York as it is from most of the continent's capitals.[113]

Not rooted in local conditions, the ministers and ministries of African governments are held in place by foreign props,[114] lubricated by graft. "Corruption," as Elizabeth Blunt, another BBC Africa analyst, tells us "is costing the continent nearly $150bn a year."[115] The Continent is indeed awash in "moral pollution."[116] To date, and on the whole, this is the actuality of independence.

Each African state has a flag which marks the geographic terrain within which the replicant strata—Francophone, Anglophone, Lusophone—live the colonial life styles they once envied. And the vast majority, damned to a wretched existence and frozen in discarded traditions, is reduced to being a political nonentity. It is held in check—as in colonial times—by violence: a servile and serving exploited mass, reduced to the status of *things*.[117]

Disillusionment and desperation are, in this situation, the order of the day. And so, in post-apartheid South Africa, for example, "According to the World Bank, the richest 10% of the population earns 58% of national income while those at the bottom, the poorest 50%, earn just 8%."[118] Economic apartheid—the reality of independence—is maintained and perpetuated by "the [replicant] elites that have shaped [and continue to shape] the new South Africa."[119] In this situation, the rather harsh memories of the colonial past are comparatively deemed. As Patrick Bond tells us, "the number of black people who believe life was better under the apartheid regime is growing."[120] South Africa is presently suffering what most of Africa has endured since the 1960s, a postcolonial condition that fosters nostalgia for the colonial era.

As in the past, when it utilized traditional chiefs to implement its policies of indirect rule, the West—and specifically the United States—is directly involved in this situation.[121] In its current politico-military strategies (e.g., AFRICOM [United States Africa Command]), the United States has outlined a militarized program of indirect rule. As Vice Admiral Robert Moeller unabashedly pointed out, in an article published in 2010,

> Let there be no mistake. AFRICOM's job is to protect American lives and promote American interests. That is what nations and militaries do. But we also have found that our own national interest in a stable and prosperous Africa is shared strongly by *our partners*. By working together, we can pursue our shared interests more effectively.[122]

As in the past (Haile Selassie, Mobutu, etc.,), the United States is to continue utilizing junior "partners" in the pursuit of "shared interests." But this time around it will do so much "more effectively." As Daniel Volman explains, according to Moeller's presentation, at a 2008 AFRICOM conference,

> [P]rotecting "the free flow of natural resources from Africa to the global market" was one of AFRICOM's "guiding principles" and [Moeller] specifically cited "oil disruption," "terrorism," and the "growing influence" of China as major "challenges" to U.S. interests in Africa. And of course Washington would prefer that selected friendly regimes take the lead in meeting these objectives, so that the United States can avoid direct military involvement in Africa . . . at a time when the U.S. military is so deeply committed to the wars in Iraq and Afghanistan, and preparing for possible attacks on Iran.[123]

This is indirect rule at its best—in effect, the re-colonization of Africa. Or, as Vattimo puts it,

> [T]he United States of Bush . . . follows today . . . in its politico-military strategies (occupation of territories as in Iraq)—the most traditional politics, those of the European states in the age of colonialism.[124]

One need only consult chapter 8 of President Barack Obama's best seller *The Audacity of Hope* to realize that this stance is not limited to Mr. Bush.[125] At the same time, the United States goes on and on about corruption, democracy, and the lack of good governance.[126] And, in this guise, effectively bolsters Africa's replicant ruling strata (i.e., "our partners").

What Aimé Césaire affirmed of Europe can be said of the United States. Its motives are transparent. "[I]t takes refuge in a hypocrisy that much more odious since it has a lesser chance to deceive."[127] Political legitimacy, in this context, depends on safeguarding U.S./Western interest. It is anchored on a willing acceptance of U.S. military-financial backing serving, as a local gendarme, in America's global gendarmerie[128]—against this kind of independence Africa has to secure itself.

VII

In view of all of the above, and beyond the expulsion of "the white man," Africa has to create the context and institute the concrete conditions—the "pre-phase"[129]—of a meaningful independence. Unlike the West, Africa experienced modernity not as the result of an internal process of historical transformation but of conquest. This, as we noted earlier with Nyerere, was nothing more than the insertion of Africa into Europe's colonial economy. Our postcolonial present, in order to measure up to what it names, has to institute a reversal of this process. It has to create a practice of economic transformation that is democratically controlled (i.e., directed, invested in, and managed) at the grassroots level. A process responsive to the needs of those engaged in it and built on the precept that mindless "imitation is suicide."[130] To be true to what it claims, our postcolonial present has to be a period of time in which independence is consolidated by the imaginative and self-reliant modernization of the formerly colonized territory, aimed at its economic viability and the establishment of participatory forms of democratic self-rule.[131]

On this point, Thomas McCarthy writes, "The question now for societies all over the world is not whether or not to modernize, but which forms of modernity to develop, in light of structural constraints and pressures emanating from the global [neo-imperial] system."[132] But, really, are there preestablished "forms of modernity" from which one "chooses"? Is it not much more a "question" of societies, devastated by European conquest, striving to recover and reclaim their differing histories? Is it not much more a question of instituting viable and sustainable economic strategies/arrangements, suited to their varied efforts at democratic self-rule, while fending off the constant "pressures emanating from the global system"?

It is imperative to keep in mind, furthermore, that these "pressures emanating from the global system" are *not* impediments or "structural constraints" imposed by concrete conditions (i.e., difficulties inherent in any process of self-transformation) but by the deliberate policies of the West executed, on its behalf, by the replicant African ruling strata: the likes of Senghor, Houphouet-Boigny, Banda, Haile Selassie, Mobutu, and so on. The "successors" of the colonial era, "who could be trusted to share" the values of the West and "be attentive to . . . [its] . . . interests."[133] In the words of Césaire, "a special class between"[134] the "global system" and those it exploits.

As if to confirm Césaire's words, Secretary of State Henry Kissinger, in a 1970 memo on President Salvador Allende to President Richard Nixon, states,

> The example of a successful elected Marxist government in Chile would surely have an impact on—and even precedent value for—other parts of the world, especially in Italy; the imitative spread of similar phenomena elsewhere would in turn significantly affect the world balance and our position in it.

After citing the above, Naomi Klein remarks, "In other words, Allende needed to be taken out before his democratic third way spread."[135] What is at stake, then, is not "which forms of modernity" to choose from, but how best to institute popular democratic forms of modernization, while fending off the violent interference and/or intervention of our former colonizers.

In this regard—the incessant needs of global capital—the drive for profits, sustained by asymmetrical relations, necessarily opposes the self-reliant (political and economic) makeover of the formerly colonized world. This "makeover" is in inverse relation to and necessarily threatens the established interests of the West. These are interests focused on maintaining global cheap labor, unrestricted access to resources and markets, the free flow and repatriation of capital and, in general, a "friendly" environ for capital and its ventures. For it is in this manner that the hierarchically structured global capitalist order reproduces itself. And so, overtly and/or covertly (under many and differing guises), Western policies, the policies of our former colonizers, go on undermining efforts at economic independence and participatory forms of democratic self-rule.[136]

Forms of democratic self-rule that are transparent and that utilize procedures and methods grounded in the specifics of our differing histories. Forms of self-rule focused not merely on formal political democracy,[137] but a holistic approach aimed at the social, political, and economic empowerment of those who have taken charge of their own political affairs. The formerly colonized cannot allow themselves to be held hostage by the threat of foreign—direct or indirect—intervention.[138] In conjunction with economic self-transformation, the concrete political self-institution of the formerly colonized has to find ways of establishing itself.

The *independent* self-expression of the political will of those who made independence possible—rural and urban ordinary folk (i.e., peasants, nomads, workers, shopkeepers, students, maids, servants, etc., those whose children swelled the ranks of the liberation army and/or the membership of the political movements that brought about independence)—is the true measure of this transformation. Those in control of the bureaucracy, the post-colonial state apparatus (i.e., the leadership and cadres of the liberation army and/or the political movement that confronted colonialism and is now the government), cannot allow themselves to be held hostage to the threat of intervention and—in fear of this threat—suffocate and effectively hold-back the will, *the political self-expression*, of the formerly colonized. For this is to concede defeat!

In spite of this—very real—threat, the liberation movement in power has to activate and institute the concrete forms of democratic self-rule that actuated and motivated the struggle for independence. The exploration and thematic articulation of this politico-economic project, on the level of concepts and ideas, is the task of African philosophy. All this means probing, searching, questioning, and undermining the hegemony that binds us to the colonial past, in tandem with seeking the sense and meaning of independence. And, in this process, conceptually articulating the "pre-phase" needed to concretely consummate its possibility. For, as Said has observed,

> to be an independent postcolonial Arab, or black [African], or Indonesian is not a program, nor a process, nor a vision. It is no more than a convenient starting point from which the real work, the hard work, might begin.[139]

This "convenient starting point" was taken as the final moment of Africa reclaiming itself. The subsequent "real work, the hard work" of socio-economic-political restructuring and rethinking the character and substance of independence was never undertaken. And yet, the end of foreign rule ought to have unleashed—to the measure of independence—the transfiguration of the human-material reality that had become "independent." This is indispensable if we are *not* to remain "formerly colonized" *thingified beings*—like "crabs in a basket" (note 103)—falling over each other, in replicant imitation of the West.

On the level of ideas and concepts, this "real work" is the critique of the Occidental tradition in tandem with a sifting and exploring of traditions—European and African—aimed at a new synthesis: "a selective analysis of the values of the culture within the framework"[140] of contemporary exigencies. In this, our efforts would be focused on digging deep into our hybrid heritage and excavating—out of our needs and contemporary concerns—the possibilities of our future entombed by the stasis of the present. It is in confronting this entombment, in this interplay of seeking a viable future out of our hybrid heritage, that we can tangibly reclaim the lost possibilities of our postcolonial present.

The aim in all of this is not to reject the West. Nor is it merely to embrace our indigenousness. Our objective is to cultivate a synthesis and, in doing so, displace the ideas and concepts—the prejudices and presuppositions (i.e., "the epistemology of imperialism") in and through which Western hegemony holds us captive. Our reflections will thus not be oriented by "Africanité," à la Senghor, but by the *practical pragmatic utility* of the resources of our heritage. In this our efforts would be focused on the sense and meaning, in the way of implementing popular democratic forms of governance, in and out of our various hybrid heritages.

In and out of these legacies to invent the politico-economic forms of organization whose establishment would constitute the re-insertion of Africa—into the modern world—on its own terms, this is our task. As the Angolan philosopher Afonso Mário Ucuassapi puts it,

> Doing philosophy [Fare filosofia] means interrogating one's own historical temporality, in terms of a particularity that touches us; not to conceptualize anymore our political life, our democracy and our institutions as imitations of the Occident, but to invent a democracy to the measure of our peoples, in keeping with their reality.[141]

In this regard, Kwame Gyekye dedicates the last chapter of his book *Tradition and Modernity* to a discussion of similar concerns, in the present context of Africa, and manages to cover many interesting issues/topics without ever engaging the central question of how modernization, in Africa, has been nothing more than a subjugated mimicry of the West. But isn't this the central problem of modernity in Africa? For, as Thomas S. Kuhn tells us, questions in the realm of theory (i.e., problems, themes, concerns, etc.,) are not "had for the asking,"[142] they arise out of the subject matter itself—that which presents itself for thought and/or questioning.

VIII

Just as, in the past, Christianity and civilization served the purposes of conquest and colonialism, in like manner, today "good-governance," "global/regional stability," "food aid," "development aid," "modernization," "economic growth," "the fight against terrorism," "human rights," "women's rights," "the rights of minorities," "democracy," "the rule of law," and so on are the *code-words* implicitly linked to the setup in and through which the West holds us captive.[143] The challenge for African philosophy is to think beyond these snares.

We, those of us engaged in the practice of African philosophy, have to reimagine the democratic ideals that fueled the political and armed struggles for independence in and out of the context of the present and, in doing so, formulate the concepts and ideas that can help actuate them. The challenge is to articulate counter-discourses aimed at novel ways of comprehending and arranging social-political existence.[144] We have to be able to contest the established hegemony while inventing (i.e., conceptualizing) the forms of a truly postcolonial democratic existence that emerges out of the real concerns masked by the code-words of the West.

To "invent" here means to come upon—to discover from within the limits and needs of the present—the way, or ways, for consolidating our independence. Like scientists engaged in "extraordinary science," our only concern will thus be to see "what works," what can help us overcome our postcolonial stasis: the replicant perpetuation of colonial "chosification."[145] In this regard, the only thing that we can say categorically, borrowing the words of the young Marx is that, "we do not anticipate" the future "with our dogmas" but rather "attempt to discover the new world through the critique of the old."[146] Indeed, to reimagine—invent, rediscover, retrieve—the lost possibilities that were, at one time, the raison d'être of the independence struggle: this is the task of contemporary African philosophy. Our stance will thus be a self-reliant and critical posture: a perspective that tangibly confronts its situation with its own arsenal of conceptual tools and theoretic frameworks.[147]

The importance of all of this derives from the understanding that, at the end of the day, what really matters in the practice of African philosophy is the character of the lived existence we strive toward and help to bring about. For as Herbert Marcuse noted, not so long ago, our postcolonial condition—our present,

> is not the old colonialism and imperialism (although in some aspects, the contrast has been overdrawn: [for] there is little essential difference between a direct government by the metropolitan power, and a native government which functions only by grace of a metropolitan power). The objective rationale for the global struggle is not the need for immediate capital export, resources, [or] surplus exploitation. It is rather the danger of subversion of the established hierarchy of Master and Servant, Top and Bottom, a hierarchy which has created and sustained the have-nations, Capitalist *and* Communist.[148]

At present we need not worry about "actually existing socialism,"[149] the fading memory of a mangled vision. What remains is the capitalist West, the "have-nations," which under the guise of always changing new code-words aim to keep this "hierarchy of Master and Servant, Top and Bottom" in place and in perpetuity. It is the hegemony of this "hierarchy" that needs to be confronted, in our efforts to retrieve our ideals and actuate their possibility.

The challenge for African philosophy (i.e., for that discourse that incessantly assesses and reassess itself in light of "all that which happens in human reality" and goes on, and on, about "how can you still say this?") is to persuasively think through the questioning of this "hierarchy," the questioning of the prejudices and presuppositions (i.e., the structuring substance of replicant Africa) that sustain the hegemonic hold the West has over us. Short of this, the discourse of African philosophy will be "quelque chose d'extérieur au sérieux de la vie"[150] and nothing more. We now turn to the larger context, the contemporary philosophic state of affairs, in and out of which this project is to be engaged.

2

Continental and African Philosophy

Dialogue at a Distance

> Then one day the rumor spreads: a student has killed the English governor of the Indies, or: the Italians have been defeated at Dogali, or: the Boxers have exterminated the European missionaries; and then horror-stricken old Europe curses against the barbarians, against the uncivilized, and a new crusade is undertaken against those unfortunate people. And notice: the Europeans have had their own oppressors and have fought bloody struggles to liberate themselves and now they erect statues and marble memorials to their liberators, to their heroes, and they exalt to national religion the cult of those who died for the country. But don't say to Italians that the Austrians came to bring us civilization: even the marble columns would protest. We, of course, have gone forth to extend civilization, and in fact now those people love us and thank heaven for their fortune.
>
> —Antonio Gramsci[1]

> Another man's corpse seems to us like a log of wood.
>
> —Igbo proverb[2]

I

In 1957, the same year the Gold Coast secured its independence and appropriated the ancient name of Ghana as the designation for its newly won freedom, Emmanuel Levinas penned an article approvingly exploring Lucien Lévy-Bruhl's notion of "primitive mentality."[3] At the very moment when

Africa was commencing to rid itself of the political shackles that held it in subjection[4] it was tacitly, on the level of reflection and ideas, being penned into a subordinate status. For, indeed, as Levinas has jovially noted in friendly conversation with an interviewer, "I often say, though it's a dangerous thing to say publicly, that humanity consists of the Bible and the Greeks. All the rest can be translated: all the rest—all the exotic—is dance."[5]

And this by a philosopher whose philosophic reflections originate in and are focused on the theme of the "Other" (*l'autri*). A thematic grounded in the expressivity of the human *face* and in the *face* to *face* encounter of *the Other.* For, as Levinas puts it, "Free beings alone can be strangers to one another. Their freedom which is 'common' to them is [also] precisely what separates them."[6] This common freedom that also separates is, for Levinas, what calls for thinking—or *ought* to call for thinking. But his endorsement of Lévy-Bruhl and his insistence that "humanity consists" of only "the Bible and the Greeks" must mean—what else could it mean?—that this concern, of and for the Other, is limited solely and only to Europe and the West.

For, as is well known, Lévy-Bruhl's views on the mentality of "primitives," which toward the end of his life he repudiated, had nothing to do with "their freedom." The Other—the "primitive," in Lévy-Bruhl's rather myopic conception—is effectively effaced in her/his freedom and encased or en-framed in a distinctiveness that excludes him/her from the common universe of human existence. Levinas does not see that the horrors of World War II, which affected him on a personal level, originate in a brutality grounded in such exclusion, first visited upon the colonized as "primitive."[7] He does not see what Aimé Césaire had emphatically observed in 1955 that, before being its victim, Europe was the effectual accomplice of this brutality.[8] And so, for Levinas,

> Despite the end of Europocentrism [sic], disqualified by so many horrors, I believe in the eminence of the human face expressed in Greek Letters and in our own, which owe the Greeks everything. It is thanks to them that our history makes us ashamed. There is a participation in Holy Scripture in the national literatures [of Europe], in . . . the Book of Books, which all the Letters of the world awaited or upon which they comment. The Holy Scriptures do not signify through the dogmatic tale of their supernatural or sacred origin, but through the expression of *the face of the other man* that they illuminate, before he gives himself a countenance or a pose.[9]

It does not occur to Levinas, in the above, expressed in a radio interview in 1982—the year of the Sabra and Shatila massacres—that the lived experience of "the other man," the non-European, in his/her encounter of the European face and the Holy Scriptures, has been a rather darkening experience of dehumanization. It does not occur to him that "the interhuman"[10] in this context is not a transcending, in the Other, toward God,[11] but an obliteration of this very relation. It does not occur to him that equating Christianity with civilization and paganism with savagery is a destabilizing equation that undermines the "freedom which is 'common'" to us all. That it has always resulted—in the Americas, in Africa, in Asia, in Australia, and in the islands of the Pacific—*not* in the fruitful contact of differing human experiences, but in reciprocal disfigurement: That it embitters and sours the "countenance or . . . pose" of each Other.[12]

And so, unmindful of all of the above, Levinas lightheartedly explains, in another interview, "Europe, that's the Bible and the Greeks,"[13] and "Everything else in the world must be *included* in this. I do not have any nostalgia for the exotic. For me Europe is central."[14] Here, it has to be noted, Levinas is simply endorsing the age-old hubris of the Occident that sees itself as the sum and substance of all that has value in humanity. This is a view which is the sine qua non of colonialist thinking.[15]

As noted in the last chapter, writing in 1945, at the height[16] of the colonial era, Temples expressed the classic formulation of this view in stating that it is "our civilizing mission alone" that "can justify" the "occupation of the lands of uncivilized peoples."[17] This "mission" privileges the West and gives it the right and duty to subjugate and "civilize." In this it presupposes, as its epistemic underpinning, a hierarchical ordering of humankind (i.e., a knowledge) that places "the highest or Caucasian"[18] at the summit in a gradation that descends via "the various races"[19] to "the ape."[20] This "knowledge," grounded on "the epistemology of imperialism" (see chapter 1, note 92), validates Temples and the colonial project. But isn't it also the tacit underpinning of Levinas's remarks?[21]

According to Temples and Levinas, then, that which is labeled "uncivilized" or "exotic" as alien to humanity proper—"the Bible and the Greeks"—has to be shaped and molded in the image of Europe. It has to be "civilized" or "included," superseded and preserved or, in the language of the day, "assimilated." This is how James Baldwin, writing in 1959, describes this rather sinister practice of "inclusion":

> Assimilation was . . . but another name for the very special brand of relations between human beings which had been imposed by colonialism. These relations demanded that the individual, torn from the context to which he owed his identity, should replace his habits of feeling, thinking, and acting by another set of habits which belonged to the strangers who dominated him.[22]

Annul the native and conserve, or rescue, the human in the native. In other words, salvage the human "essence" incased in the "husk" of an inferior culture. This is the double action, grounded on a defunct metaphysics,[23] that Temples refers to as "our civilizing mission," which is—in substance—the same as Levinas's view that "Everything else . . . must be included," or subsumed, within Europe.

Odd as it may seem, this is the candid and nonchalant view of Levinas, a philosopher who has himself suffered, in the tragedies that befell his family, the horrific effects of such racist labeling. And, as he himself tells us in 1990, five years before the end of his exceptionally prolific life,

> racism is not just opposed to such and such a particular point in Christian and liberal culture. It is not a particular dogma concerning democracy, parliamentary government, dictatorial regime[s], or religious politics that is in question. It is the very humanity of man.[24]

In other words, racism puts "in question . . . the very humanity of man." But then, when Levinas labels all that which is other than "the Bible and the Greeks" as "the exotic" and as having to be "included in this" (i.e., Europe) is he not putting "in question . . . the very humanity" of all that which lies beyond Europe? Is he not tacitly endorsing—in the name of "the Bible and the Greeks"—the violence and the fabrications that, since the fifteenth century, have validated the decimation of "All the rest"? Is he not repeating a gesture and—in substance—validating a stance that calls to mind the horrors of World War II?

II

These horrors, and the political shakeup of the colonized that they in part triggered, created the auspicious setting that made the idea of the European mission to civilize the world questionable. The colonized, in rejecting the old assumption of the Occidental mission to civilize, recommenced[25] the struggles that had defined their existence prior to the brutal "pacification campaigns" that sealed their subjection. And so, those whose humanity had been deemed to be devoid of history forced themselves into it.

As Basil Davidson has noted, after "1945 the colonial powers could still resist" the process of decolonization but "they could not stop it."[26] Thus, the direct domination of the globe, by Europe, had started to come undone.[27] Bit by bit, Africa, and the rest of the non-European world, secured its political independence. As Jean-Paul Sartre points out, in his preface to Frantz Fanon's *Les damnés de la terre*,

> Not so long ago, the earth numbered two thousand million inhabitants, five hundred million men, and one thousand five hundred million natives. The former had the World, the others only its use.[28]

The attainment of formal independence effectively reestablished Africa, and the formerly colonized world, within the confines of history. It instituted—beyond segregators and the segregated, colonizers and the colonized—a shared world of human existence. On a formal level it nullified the violent and odious distinction between "human beings" and "natives"—Western Man and the Primitives; or, in Levinas's rather crassly quaint formulation, the "Bible and the Greeks" and "All the rest."

By mid-twentieth century, Levinas notwithstanding, the belief or bias—the bigoted stance—that "the Bible and the Greeks" constitute humanity, and that, "[e]verything else in the world must be included in this" was beginning to crumble. Those who were to be trounced, subsumed, and preserved,[29] in rejecting[30] this inclusion or assimilation,[31] commenced to reclaim their history (i.e., their proper visage). They tangibly established the concrete conditions within which the Occident could no longer see them as "raw material" for a humanity, yet to be formed.

On this side of the Atlantic, as Baldwin writing in 1961 tells us, the "emergence of Africa"[32] had an electrifying effect which led to the political-existential situation in which "the American Negro can no longer, nor will he ever again, be controlled by white America's image of him."[33] In this regard it ought to be noted, at least in passing, that the shattering of this image was, in part, a concrete antecedent to developments that have made possible the election, and reelection, of an African-American president, in the dawning years of the twenty-first century.

Thus, despite shortcomings and contradictions, explored in chapter 1, the achievement of independence fulfilled a felt minimal need in the Black world. It established the historical visage of the formerly enslaved and colonized, engaged in bypassing the disfigurement imposed on them by Europe's conceited self-image.[34] It constituted a new *étape* from which more complex and protracted struggles could commence. It did so by reinserting Africa into history.[35] It reestablished Africa and the Black world, in general, within the compass of human historical existence from which the darker portion of humanity had been expelled by racist and colonial terror.[36] In this way a hybrid, or intermixed, world of shared existence has been tangibly instituted.

In view of all of the above, and what was said in chapter 1, we need now to ask the crucial question: What is the present philosophic standing of the *ideas* and *concepts* (i.e., the prejudices/prejudgments and presuppositions), that until recently sanctioned and authorized European supremacy and colonialism? And how is this related to what I have named the "dialogue at a distance" of Continental and African philosophy?[37]

III

Today, in the second decade of the twenty-first century, a great deal has changed and a much more encouraging situation prevails. Reflecting on the contemporary scene that defines the climate of critical self-awareness, for example, Charles Taylor, writing in 2002, at the dawn of our present century, states,

> The days are long gone when Europeans and other Westerners could consider their experience and culture as the norm towards which the whole of humanity was headed, so that the other could be understood as an earlier stage on the same road that they had trodden.[38]

In the same vein, Hans-Georg Gadamer in 2001 categorically affirms,

> "[W]e . . . need to accept our worldwide heritage not only in its otherness but also in recognizing the validity of the claims this larger heritage makes on us."[39]

These "claims" of a "larger heritage" grow stronger the more we come to see the odd notions of a "retarded" and an "advanced" humanity[40] as oddities of a myopic past, that of *The Age of Enlightenment* and the nineteenth-century colonial project, which globalized Europe in the belief that its heritage was coequal with the human heritage as such. Indeed, strange relics of a residual past, of a time in which Europe took itself to be humanity in toto. Nowadays *narrow-minded* is the term that best describes these views.

The present constructive understanding of the relation of the non-Western and Western world (Taylor) and the openness to our "worldwide heritage" (Gadamer) are themselves theoretic effects of political developments generated out of the protracted rebellion of the non-European world. These developments have instituted a global situation in which the idea of a *singular true history* of humankind has been rejected, its claim to validity having been surpassed. Indeed, as Gianni Vattimo has observed,

> history [la storia], after the end of colonialism and the dissolution of Eurocentric prejudices, does not have any more a unitary sense, it has been fractured into a number of stories [di storie] irreducible to a single guiding thread.[41]

The demise of colonialism thus makes possible rethinking the character of our common humanity. In fracturing the linear conception of history, it undermines the thinking and terminates the age in which violent colonial effacement—or the erasure of difference—was normative in intercultural or interhistorical relations. It constitutes and opens the way for the possibility of a shared and interdependent human existence.

What these noted thinkers—Taylor, Gadamer, and Vattimo—endorse, against the grain of Occidental traditions, is the variegated multiplicity of our shared existence. Thus, and concretely, using for this purpose the spokesmen of a hermeneutically self-aware and critical reason,[42] the splintered multiplicity of human existence reaffirms itself. Indeed, as Jacques Derrida has noted, "Deconstruction in general is an undertaking that many have considered, and rightly so, to be a gesture of suspicion with regard to all Eurocentrism."[43]

From the centrality of "Europe" as the "Bible and the Greeks," to "a number of stories" constitutive of a "larger heritage," which is "irreducible to a single guiding thread," to "a gesture of suspicion with regard to all Eurocentrism," we have come full circle back to the variegated multiplicity of human existence, prior to the modern age. This coming back, furthermore, this fracturing, is with a difference, that of the hybridity of the formerly colonized and colonizing worlds, the dialectically propitious effect of the dual experience and overcoming of formal colonialism.

And so, a long muted multiplicity, using for this very purpose the spokesmen of a reformed reason critical of *Enlightenment Reason*, in whose name it was suppressed, is presently reaffirming itself.[44] Analogously, developments that, in effect and retroactively, put in question the raisons d'être for this "enlightened" colonial suppression, have also come to occupy center stage in contemporary Continental philosophy. As Vattimo puts it,

> Philosophy follows paths that are not insulated or cut off from the social and political transformations of the West (since the end of metaphysics is unthinkable without the end of colonialism and Eurocentrism) and "discovers" that the meaning of the history of modernity is not progress towards a final perfection characterized by fullness, total transparency, and the presence finally realized of the essence of man and the world. It comes to see that the emancipation and liberation that mankind has always sought are attainable through a weakening of strong structures, a reduction of claims, and that implies, in general terms, that quality counts for more than quantity, that listening to what others have to say counts for more than measuring objects with precision.[45]

The above pronouncements indicate that, in principle, the days of Occidental arrogance and domination are passé. They indicate that the missionary stance, of converting heathens and civilizing savages, has become obsolete. Today, it rings hollow, just as at one time it commanded "enlightened" public opinion.

These pronouncements indicate that our contemporary world—that does not have any more formal empires on which the sun never sets—calls for and makes necessary, in view of our common survival, a stance of openness and a predisposition to seriously engage and cultivate shared values. They indicate that the belief that "humanity consists of the Bible and the Greeks" is merely a negative and narrow-minded unproductive prejudice[46] that *we*, humanity, can no longer afford. The kind of prejudice which, as Gadamer tells us, "it is the undeniable task of critical reason to overcome."[47] Openness to shared, viable, and livable possibilities, this seems to be the prevailing predisposition, the lived sensibility (i.e., the enabling/positive prejudice) of our postcolonial present.

And so, the "Eurocentric," "single guiding thread," to borrow Vattimo's words, with which the Occident had firmly bound the world, is de facto unraveling. The above pronouncements call for the hastening of this unraveling by the tangible articulation of de jure philosophic self-validations of our present situation. They call for the cultivation of "justified prejudices productive of knowledge"[48] in view of our current understanding that difference, variance, diversity, and so on are a common treasure-trove: values that preserve our shared humanity. In this sense, "the meaning of the history of modernity," as a "weakening of strong structures," is a resolute openness to a concrete predisposition for ongoing dialogue, a willingness to turn away from the missionary stance that takes its truth as *The Truth* that has to be globalized—by force, if need be. It is an embracing of our varied/variegated humanity as the possibility for a shared global future.[49]

To be sure, until recently, such a view regarding modernity and the attitudes articulated by Taylor, Gadamer, Vattimo, and Derrida were not acceptable in Continental philosophy. In fact, Levinas's remarks noted earlier express a kind of residual lingering nostalgia "for the good old days" when the Occident saw itself—and more important, was seen by Others—as the *True* gauge of all that has value in humanity; bygone days, not so long ago, when "measuring objects with precision" was all the craze. All this has now become stale and not in keeping with the Zeitgeist of our postcolonial world.

But, it ought to be remembered that, not so long ago, it was by clinging to "a single guiding thread"[50] that Kant, for example, could assert that the Occident "will probably give law, eventually to all the others."[51] And why, pray tell, should this be the case? Because, as Kant puts it, unlike animals, human beings need discipline (*Zucht*) in their tender years and cultural formation (*Bildung*) as they mature into adulthood; this is what completes their humanity. And, he adds, for good measure,

> We see this also among savage nations, who, though they may discharge functions for some time like Europeans, yet can never become accustomed to European manners. With them, however, it is not the noble love of freedom which Rousseau and others imagine, but a kind of barbarism—the animal, so to speak, not having yet developed its human nature.[52]

Today, such views which narcissistically equate humanity with "European manners" and non-European peoples with "savage nations" are no longer tolerable. It is no longer acceptable, in polite company, to refer to non-Europeans as "the animal."

And yet, Gadamer, the self-same Gadamer, who I quoted just now (note 39), urging us in 2001 to be open to "our worldwide heritage," writing in 1978, refers to Kant as "the greatest thinker of the idea of freedom who ever lived."[53] It is clear that we are here facing an inconsistency that is not, and yet needs to be, accounted for because philosophy is a mode of reflection that incessantly calibrates itself in view of "all that which happens in human reality."[54] And, as Gadamer is well aware, in our words and deeds, consistency and rigor are indispensable for such attunement.[55]

Kant, furthermore, does not stand alone in holding and expressing the kind of views quoted above. As indicated in chapter 1, a de-structive reading of the major figures of the Occidental tradition shows how this Eurocentric "single guiding thread" substantially structures their thinking and—as a core component—constitutes or frames the Otherness of the Other in terms of the Occident's own narcissistic universalizing of itself. For, in the eyes of the icons of the modern tradition, Europe is humanity and humanity is Europe. The Occident is both *model* and *instance!* This "double game" enshrines the "happenings" of European history as the *Truth* of humankind as such. And thus, beguiled by its own noble image of itself, Europe subjugates the globe.

That today major thinkers openly disavow this Eurocentric stance and endorse its critique means, among other things, that Continental philosophy has come to the sober and salubrious realization that its picture of reality is but *an image* in a mosaic constituted by the multiple variance of our shared existence. It also means that the de-structive and/or critical philosophizing of those of us who labor at or in the margins of this tradition has had a direct and/or indirect effect of deflating, or corroding, this stance. In contrast to the myopic past, this situation makes for promising possibilities.

IV

It seems, then, that there is a confluence, an unplanned fortuitous convergence of shared concerns in contemporary Continental and African/Africana philosophy. This flowing together, of critical concerns deriving from a shared global situation, constitutes the "dialogue at a distance" of these two areas of contemporary discourse. We need to further cultivate this dialogue. We must engage ourselves in shortening this distance in view of our "worldwide heritage" (note 39) and what it calls for.

We have here an opportunity, as never before, to foster and cultivate the promise of minimally alienated intercultural relations.[56] This situation offers us the possibility of engaging concerns deriving from a shared global historicity variedly refracted by our differing positions and attitudes in the spectrum of contemporary intellectual work. In my view, this is a key asset of our shared and variegated postcolonial heritage.

To be sure, beyond the realm of European and African philosophizing, this promising theoretic situation of the present, avowed by the above noted Continental philosophers and which is the reflective space in and out of which African philosophy articulates itself, was created—when all is said and done—by the armed and political struggles of the formerly colonized. The critically self-aware stance of prominent Continental philosophers and the de-structive/critical efforts of African/Africana philosophers are both auspicious theoretic effects of the struggle against—and the final demise of—unmitigated Western dominance. As Vattimo has noted,

> Many and more diverse things have come to pass: the "primitive" peoples, labeled as such, [and] colonized by the Europeans in the name of the right of "superior" and more evolved civilization [to colonize], have rebelled and rendered problematic de facto a unitary centralized history.[57]

This is what has made it possible for non-European voices in the field of philosophy, as in many other fields, to become audible. In reclaiming their historic visage, differing peoples, who were deemed to be without one, gave voice to and manifested the varied aspects of the actuality of being human.[58] By freeing themselves they brought about a new understanding of the character of our shared existence. In effect, they established the political-ethical context within which variance and multiplicity have become the norm.

The interplay of this multiplicity, which constitutes our present world, requires a rethinking of our shared—unequal—past. For, the fracturing of "a unitary centralized history," the end of the colonial empires of Europe, when looked at from the Other side (i.e., the side of the newly sovereign peoples), is the reestablishment of our differing humanity: a diversity the West once cohabited along with the rest of *us*. This splintering of "a unitary centralized history," the demise of the inglorious empires of Europe, gives us a glimpse of the *face* of the Other. It resurrects the variance that is our shared world by reclaiming the "*being-history*"[59] of the formerly colonized. It thus makes room for the visage of the Other by curtailing/bypassing Euro-centrism. Ultimately this tangible reaffirmation of multiplicity is the most important net gain of our postcolonial present.

It is the ontic historico-political lived reaffirmation of the ontological truth that, "Existence is revealed in many ways."[60] In rejecting colonization and its violent assimilationist project (i.e., "a unitary centralized history") what is rejected, in effect, is the claim of a singular humanity; what is affirmed is the varied ways in which *human being* reveals itself. This ontological truth of what it means to *be* human necessitates, on the ontic-political level, a reciprocal acknowledgment of variance and difference. In this recognition of each in the Other, of a similarity in being dissimilar—in this variedness—conflict can be avoided only by curtailing the relative partiality (for itself) of each of the components of this lived variedness. In other words, as Vattimo puts it,

> The "other" cultures are finding their voice and asserting themselves as autonomous visions of reality, with which Europeans have to start a dialogue, which they can no longer simply "civilize" or "convert."[61]

The words *civilize* and *convert*, which Vattimo places in double quotation marks for emphasis, describe the violent operations through which the European colonizing venture nullified the Otherness of the differing peoples it conquered and whose existence, in some cases, it succeeded in eradicating completely and in others it substantially hybridized. This is the dialectic of global historical existence, with all of its negativity, the destruction of peoples and cultures and also, with all of its positive possibilities, the concurrent formation/creation of new peoples and cultures.[62]

Thus, within the discourse of contemporary Continental philosophy, a new awareness and recognition has come to the fore regarding the historicity of the Occident and its negative violent effects on the rest of the globe. This recognition is not, and it should not be, a trite atonement for past "sins." Rather, it should see and constitute itself as the opening of a possibility for the West to seriously engage itself on an equal footing with all the Other cultural-historical totalities that comprise our world; the differing facets of our intertwined heritages; the multiple visages that compose the historical actuality of our existence. This is what Vattimo is pointing to when highlighting the possibility of "start[ing] a dialogue"[63] between and among former colonizers and colonized. This, too, is what Gadamer—in spite of his inconsistency—affirms when he says that we need to recognize "the validity of the claims this larger heritage makes on us" (note 39).

For, indeed, this "larger heritage" is largely that of the formerly colonized, that of "most of the earth" which by "the beginning of World War One, Europe and America held . . . in some form of subjugation."[64] And, the "validity of the claims," that still need serious consideration, are of those who until recently were subject peoples. In all of this, it seems that, *grosso modo*, Continental philosophy is coming to the welcome realization that "It is a terrible, an inexorable, law that one cannot deny the humanity of another without diminishing one's own; in the face of one's victim one sees oneself."[65]

V

Now, as Derrida has emphatically noted, all of the above should not be and is not aimed at "condemning Europe as if it were but the scene of its crimes."[66] Europe, the West in general, is a great deal more than "the scene of its crimes." Indeed, as Fanon remarked, in the early years of the anticolonial struggle, "This colossal task which consists of reintroducing humanity into the world" can be brought about only with the "decisive help of the European masses."[67] But, for this to be possible, the European peoples must "decide to awaken" and "cease playing the irresponsible game of sleeping beauty."[68] The burden of the past should not unstill them.[69]

In the past "on colonial issues [sur les problèmes coloniaux]" they took the "positions of our common masters."[70] To "awaken," here means, to go beyond the residual past and heed the call of our shared "larger heritage." To meaningfully accept the claims of this Other humanity, as part of "our worldwide heritage." To be open to and receptive of this humanity—beyond its Otherness—to accept, in other words, the enlargement and enrichment of our shared human existence/heritage.

It means that the West has to come to terms with itself and see that, it, itself, is not the limit of what it means to be human. It means that it accedes to, and accepts the demise of the European empire of the mind and tangibly welcomes the counter-discourse of a variegated humanity. As noted above—in contrast to Levinas—Taylor, Gadamer, and Vattimo are open to such a possibility and Derrida enlists the perspective attached to his name, and developed out of his work, to this end. In this context, the Occident would become, once more, an interlocutor among equal interlocutors. In refusing to see itself in the "face" of its "victim[s]," the West/Europe would open itself up to the possibility of coexistence in deference to our shared but differing ek-sistence. In this regard Philippe Nemo's bunkering[71] of the West, in a defensive stance, against all that which is considered to be beyond it is a dangerous throwback to bygone days, to a past when the West—blinded by hubris—constituted its humanity in the denial of its "victim['s]."

What has to be noted in all of the above is that what is possibly coming to pass is the dialectical reinstatement, on a more concrete level, of the multiple voices that constituted our shared humanity prior to the coming of the modern age. For it ought to be remembered that in the days of Marco Polo and/or the Crusades, our globe was multiple worlds in war and/or peace and in a constant process of cross-fertilization.[72] What is possibly coming to pass is a return of this multiple existence, in full recognition that this is the more suitable condition for our mutually dependent, and differing, humanity. A differing dependent humanity, on both the individual and collective level: a limited and dependent existence defined by its variegated finitude.

This is what Aimé Césaire means when he states, "My conception of the universal is that of a universal rich with all that is particular, rich with all the particulars, the deepening and coexistence of all the particulars."[73] For "tout le particulier" in all of their limitedness, possibilities, specificity, dependence, and finitude are the concrete actualities of our shared and yet differing humanity. A postcolonial globe constituted by variance in deference (i.e., a totality of particulars), a perspectival world keenly and concretely aware of its perspectival-ness, a world lived in differing interpretations of a shared existence, akin in being different.[74]

African philosophy is thus a focal point, and a situated source of dialogue, a concrete component of this multi-vocal dialogical state of affairs, the voice of a specific historical-cultural *particulier*. It is the philosophic voice of the formerly colonized that seeks "coexistence" focused on shared venues and reciprocal concerns. Putting colonialism behind us—and as a tangible effect of this putting behind—it is high time to explore our lived circumstances aimed at bettering our mutual earthly condition.

VI

The colonial empires, in receding into the dead-past, have left behind a multitude of cultures and histories that, fraught with all kinds of difficulties, are in the protracted process of forming a new global community. This situation harbors within itself, as a core organic component, aspects of the European heritage, imposed at one time, which have now become indispensable to this process of self-formation. For, what is left, after the end of colonialism, is a hybridized world that in rejecting colonialism is, at the same time, keenly aware and critical of its own indigenous pre-colonial past.[75]

Africa hopes to consolidate its regained freedom out of a critique and reassessment of its own indigenous past and its more recent colonial experience. In both directions what we have is not mere rejection, but the critical sifting/sieving of what can be beneficial for enhancing the possibilities of our shared world. In this effort, the heritage of modern Europe and that of the African indigenous past have much to offer.[76] For, in spite of failings and frustrations (explored in chapter 1), what struggles to reinstate itself, after the end of colonialism, is *not* pre-colonial Africa—"a radical Otherness"[77]—but what Fanon hoped for and referred to as "Cette Afrique à venire."[78]

> [A]n auto-centric Africa having in itself [elle-même] its centers of conception, of decision and of realization for the totality of its spheres of essential activity: political, economic, and spiritual [cultural]: a fraternal Africa respectful of this same principle of auto-centration [d'auto-centration] as regards its own institutions and those of other peoples.[79]

In reclaiming itself in "the totality of its spheres of essential activity," Africa can do so, as evinced by the political stance of its most noted leaders—Nkrumah, Nasser, Cabral, Nyerere, Lumumba, Biko, and others—not in conflict, or subservience, but in tangible efforts at cooperation with the rest of the globe.[80]

Indeed, the demise of colonialism has de facto opened up a situation in which the words of Fanon—"For Europe, for ourselves and for humanity, comrades, we must make a new skin, develop a new thinking, attempt to put afoot a new humanity"[81]—could possibly be actualized. For what these words call for is the de jure acceptance of the hybrid de facto multiplicity of our present. The practical and meaningful recognition and concrete acceptance of "the claims" our shared "larger heritage makes on us" all.

VII

In view of all of the above, the confluence of concerns that constitute what I have named the "dialogue at a distance" of Continental and African philosophy needs to be further cultivated and the distance shortened. For what African/Africana philosophy questions, from "the Other side," is the same metaphysics whose critique is now a cornerstone of the current discourse of Continental philosophy. As Vattimo puts it,

> That which we have learnt, from Heidegger, but also first, from Nietzsche, to call metaphysics is none other than the principle of authority that pretends [pretende] to legitimate itself with the "objectivity" and the rationality of its own theses.[82]

The critical deflation of this self-referential authority, the de-structive querying of its pretense, of its narcissistic[83] metaphysics—the theoretic linchpin of colonialism and racism—is also a central preoccupation, the critique of Eurocentrism, of African/Africana philosophy. For, as argued above, the end of colonialism calls for a re-thinking of the pretense (i.e., ideas and concepts, the prejudices and presuppositions) that *authorized* its practice. Or, as Derrida puts it, from "the Other side,"

> What I call 'deconstruction,' even when it is directed toward something from Europe [i.e., Eurocentrism], is European; it is a product of Europe, a relation of Europe to itself as an experience of radical alterity. Since the time of the Enlightenment, Europe has undertaken a perpetual self-critique, and in this perfectible heritage there is a chance for a future."[84]

I hope it is clear, from all that has been said thus far, that what I have proposed in this chapter, as in the book as a whole, is the furthering of this "perfectible heritage," not merely as European but, as the patrimony of a common hybrid humanity, as *our* "chance for a future." For Europe, as I am sure Derrida would willingly concede, became Europe—this vibrant and dynamic site of "a perpetual self-critique"—not in isolation but in and through an ongoing and incessant interaction with all the rest of *us*.

From both sides, then, what we need to cultivate in our shared heritage is this enabling contact, but this time around focused on dialogical and peaceful venues. For, as Gadamer reminds us, "Only through others do we gain true knowledge of ourselves."[85] It is this which fosters a reciprocal and "perpetual self-critique." And, in and through this critique, "Precisely through our finitude, the particularity of our being, which is evident even in the variety of languages, the infinite dialogue is opened in the direction of *the truth that we are*."[86] But, as we noted earlier, isn't this what Césaire is also calling for with his conception of "a universal rich with all that is particular, rich with all the particulars, the deepening and coexistence of all the particulars"?[87] Isn't this dialogical and reciprocal enrichment of "tout le particulier" indeed "the truth that we are"? And, isn't this what Fanon is also calling for when he states, "For Europe, for ourselves and for humanity . . . we must make a new skin . . . attempt to put afoot a new humanity."[88]

All of the above follows from the understanding that the end of colonialism calls for a critical debunking of the metaphysics—the ideas and concepts—that, for so long, sanctioned its practice. The remarks of Taylor, Gadamer, Vattimo, and Derrida which engaged us throughout this chapter are themselves effects of this critique that need to be further developed and expanded. Thus, those of us engaged in African philosophy need to fan these flames, far and wide. We need to become arsonists of the Idee![89]

Fires, as forestry experts tell us, have a beneficial effect in the economy of nature: they clear the ground for new and more vigorous growth. In this clearing, in this making room for new growth, "The challenge is to be able to acknowledge the humanity of their way, while still being able to live ours."[90] To recognize, in other words, the acuity of the Igbo proverb, that "another man's corpse" might *seem to be, but is not* "a log of wood."[91] This is what is at stake in the ongoing effort to shorten the "distance" in the "dialogue" between Continental and African/Africana philosophy—consciously sharing analogous concerns out of differing and yet interlaced thematic engagements.

VIII

In this spirit and manner, in the second half of this book I will explore aspects of the thinking of Kant, Gadamer, Heidegger, and Marx in relation to concerns focused on postcolonial Africa. The intent is to suggest ways—utilizing these thinkers—toward ameliorating our shared existence and contribute towards the enlargement of our hybrid heritage. And, in so doing, fuel further the timely and worthwhile project of shortening the distance in the dialogue between Continental and African philosophy, in engaging the concerns of our shared postcolonial world. Indeed, this project is itself grounded in and originates out of the lived experience of our postcolonial condition, whose core concerns it hopes to articulate and tangibly tackle on the level of ideas and concepts.

Part II

Encounters

3

Post-9/11, Perpetual Peace?

A Reading of Immanuel Kant[1]

In essence, we are headed directly toward a global crisis.

—Hans-Georg Gadamer[2]

I

In the introduction to the *Basic Writings of Kant*, published in 2001, Allen W. Wood affirms that Kant's *Perpetual Peace*, originally published in 1795, is "the chief statement by a major figure in the history of philosophy that addresses the issues of war, peace, and international relations that have been central concerns of humanity during the two centuries since it was written."[3] Indeed, *Perpetual Peace*—in a very direct and focused manner—speaks to the central concerns of international relations that have confounded, and still perplex, humanity. In the second decade of the twenty-first century an exploration of this text should be beneficial not only for understanding Kant's international political perspective but also, and more important, for grasping the sense and character of our postcolonial present.

In this chapter, I will explore Kant's text in view of the unpredictable global situation that prevails since September 11, 2001. In this regard, the Chilean disaster of September 11, 1973, which claimed the life of President Salvador Allende and the lives of thousands of citizens of democratic Chile, should also be kept in mind. For, both of these cataclysmic events were brought about by fanatical unlawful forces fixated on brutally imposing their political will—by terror—on the international community.[4]

My aim, in all of this, is to see if Kant's stance in international relations makes possible avenues for overcoming the dangers of the present or, *au contraire*, gives philosophic succor to the very forces that are responsible for our present predicament. Kant's enlightened "good intentions" notwithstanding, it is necessary, if one is to take him seriously, to critically explore this question and to scrutinize that which Wood and other liberals[5] take for granted. For, in philosophy as in life, "good intentions," no matter how enlightened, do not amount to much if they exacerbate the very problems they seek to overcome. It is in this spirit then that I will engage Kant's *Perpetual Peace* by pointedly confronting it with the question, Is it helpful in the present situation or does it compound, by philosophically authorizing the imperious attitude of major powers, the very dangers it purports to overcome?

In this regard, it has to be emphasized that Kant was himself an ardent advocate of critical work along these lines. Indeed the stance of critique, as the proper temperament of philosophy, is one of his most enduring contributions to the modern Western tradition. The hope is thus to emulate Kant in furthering critique and, to that of pure and practical reason and the critique of judgment, add a modest contribution toward articulating a much less pure—in fact a rather worldly—critique of our Janus-faced post-9/11 world of international relations.[6] And so, in what follows, I will explore pivotal sections of Kant's *Perpetual Peace* in light of what I take to be crucial concerns, past and present, in international political affairs.[7]

II

In the "Second Definitive Article for a Perpetual Peace," titled "The Law of Nations Shall be Founded on a Federation of Free States," Kant considers systematically the possible way in which such "a federation" can be brought about. He begins by noting that nations, unlike individuals, cannot be brought under the rule of one state for this would violate the freedom of each and "many nations in one state would then constitute only one nation."[8] As Kant correctly points out, what is at stake here is the "rights of nations against each other so far as they are distinct states and not amalgamated into one."[9] This, then, is what he approvingly refers to as "a league of nations"[10] that relate to each other in a non-bellicose manner.

As things stand now, "each [state] is a judge of its own case" and so "war alone is their way of bringing suit."[11] In other words, in any confrontation or conflict, each state is concerned only with itself and does not see, in its practical-political conduct, that each other state stands in the same relation that it, itself, occupies vis-à-vis the aggregate of states within which it exists as a sovereignty, a particular state. And yet, says Kant, in spite of this awful situation and practice,

> the homage which each state pays (at least in words) to the concept of law proves that there is *slumbering in man* an even *greater moral disposition* to become master of the evil principle in himself (which he cannot disclaim) and to *hope* for the same from [all the] others.[12]

What Kant aims at is a theoretical elucidation of the framework in which this "greater moral disposition" of humanity could possibly be actualized. "Otherwise" says Kant "the word 'law' would never be pronounced by states which wish to war upon one another; it would be used only ironically."[13] His intent is to avert this calamitous irony and to cultivate the ground for the possibility that "man" will "become master of the evil principle in himself" and "hope for the same from others." Thus, "a league of nations" is to be the incarnation of the "greater moral disposition" that is "slumbering in man." Kant's aim is to articulate the way this "greater moral disposition" can be awakened, and tangibly instituted, as the ground for inter-state relations. He wants to concretely ground this "hope" of humanity, which humanity has of itself.[14]

For "a federation" or "a league of nations," which Kant also refers to as "a league of peace," is different from a "treaty of peace" for such a treaty ends "only one war" in contrast to "a league of peace" which would end "all wars forever."[15] This, furthermore, does not require that "states in league" should "submit to civil laws and their compulsion, as men in a state of nature must submit."[16] The league is not to be a "dominion" or a central authority. Unlike "men in a state of nature" who exit, the given conditions of nature, only by submitting to "civil laws," the league is to be an external interstate regulatory organization focused on the "maintenance and security of the freedom"[17] of each of the states which, in aggregate, constitute the actuality of the "league." In other words, the "league" protects the freedom of each by thwarting the possible aggressiveness of a strong state or a combination thereof.

Kant next considers the "practicability (objective reality) of this idea of federation."[18] In view of the very careful way in which he insists on the freedom of each state, in the "federation" or "league," it is clear that he has in mind completely independent or sovereign states. But how is this interstate organization, which Kant hopes will "spread to all states and thus lead to perpetual peace,"[19] to be established? This is how he puts it:

> For if *fortune* directs that *a powerful* and *enlightened people* can make itself a republic, which by its nature must be inclined to perpetual peace, this gives a *fulcrum* to the federation with other states so that they may adhere to it and thus secure freedom

> under the idea of a law of nations. By more and more such associations, the federation may be gradually extended.[20]

But is it ever prudent to entrust all of this to "fortune"? For, as Aristotle has noted, "what is greatest and most beautiful [i.e., global harmony] to be left to chance [i.e., fortune] would be too discordant."[21] Moreover, as Machiavelli points out, "fortune," especially in politics, is seldom accidental. The fortunate is not the unplanned. As Machiavelli explains,

> I compare fortune to one of those dangerous rivers that, when . . . enraged, flood plains, destroy tress and buildings, move earth from one place and deposit it in another. Everyone flees before it, everyone gives way to its thrust, without being able to halt it in any way. But this does not mean that, when the river is not in flood, men are unable to take precautions, by means of dykes and dams, so that when it rises next time, it will either not overflow its banks or, if it does, its force will not be so uncontrollable or damaging. The same happens with fortune, which shows its power where no force has been organized to resist it, and therefore strikes in the places where it knows that no dykes or dams have been built to restrain it.[22]

As should be clear from the earlier citation (note 20), Kant is not taking any precautions against calamitous possibilities; he merely places himself in the position of a helpless victim. He writes as if "fortune" just befalls us! He fails to recognize, as Machiavelli points out, that *fortuna*—especially the unfortunate or bad fortune—comes to pass "where no force has been organized to resist it." And so, the sense of Heraclitus's judicious aphorism "Character for man is destiny"[23] escapes him, for the fortunate and/or the unfortunate, in large measure, are the effects or outcome of human conduct. As Machiavelli puts it, "I am disposed to hold that fortune is the arbiter of half our actions, but that it lets us control roughly the other half."[24] And, further, likening fortune to a beautiful woman, he states that she favors those who in a manly manner are focused on controlling her.[25] Leaving the out-of-date chauvinistic notions about women aside, what we are being told is that *fortuna* does not just happen but is made to happen by our actions and/or inactions. In his omissions, blunders, and/or effectual actions or inactions, the human being controls "roughly the other half" of what may or may not come to pass.

Kant is himself well aware of the problematic nature of his position. For the community of nations cannot guard against the possible, if not probable, impetuous and imperious ambitions of "a powerful and enlightened people" since this very "powerful and enlightened people" is itself the "fulcrum" or grounding post, of the hoped for "federation." The very way in which Kant formulates the question—as he himself is well aware—makes clear this inbuilt difficulty:

> But when this state says, "There ought to be no war between myself and other states, even though I acknowledge *no supreme legislative power* by which our rights are mutually guaranteed," *it is not at all clear* on what I can base my *confidence* in my own rights unless it is the free federation, the surrogate of the civil social order, which reason necessarily associates with the concept of the law of nations—assuming that something is really meant by the latter.[26]

Without a doubt, "it is not at all clear" on what one can base one's "confidence" in such an arrangement. To be sure, Kant places his hopes on a "republic, which by its [very] nature must be inclined to perpetual peace" (note 20). To his credit, Kant puts his trust in a republican constitution, the spirit of a free people. And, writing in 1795, the phrase "a powerful and enlightened people" is most certainly a reference to revolutionary France.[27] But, republics have been known to turn imperial. Rome, after all, started out as a republic and the Napoleonic sequel to the French revolution is not very reassuring.

As is clear from the last citation (note 26), Kant is well aware of the problem. Just as a powerful "people" can guarantee, it can also undermine the hoped for community of states. A state powerful enough—politically and militarily—to be the "fulcrum" of a global regulatory interstate organization and which does not acknowledge, between itself and other states, a "supreme legislative power" is, in a very real sense, itself this very power. And yet, Kant hopes to establish the "league" or "federation" by pinning its prospects on the good will of a "powerful and enlightened people" (note 20). But then, what is the "league" or "federation" to guard against? In the hope of averting the perpetual "peace" of the grave[28] Kant ends by endorsing the very thing that could possibly bring it about. He is stuck in a circular quagmire that leads him to endorse the very thing he hopes to avert. In view of all of the above then, let us now take a quick glance at our contemporary world-political situation.

III

Speaking on June 1, 2002—to a West Point graduating class—President George W. Bush candidly, and rather forcefully, asserted that

> America has, and intends to keep, *military strength beyond challenge*, thereby making the destabilizing arms races of other eras pointless, and limiting rivalries to trade and other pursuits of peace.[29]

President Bush was right. We, the United States, can indeed do what he claimed, to the extent that it coincides with our interests, or when we see fit, we can do the opposite of the above—for we do not recognize any power contrary to our interests. In the very act of affirming the "pursuits of peace" as the *peaceful* intent of his policies, President Bush expressed the bellicose nature of his stance. His actions—be they peaceful or belligerent—depend solely on the self-perceived interests of the United States, based on its own assessment of its options, actions, and situation. For it is the "military strength beyond challenge" of a single state that is to limit "rivalries . . . to pursuits of peace."

Indeed, in Kant's words, the United States "is a judge of its own case" (note 11) precisely because, as Bush tells us, it acts based on "military strength beyond challenge." But isn't this the very danger and/or problem that Kant is striving to overcome? And yet, the United States is the kind of state (note 20) that Kant pins his hopes on. In this respect, furthermore, President Bush's soft-spoken and genteel successor, President Barack Obama, presents the same stance in a less overtly bellicose but equally self-righteous and aggressive manner.[30] Indeed, for President Bush as for President Obama—and all U.S. presidents since 1945 and before—the unchallengeable might of the United States is and has been the ground of its relations with the rest of the world.

As the above illustrates, by relying on a strong state in his efforts to theoretically establish "a federation of free states" which would awaken the "greater moral disposition" that is presently "slumbering in man" (note 12), Kant ends with the de facto supremacy and/or dominance of "a powerful and enlightened people." What he has achieved is to place the "federation of free states" at the mercy of the good will of the strongest state amongst them. But is it ever prudent to count on the good will of a strong state? In fact, isn't this the very danger and/or problem that needs to be overcome?

It has to be emphasized, furthermore, that good will has nothing to do with rights as such or with "the rights of nations against each other so far as they are distinct states."[31] Good will comes into play only when rights cannot be upheld or are not recognized. Rights and recognition among states implies mutual and reciprocated acknowledging of each other. It is akin to what Hegel refers to as the principle of abstract right. "Be a person and respect others as persons"[32] which, properly rephrased in our context, would read "Be a state and respect others as states."[33] The problem with powerful states, as exemplified by the United States, is that they see fit to replace "respect" with "military strength beyond challenge."

Ultimately, for powerful states (i.e., major powers) international relations are grounded on strength. And so, being "mindful not to succumb to utopian thinking,"[34] it is clear that when critical interests come into play (i.e., oil, national security, etc.) a "powerful and enlightened people" will always act in the manner in which the powerful act,[35] as "a judge of its own case." For, if it fails to do so, it might remain "enlightened" but it most certainly will not remain, for long, a "powerful" state. Even when such a state restrains itself it still remains answerable only to itself and is not subject to any control, beyond its own sense of right and wrong.

And so, despairing of a solution and leaving aside his earlier scruples regarding the complete independence, or sovereignty, of the states to be federated (i.e., completely reversing himself on this crucial point) Kant asserts,

> For states in their relations to each other, there cannot be any reasonable *way out* of the lawless condition which entails only war except that they, like individual men, should give up their savage (lawless) freedom, adjust themselves to the constraints of public law, and thus establish a continuously growing state consisting of various nations (*civitas gentium*), which will ultimately include all [the] nations of the world.[36]

Unlike what we have seen thus far, in the above quotation, Kant is not anymore considering an external regulatory interstate league, but is advocating for a world state or government. For a civitas gentium is a community of citizens, or a state, and not a "federation" of states. This, for Kant, would be the optimal scenario in which states would "give up" their "freedom" and become part of "a continuously growing state consisting of various nations." Or, better still, a single state composed of "all [the] nations of the world." According to Kant, this is the only "way out" of a situation of perpetual tension and conflict among states.

"But" says he, "under the idea of the law of nations *they* do not wish this, and reject in practice what is correct in theory."[37] But to whom, in the above quote, does "they" refer to? Kant does not say, but it most certainly cannot refer to small insignificant states, but strong and powerful states which consider themselves the embodiment of the will of an "enlightened people." Such strong states—unlike small insignificant states concerned only with survival—are always focused on and jealously guard their "majesty"[38] and prestige and, to this end, sacrifice their citizens in war and are most certainly not inclined, or willing, to subsume their freedom and sovereignty under, or within, the domain of a single "world republic." Again, despairing in his reflections—and hoping to salvage something from all of this—Kant writes,

> If all is not to be lost, there can be, then, in place of the positive idea of a world republic, only the negative surrogate of an alliance which averts war, endures, spreads, and holds back the stream of those hostile passions which fear the law, though such an alliance is in constant peril of . . . breaking loose again.[39]

In the above Kant does not indicate, nor scrutinize, the source of "those hostile passions." But it is clear that they must emanate from the feeling of grandeur and self-confidence—"from pride in their independence,"[40] as he puts it—that constitutes "powerful" strong states, in their own eyes, and in their relations with other states. Now, in confronting a small weak state, such a stance necessarily produces timidity, mollification and leads to accommodation.

On the other hand, in facing "a powerful and enlightened people," such a posture provokes a similar disposition—"hostile passions"—on the other side and thus a generalized state of hostility, emanating, in Kant's words, from "pride in their independence." For each "powerful and enlightened people," in any conflict, sees itself as equal—if not superior—to any other and this not by choice but because this is precisely what it means to be "a powerful and enlightened people." After all, aren't the "powerful," in their own eyes, always "enlightened"? It seems then that, in seeking perpetual peace Kant has stumbled upon the source of perpetual war.

IV

As Jean-François Lyotard has noted, in philosophy one always asks "where what he reads goes wrong."[41] Where then does Kant go wrong? In spite of his rigor Kant fails to note, when looking at the "practicability (objective reality) of this idea of federation" (note 18), that all states do not relate, each to the other, in the same manner. What he refers to as "correct in theory" (note 37) fails to consider, concretely, the practical actuality of interstate relations.

Weak, militarily and politically insignificant states, by virtue of their weakness, are compelled (by prudence, necessity, fear, etc.) to be submissive and servile. On the other hand, "powerful" states, to the extent that they are and wish to remain powerful, see themselves as the will of an "enlightened people" and exude a bellicose arrogant self-confidence. The vice of the weak is servility that of the strong, or "powerful," is a felt and abiding sense of superiority. It is this pride which constitutes such a state or people—in its own eyes or national imaginary—as a "powerful" state. Its hubris, its sense of itself as a *major player*, is the very emblem of such a state's sense of self (i.e., its identity) as a powerful state and people.

It has to be noted that Kant is well aware of all of this, for it is only from a position of strength that a state could possibly declare that "There ought to be no war between myself and other states, even though I acknowledge no supreme legislative power by which our rights are mutually guaranteed."[42] For such a declaration coming from a weak, or even moderately strong, state is merely laughable at its own expense. Indeed, as Kant himself points out, "it is not at all clear" how one can have "confidence" in such a unilateral declaration of "what is right" for it does not rest on "universally valid public laws which restrict the freedom of each one."[43] Such a declaration, in fact, is evidence of the unrestrained freedom that a powerful state enjoys in its relations and dealings with other states. It is evidence of its prowess, its capacity for moderation and/or immoderation, as it alone sees fit to determine. As we saw earlier (note 29) this is what President Bush affirms and President Obama, in his own genteel and soft-spoken manner, upholds for the United States in its international relations.[44]

V

In view of all of the above, then, the only way out of the circuitous quagmire that Kant finds himself in is to conceptualize the "fulcrum" of this hoped-for "federation" as a strong alliance, or contract and solidarity, of small states whose interest in such a federation is a question of survival and not prestige. A "powerful" state can reverse its stance, vis-à-vis other states, in accordance with the changing requirements of its "majesty" and/or self-interest. Weak states, on the other hand, cannot afford the luxury of such reversals without jeopardizing their very existence. Such states know from bitter experience that mutual recognition, tolerance, and international legality are their sole safeguards. For the "majesty" and/or prestige of such states—weak, small states—is their very existence.[45]

But how exactly is this "contractual solidarity of the weak," which I am proposing, contra Kant, as the "fulcrum" of a possible "federation of free states," to be understood? This is how Amilcar Cabral, the key figure in the history of one of the smallest and weakest countries of West Africa, puts it. Addressing the United Nations General Assembly in 1962, he states,

> When in our country a comrade dies under police torture, is assassinated in prison, is burned alive or falls under the bullets of Portuguese guns, for which cause is he giving his life? He

> is giving it for the liberation of our people from the colonial yoke, and hence for the UN. In fighting . . . for the liberation of our countries we are giving our lives, in the present context of international legality, for the ideal which the UN itself has defined in its Charter, in its resolutions, and in particular in its resolution on decolonialisation [sic].

And again:

> For us, the only difference between the Indian soldier, the Italian pilot or the Swedish administrator who dies in the Congo and our comrade who dies in Guinea or the Cabo Verde Islands is that by acting in our country for the same ideal we are simply *anonymous soldiers for the United Nations*.[46]

Cabral presents the cause of his people in terms of the UN Charter and in the "context of international legality." He is well aware that his country's soon to be won independence can only be guaranteed by such an international arrangement. The interests of his small and weak country, without effort, coincide with the possibility of global peace. This is so precisely because it is only in this manner that a small country (or state) can possibly maintain its sovereignty. Cabral's stance derives from the harsh consequences that would befall his weak and small country in the absence of "international legality." The stance he adopts, congruent and compatible with the safety and self-preservation of other states, is thus vouched for (i.e., guaranteed) by the need to survive, which cannot be neglected with impunity. In contrast to Cabral, let us now listen to the words of a representative of a great and powerful state. The kind that, according to Kant, could be a "fulcrum" for the federation and ultimately for the world government he envisions.

Addressing the same august body, the United Nations, in 1952, John Foster Dulles, then Secretary of State of the United States—which at the time was, and to this day is, the dominant nation on earth and *in its own eyes* the embodiment of the will of "a powerful and enlightened people"—had the following to say in the deliberations on the fate of Eritrea, a small African territory and former Italian colony:

> From the point of view of justice, the opinions of the Eritrean people must receive consideration. Nevertheless, the strategic interest of the United States in the Red Sea basin and considerations of security and world peace make it necessary that the country has to be linked with our ally Ethiopia.[47]

Unlike Cabral, Dulles's thinking is not concerned with the Charter of the United Nations or with the idea of the right of nations to self-determination. His only concern is the "strategic interest" of the powerful state he represents. Cabral, even if he wanted to, cannot afford the arrogant and callous demeanor of Dulles. Dulles, on the other hand, could not endorse, in his pronouncements on the case of Eritrea, for example, the kind of concerns voiced by Cabral and still uphold the interests "in the Red Sea basin" of the strong and powerful state he represents.

To be sure, Dulles tacitly recognizes "the point of view of justice" in the very act of breaching it. For him "the point of view of justice," the aspiration of "the Eritrean people," ought to be considered, but they can also be thwarted. When convenient "justice" should be upheld, when not expedient, however, it can and should be abrogated. Cabral does not have the luxury of such leeway and is bound to see, the fate of his own country, in the callousness meted out to other small weak nations. Similar trepidations cannot be imagined to council the judgment of Dulles, or of any other envoy of "a powerful and enlightened people." Indeed, power has blinding benefits! The strong are sightless in the concerns of the weak.

Interestingly enough, Kant disapprovingly cites a Gallic Prince, who expresses a view similar to that of Dulles—a view that could only be endorsed by "a powerful and [in its own eyes] enlightened people." The Gallic potentate states, "It is the prerogative which nature has given the stronger that the weaker should obey him."[48] The League of Nations (1919) and the United Nations (1945) were both established to counter such bestial logic. Even in his counter-examples Kant ends up with the opposite of his "good intentions." For this logic of violence, as we saw with Dulles and Bush, is what bluntly directs the conduct of powerful states, the kind Kant thinks can serve as a fulcrum for a "league" and/or a "federation" of states.

In this regard, it ought to be remembered that the 1935 invasion of Ethiopia—the sole African member state of the League of Nations—by Italy which, along with Japan's invasion of Manchuria, heralded the Second World War, was the direct effect of such violent logic. When Italy, using a contrived pretext, confronted Ethiopia, the latter, a nonindustrial weak state, was mollified, gave way, and put its trust in the League of Nations. Italy, on the other hand, an industrial European power, the equal of any other, felt that it had been deprived of a colonial empire ("from pride . . . [in its] . . . independence," in Kant's words [note 40]), and invaded a member state of the League of Nations. This it did disregarding established international legality, by which it was bound, and with the implicit and racist complicity of the other great powers.[49]

Thus, and with a great deal of realism we can say, *grosso modo*, that in a contracting world of politico-economic interdependence, weak countries can survive only to the extent that the norms of international legality (i.e., the contractual relations that guarantee mutual justice and recognition) nullify the permanent threat embodied in the military-political might of "powerful" states. Here, it has to be noted and emphasized that the struggles for national liberation in Africa and Asia, starting from the mid-1940s to the end of the twentieth century, were all aimed at establishing the mutual recognition of former *colonizers* and *colonized*. These struggles, their differing local slogans notwithstanding, were all focused on the principled parity of all peoples and the right of every people (disregarding race, color, creed, etc.) to equality, justice, and recognition. At their very core, the "ethical content" of these struggles was grounded on the ardent belief in the equal rights of all peoples to "self-determination."[50]

As attested to by the opening declaration of the Bandung Conference of 1955, peaceable relations among sovereign states was the core concern of these struggles.[51] And, for the most part, these struggles have produced, relatively speaking, "small" and "medium"-sized states, whose relative weakness (if nothing else!) inclines them toward peaceful avenues in interstate relations. In other words, these states, precisely because of their "limited capabilities" or "relative weakness," are inclined toward international order, peace, and stability, in contrast to "powerful states" who, because of their might, are less inclined in this direction.

Contra Kant, then, it has to be maintained that it is the "weak" and not the "powerful" that can possibly serve as a "fulcrum" for "a federation of free states." In the manner of the six-inch-tall Lilliputians, these states have to be able to overpower the Gulliver nations that dominate the international scene and threaten collective security. But how is this to be achieved? Within the scope of this chapter I can only suggest the possible avenues through which the spirit, if not the letter, of Kant's thinking can be further explored, engaged, and appropriated.

VI

In this regard, it should be emphasized that the term "weak" is a relative term, which does not necessarily mean "helpless." Weak, or "relatively" strong, states can guarantee their safety, sovereignty, and independence only through a solidarity grounded on mutual recognition and respect. And this is not only or primarily because of their "good will" but because of the concrete actuality of their stature (i.e., size of territory, limited population and resources, limited military capabilities, etc.) which, in its limitedness, inclines them, out of self-preservation, toward peaceful venues. It inclines them toward mutual solidarity and a system of reciprocal protections and assurances. And so, in keeping with Machiavelli's advice, by "means of dykes and dams" (i.e., regional and/or continental political-economic organizations), small and medium-sized member states of the international community need to keep in check the torrential might of powerful states or major powers. Utilizing mutual solidarities, these states need to employ and strengthen the structures of global and regional institutions.

Here it has to be accentuated that the international legality enshrined in the United Nations, for example, is not, for the formerly colonized and now "relatively" weak member states, merely an ideal or an abstract concern for "justice." Starting from the days of their struggles against colonialism, these states have seen, in the principles of the United Nations, the content and assurance of their sovereignty and independence even, in some cases, as the United Nations itself refused to acknowledge their rights and their very existence.[52] On the other hand, for "powerful" states, which see themselves as the will of an "enlightened people," the United Nations has always been a limiting structure made necessary—and not desirable—by their mutually bellicose tendencies.

Each powerful state suspects other powerful states of the intentions that it harbors toward the other member states and, on this alleged reason, wants them checked and limited, while trying to preserve, for itself, a privileged special status without restrictions. The United Nations is thus a curbing structure whose restrictions are grudgingly accepted by powerful states, always intent on circumventing its restrictive controls. And so, President Bush coins the phrase "coalition of the willing"[53] and nicely evades UN restrictions and presents the Gulf War as in the collective interest while bribing and/or threatening into acquiescence the "weaker" members of the community of states. Bribery, corruption, and the use or threat of force (the "carrot and/or the big stick") are the trademark tools in this arena. International diplomacy, in the view and conduct of powerful states, is the field in which "intelligence agencies" ply their trade: crafty/devious political maneuvering calculated to impose the will of the powerful, in the guise of the collective interest and in the name of international legality and justice.[54]

In Plato's *Republic*, Glaucon, in trying to elicit the most complete response from Socrates on the question of justice, articulates the implicit conception of "the nature and origin of justice" that accurately describes the conduct of international relations as dominated by the thinking and strategic conduct/maneuvering of strong powerful states. As Glaucon puts it,

> They say that to do wrong is naturally good, to be wronged is bad, but the suffering of injury so far exceeds in badness the good of inflicting it that when men have done wrong to each other and suffered it, and have had a taste of both, *those who are unable to avoid the latter and practice the former* decide that it is profitable

> to come to an agreement with each other neither to inflict nor to suffer it. As a result they begin to make laws and covenants, and the law's command they call lawful and just. This, they say, is the origin and essence of justice; it stands between the best and the worst, *the best being to do wrong without paying the penalty and the worst to be wronged without the power of revenge*. The just then is a mean between two extremes; it is welcomed and honoured because of men's lack of the power to do wrong.

In the next sentence he explains the crucial point, for that which concerns us:

> The man who has that power, *the real man*, would not make a compact with anyone not to inflict injury or suffer it. For him that would be madness.[55]

Indeed, if we recall President Bush's statement (note 29), this is the basic message it conveys. The United States has "military strength beyond challenge," which it is willing to put to the service of "limiting rivalries to trade and other pursuits of peace." And this it does on its own terms, without entering into an agreement and/or "compact with anyone." On the other hand, the vast majority of the states that compose the international community, unlike "the real man" in Glaucon's example, occupy a position similar to "those who are unable to avoid the latter [i.e., suffer wrongs] and practice the former [i.e., to do wrong with impunity]." Their interest in mutual protection is not concerned with the *ideal* of justice but with survival (i.e., with the practical possibility of securing their continued existence).

In view of the threat embodied in the unilateralism of "the real man," therefore, what needs to be focused on is the "practicability" of how we are to conceptualize the possibility of peace in defense against the Gulliver nations of our world and in view of our shared historical experience. An experience marred by two catastrophic world (i.e., European) wars whose lessons are that the relative stability of our world has, thus far, been maintained by the sacrifices, from differing nations, of those who have effectively acted as "anonymous soldiers for the United Nations." In this respect, what we need to cultivate is a "national consciousness, which is not nationalism"[56] and which, in recognizing its own partiality gives allegiance to a larger whole and in this way makes room for, or renders possible, "an international dimension."[57]

This released and compassionate disposition, this concrete "international dimension" which, in effect, directed even Kant's thinking is what needs to be seriously explored and nurtured. In this regard, as Glaucon points out, most men or states analogously, are in the situation in which they "are unable to avoid the latter [to be wronged] and practice the former [to do wrong]" with impunity. It is this, a rather compelling state of affairs, which basically inclines Lilliputian nations, unlike Gulliver nations, toward non-bellicosity and peaceful venues in their international conduct. In this regard, the optimal way of fostering this non-belligerence—in our present postcolonial world and within the confines of the international legality established by the United Nations—is to encourage, strengthen, and give weight to the General Assembly in tandem with curtailing, or finding ways of curtailing, the veto power of the Security Council. This, indeed, has been the general direction of the efforts of "smaller" nations in the UN.[58]

For the Security Council, composed until recently (i.e., the entry of China) by former colonial powers, is the site in which the power of the powerful is exercised to thwart the will of the international community. The veto power of the Security Council is utilized to frustrate the will of the majority and to push the "special" agendas of "favored" states. It is utilized to impose the agendas of major powers as the concern of the community of states. The effort to curtail this power is thus a democratic affirmation of the interest of the community of states, as a whole.

VII

To Kant's credit, the problem he confronts, and leaves us with, is the very problem the international community—in the second decade of the twenty-first century—is facing. In tackling this problem we need to be open to "our worldwide heritage."[59] To be open to this "heritage" means to recognize the "validity of the claim[s]" of the formerly colonized. To recognize, that is, that our shared possible future of peace can only be grounded on the legitimacy of these claims. For the formerly colonized world—in all of its struggles and strivings—to this very day, seeks only its *human due* as a legitimate progeny of the earth. It seeks only to cash-in the promissory note in whose guise Europe conquered the globe. In the words of Patrice Lumumba,

> We hold out a fraternal hand to the West. Let it today give proof of the principle of equality and friendship between races [i.e., peoples] that its sons have always taught us as we sat at our desks in school, a principle written in capital letters in the Universal Declaration of the Rights of Man.[60]

Lumumba invokes the Universal Declaration of the Rights of Man. In so doing, he openly endorses the marrow of Europe's social-democratic heritage. As we saw in chapter 2, this openness is an auspicious outcome of our postcolonial present. And so, in being open and receptive to that which is disclosed in our postcolonial present, we just might, in the spirit of Kant, all of us and together, surmount the dangers signaled by 9/11—2001 and 1973.

As Lefort has noted, a lasting "peace can be based only on the idea that the relationship among men [or states] are relationships among fellow men [or fellow states]."[61] In other words, "A permanent peace cannot be prepared by threats but only by the honest attempt to create mutual trust."[62] Which means that "military strength beyond challenge" (note 29) and/or "strategic interest" (note 47) cannot be, any more, the ground on which we base our thinking. We have to counter, to the nature sanctioned logic of brute force, a logic of *recognition*, *respect*, and *dialogue*—a logic grounded in the finitude, or humanness, of our shared existence.

In this way, by "Inject[ing] the voice of reason into world affairs"[63] we can possibly avert catastrophe and think, or envision, a global political reason, beyond might, violence, and brute force. A dialogical political reason grounded on species-wide obligations, concerns, and responsibilities. This responsiveness, the challenge of the present, is the possibility that we need to nurture and project into and as our future, for indeed, "Höher als die Wirklichkeit steht die Möglichkeit."[64] Ultimately, this might be—as the Bible tells us—the way that "the meek [i.e., the weak] shall inherit the earth" (Mathew 5:5).

4

Hermeneutics and Differing Traditions

A Reading of Hans-Georg Gadamer[1]

Whether our coming to the Big Chief's compound will do any good we cannot say. We did not see him . . . But we can go back to our people and tell them that we have struggled for them with what remaining strength we have . . . Once upon a time the leopard who had been trying for a long time to catch the tortoise finally chanced upon him on a solitary road. "Aha" he said; "at long last! Prepare to die." And the tortoise said; "Can I ask a favour before you kill me?" The leopard so no harm in that and agreed. "Give me a few moments to prepare my mind," . . . But instead of standing still as the leopard had expected the tortoise went into strange action on the road, scratching with hands and feet and throwing sand furiously in all directions. "Why are you doing that?" asked the puzzled leopard. The tortoise replied, "Because even after I am dead I would want anyone passing by this spot to say, yes, a fellow and his match struggled here." My people, that is all we are doing now. Struggling. Perhaps to no purpose except that those who come after us will be able to say, "True, our fathers were defeated but they tried."

—Gray-bearded Elder[2]

We must rid ourselves of the habit, now that we are in the thick of battle, of minimizing the actions of our fathers . . . They fought as best they could, with the arms they possessed, and if the echoes of their struggle have not resounded in the international arena . . . the reason for this lies less in their lack of heroism than in a fundamentally different international situation.

—Frantz Fanon[3]

Every Winter has its Spring.

—Palestinian Proverb

I

As Gianni Vattimo has noted, the "current configuration [of hermeneutics] is mostly the result of Gadamer's work."[4] In this chapter, I will engage this "work" by exploring its value for the contemporary discourse of African philosophy. The aim will be to display the significance of this "work" by laying out its core self-understanding. In this my main concern will be to show how "Gadamer's work" articulates a practice of philosophy that is open to and welcoming of Otherness, just as the past is "allowed to speak"[5] and is heard, or encountered, in and out of itself. In other words, just as the past "speak[s]" autonomously in the *consciousness saturated with history*,[6] in like manner, different/differing traditions can possibly "speak" and come into contact, each with the Other, in a self-standing sovereign way.

We will thus explore this way and, in so doing, reveal the value of Gadamer's hermeneutics for the interpretative practice of contemporary African philosophy.[7] This we will do as it relates to African philosophy's own past and its hermeneutical encounter of Other traditions. For to explore the possible ground of encounters in and among differing traditions is an interpretative undertaking, if ever there was one, whose truth[8] needs to be properly engaged.

II

In an interview given toward the end of his long and productive life, in responding to a question posed by Glenn Most, a professor of classical philology, Gadamer makes the following insightful remarks. Most comments and goes on to ask,

> For you, then, the Greeks seem to form a vanishing point at which the unity of natural science, ethics, and aesthetics, as objects of reason, could be rescued. But in today's culture the subdivided realms of knowledge fall apart, and at the same time the Greeks are increasingly disappearing as a basis of our culture. Do you see other possible resources than the Greeks that would be able to preserve the rational unity of these other realms?[9]

To these stimulating remarks and the concluding question, Gadamer responds in kind:

> In spite of all this, it is also the case today that the modern world is gradually coming together into a functional unity through science and technology, although this is taking place against the backdrop of highly different cultural centers and forms. We still do not really know anything about what our civilization with its skyscrapers and powerful machines means for human beings living in other parts of the world. Who knows, perhaps we will come to see that the relaxed conversation of a Chinese [or Arab, or African, or Indian, etc.] wise person with his disciples also has something to contribute, something that is quite different from the logic and desire for proof we first learned from the Greeks and which we have developed into an instrument to *dominate* the world and thereby perhaps have also disfigured [denaturiert] it.[10]

What is of interest to us in the above passage is that for Gadamer "the relaxed conversation of a Chinese wise person with his disciples" can teach us, or "contribute, something that is quite different" than what *we* (i.e., the West) have appropriated from the Greeks and "developed into an instrument to dominate the world and thereby perhaps have also disfigured it." For Gadamer, then, the specificity of Chinese culture is *different,* not grotesque or bizarre, as it was for Kant, for example,[11] and it "has something to contribute."

It has to be noted that this explicit recognition of difference and the possible contributions of Other cultures/histories presupposes a rather radical curbing, on Gadamer's part, of his own interpretative projection. It is in this way that it is "open"[12] to encountering Otherness. For what is called for, as Gadamer tells us in *Truth and Method,* is that we "remain open to the meaning [or opinion] of the other person or of the text" and that this "openness [Offenheit] always includes our placing the other meaning [or opinion] in relation with the whole of our own meanings or ourselves in a relation to it."[13] This "openness" is thus the tangible stance of a seeking that consciously owns up to and is aware of its own finitude and specific distinctiveness. This stance (i.e., this "openness") allows the person who incarnates it—as it allows Gadamer in the above citation (note 10)—to concretely recognizing the partiality and/or flaws (i.e., "an instrument to dominate," "perhaps [we] have also disfigured it") of his own historical heritage. It is this that institutes the space for the Other (i.e., the hypothetical "Chinese wise person with his disciples") to be a possible, or imaginable, source of a *different,* or countervailing, truth.

And so, read generously,[14] "a Chinese wise person" can be a placeholder for a sage and/or a philosopher from any Other culture. Gadamer himself suggests such a "generous reading" when elsewhere, in the same book of interviews, he states that we need to be open and receptive to "what has come down to us from world cultures, not just the European!" In the next sentence, stressing this same point, he further notes, "Indeed, we . . . need to accept our worldwide heritage not only in its otherness but also in recognizing the validity of the claim this larger heritage makes on us."[15] All of this indicates, and very strongly in my view, the receptivity of Gadamer—and of contemporary philosophical hermeneutics—to that which Other cultures and peoples have to offer. It is, in this respect, a critical stance that counters—in effect—the haughty European demeanor that subjected the world, charmed by its own *idea* of itself.[16]

It is imperative to note, furthermore, that this is a rather radical break with the heritage of Plato and Kant to which Gadamer is tied, even as he goes beyond it.[17] In a way, what I hope to do in this chapter is to enlarge this fissure and appropriate the fruitful space it makes possible by systematically unpacking what, in *Truth and Method,* Gadamer names "effective-historical consciousness."[18] Based on this, I will argue that his remarks cited above and expressed toward the end of his life, with his magnum opus behind him, are not merely supplemental and/or casual off-the-cuff interview remarks but firm indications, grounded in his main work, of his conception of hermeneutics as a *radical openness.* Arguably this is the central—if not the most important—contribution of his work to the emerging receptivity of Occidental thought to that which Other traditions have to offer: a propitious and welcome achievement of our postcolonial present.

This receptiveness was a central theme that we explored in chapter 2, in stark and sharp contrast to Levinas's rather myopic perspective and by way of relating it to the analogous stance/orientation of contemporary African philosophy. By the end of this chapter, the value of "Gadamer's work," for the contemporary discourse of African philosophy/hermeneutics should be, if my efforts are successful, obvious. For, as already indicated in the Preface and the Introduction and specified in chapter 2, my concern—focused on nurturing the fruitful entwining of contemporary existence made possible by our hybrid and interlaced heritage—is aimed at shortening the distance in the dialogue of Continental and African philosophy.

In this regard, preliminarily and in view of what has been said thus far, we can begin by observing that Gadamer's stance is open to and welcoming of the seventeenth-century Abyssinian philosopher Zär'a Ya'əqob, who defines his work as a *hatäta*—a "[critical] examination"[19] of sedimented traditions. This would be a *contribution* (note 10) focused on the critical and interpretative sifting and sieving of that which "people hastily accept . . . from their fathers."[20] For, as I have shown elsewhere by an explorative explication of Zär'a Ya'əqob's work,[21] for him—as for Gadamer—the task of interpretative reflection (i.e., hermeneutics) arises out of the need to make sense of one's heritage. Or, as Gadamer puts it in *Truth and Method*, "understanding becomes a special task only when . . . misunderstandings have arisen."[22] Indeed, for Gadamer—as for Zär'a Ya'əqob—the originary source of interpretative reflection is the need to overcome, or bypass, the alienation of meaning in one's heritage. What, then, are the specific characteristics of this stance? This is the basic task of the present chapter: an orderly explorative explication of Gadamer's conceptualization of the "effective-historical consciousness."

III

In the second section of *Truth and Method*, in contradistinction to Wilhelm Dilthey's efforts to harmonize life philosophy and the modern science's notion of objectivity, Gadamer articulates his notion of a "truly historical consciousness"[23] by taking a critical stance toward the Cartesian postulate of "methodic doubt." Gadamer begins by decisively positioning himself against Dilthey's call for a similar kind of objectivity and procedure in the human sciences that one finds in the natural sciences. Dilthey's acceptance, as a whole, of the Cartesian starting point of reflection and doubt is, for Gadamer, wrong-headed. Why? Precisely because it is not congruent with, and thereby ends by falsifying, lived experience. As Gadamer points out,

> The fact that it is necessary to adopt the "attitude of reflection and doubt" and that this is what happens "in all forms of scientific reflection" (and not otherwise) simply cannot be combined with Dilthey's life philosophy. This is, rather, a description of the special ideal of the scientific enlightenment.[24]

In other words, human experience cannot be viewed in this manner without necessarily being distorted. In this critical stance Gadamer is reverting to a concern that was voiced by Aristotle in chapter 3 of Book 1 of the *Nicomachean Ethics*. Aristotle had noted there that different subjects have differing requirements and standards of exactitude and it takes "an educated person [i.e., a person tempered by experience] to look for just so much precision in each kind of discourse as the nature of the thing one is concerned with admits."[25] Again, in "The Problem of Historical Consciousness," relying on Aristotle, Gadamer argues that unlike the natural sciences, in the human sciences the role of reason cannot be that of merely applying a general rule but has to be focused on grasping and comprehending a specific situation in its concrete specificity.[26]

This, then, is the kind of tacit experiential know-how, or knowledge, that Gadamer finds useful in Aristotle's formulation of "the virtue of moral knowledge," and so he states that "Aristotle's analysis is in fact a kind of model of the problems of hermeneutics."[27] In this way, after distancing himself from Dilthey's efforts and aligning his stance with Aristotle's position, Gadamer demarcates succinctly the general direction of his project as being that of grasping or comprehending "more adequately [i.e., in concreto] the experience of the human sciences and the objectivity [that] they are able to achieve."[28] This, however, is still a limited focus, directed towards questions of method and science (i.e., the point of entry for his larger objective).

More broadly then, and in contrast to "the mode of knowledge [and method] of the natural sciences [which] appears, rather, as a variety of understanding" narrowly focused on "the present-at-hand,"[29] he is oriented to that which "Before any differentiation of understanding into different directions of pragmatic or theoretical interest, understanding is There-being's mode of being, in that it is potentiality-for-being and 'possibility.' "[30] Or as Richard E. Palmer puts it, "Gadamer is working on a preliminary and more fundamental question: How is understanding possible, not only in the humanities but in the whole of man's experience of the world?"[31] In contrast to the specific "scientific concept of objectivity"[32] of the natural sciences, Gadamer intends to delineate the "objectivity" that is germane to "understanding" as "There-being's mode of being." He further specifies, and more directly, the broader character of his concerns by stating that, "our question" is concerned with seeing "how hermeneutics . . . can do justices to the historicality of understanding."[33] The question of the human sciences is thus, for Gadamer, a point of entry. His real concern is the actuality of understanding, per se. Given the historical character of existence—taking seriously its fluid temporality and finitude—to grasp concretely and specify the acuity of understanding, this is "the core"[34] concern of *Truth and Method*.

By way of engaging this central concern, having indicated what differentiates him from Dilthey, Gadamer then turns to Heidegger's explication of understanding as the primordial and basic mode of the there-being of *Dasein* (i.e., human ek-sistence). As expounded in *Being and Time*, this is the grounding and ontologically constitutive element of the ontic existentiality of human existence. Co-primordially with mood, interpretation, and discourse (or language), it is the "there" of human existence in and through which the world is disclosed.[35] Gadamer is concerned to show how this conception of the there-being of human existence constitutes the operative actuality of human understanding. And so, in keeping with Heidegger, he displaces the question of knowledge from the epistemological (i.e., concern with method) to the ontological linguistic level. The second and third parts of his magnum opus are accordingly focused on historicity and language as elemental co-constitute ontological structures in and through which the lived event of understanding happens.

Now, in turning to Gadamer's conception of what he names "effective-historical consciousness," it is imperative to note that this conceptualization is preceded by—and is indeed composed of—an in-depth critique of the critique of prejudice which marks and constitutes "the scientific enlightenment" (note 24), as such. As Gadamer puts it, "And there is one prejudice of the enlightenment that is *essential* to it: the *fundamental* prejudice of the enlightenment is the prejudice against prejudice itself, which deprives tradition of its power."[36] A few pages further Gadamer states that this is "the enlightenment's belief in perfection."[37] In this, what Gadamer is effectively doing is elaborating and appropriating, for his notion of the "effective-historical consciousness," Heidegger's conception of "the fore-structure of understanding"[38] as *the* grounding, or generatively constitutive, element of the there-being of human ek-sistence.

In this perspective, the Enlightenment's critique of prejudice is seen as its—"essential" and "fundamental"—distinctive shortcoming or blindness: A failure to properly appreciate its immersion in history. This hubristic stance, or belief, that it is above all prejudgments, perspectives, prejudices, and so on, and that the essential task of reason is the "overcoming of all prejudices,"[39] for Gadamer, "this global demand of the enlightenment . . . [is] . . . itself a [limiting] prejudice,"[40] in effect "a pure illusion [eine reine Illusion],"[41] which needs to be removed in order to secure "an appropriate understanding [i.e., appreciation] of our finitude."[42] Finitude, for Gadamer, is not a shortcoming or a "flaw"—to be overcome—but the core constituent of our existence, internal to which, is our understanding of the world. It is in contrast to the blindness of the Enlightenment on this crucial point that Gadamer formulates, and squarely places, his conception of the "effective-historical consciousness" within the bounds of our mortality.

He does so by insisting that we restore "to its rightful place a positive conception of prejudice that was driven out of our linguistic usage by the French and English Enlightenment."[43] This, then, is the anchoring stone and basic presupposition—but also the substantive or substantiating core—of Gadamer's conception of the "effective-historical consciousness." For this "consciousness" is what it is by virtue of its acute awareness of its *situated existence*, its sensitive "openness to tradition,"[44] to the lived prejudices that constitute its finitude. Thus, our explication of Gadamer's conception of an enabling notion of prejudice—the task of the following section—is both a *basic presupposition* and a *central constituent* of how Gadamer conceptualizes the lived self-awareness of the "effective-historical consciousness." This is an important point to keep in mind because, as Palmer points out, "Gadamer's conceptions are interrelated, so that we can only gradually enter into the circle of his considerations."[45]

IV

In accord with Friedrich Nietzsche's perspectival view of the character of all knowledge[46] prejudice, for Gadamer, is that which constitutes and suffuses our awareness of the world. This is so precisely because human beings exist always and necessarily within the bounds of a lived heritage. We are constituted—in our very being—as beings of culture-history, by the prejudices (i.e., the lived presuppositions, biases, etc.) that have sedimented, in us, as the heritage that we inhabit and *are;* the very heritage "that constitute[s] our being."[47] Prejudices can be negative, restricting and/or positive and enabling—or a *pasticcio* thereof—and in this manner either restricting or enabling, or restricting in some areas and enabling in others, and so, open or closed, to the possibilities of life, as the case may be. In this, the work of "temporal distance" (i.e., of history) is to put to rest the restrictive and bring forth the enabling prejudices that allow

> the true meaning of the object [in question to] emerge [more] fully. But the discovery of the true meaning of a text or a work of art [or any other element of a tradition] is never finished [once and for all]; it is in fact an infinite process.[48]

This "infinite process," this interplay of the past in the present—in and out of the concerns that animate our lived existence—is a sieving out, a discarding and/or preserving, of the resources of our heritage in view of lived exigencies. It is in this ongoing manner, out of the sedimentations of a heritage, that the comprehension of what shows itself makes its way in the world. This, furthermore, is not a technique and/or a methodological postulate[49] but a descriptive rendition of how actually understanding is possible, and attainable, for mortal beings open to existence.

In other words, this ongoing process of filtering through in which understanding is secured is, in effect, "the reality of history and the reality of historical understanding."[50] In this, the role of the interpreter is to be open to the "effectivity of history within [her/his own] understanding itself."[51] This means that the interpreter is not a mere passive receptacle through which the elements of a heritage filter themselves. S/he is constantly utilizing his/her own conceptions and pre-understandings/prejudices to sift, examine, weigh, and consider the point at issue. This is the hermeneutic stance—in its lived tangible concreteness—as it encounters the past and/or Other traditions. It is the actuating of "the fusion of these horizons"[52] in and through which the acuity of understanding occurs, or can occur, as it sieves/sifts that which it encounters. In this way the horizons of the past and the present—in process—"combine . . . in us,"[53] fuse, or fail to do so, out of the concerns of the present and in view of a possible future.

The "effects of effective-history"[54] are thus affirmed and unfold out of an ongoing effort of filtering, sieving, and sifting-through the historical past. For "Our historical consciousness is always filled with a variety of voices in which the echo of the past is heard."[55] In this hearing a dead-past, or a dead-history,[56] is pushed aside and discarded just as, and concurrently, in this very process, the "effects of effective-history" are "heard" and—in this hearing—affirmed. As Gadamer puts it, in "The Problem of Historical Consciousness,"

> Every experience is a confrontation. Because every experience sets something new against something old and in every case it remains open in principle whether the new will prevail—that is, will truly become experience—or whether the old, accustomed, predictable will be confirmed in the end. We know that even in the empirical sciences, as particularly Thomas Kuhn has shown in the meantime, not every new recognition is accepted without resistance. Rather, it is set aside as long as possible by the prevailing "paradigm." So it is basically with all experience. It must either overcome tradition or fail because of tradition. The new would be nothing new if it did not have to assert itself *anew* against something.[57]

This, then, is what Gadamer means, when he states that the "historical movement of human life consists in the fact that it . . . can never have a truly closed horizon."[58] The interpreter, s/he who is engaged with history, has an active-passive stance or disposition in which, as much as possible, her/his own "choices" and "inclinations" are examined, preserved and/or curtailed and, in this, one becomes an active-passive vector through which what is to show itself comes forth. For "Even the most genuine and solid tradition does not persist by nature because of the inertia of what once existed. It needs to be affirmed, embraced, [and] cultivated."[59] This affirming is the only gauge or standard, the internal cohesion—of what is at issue—in view of the projected questioning that solicits its coming forth. And so "The only 'objectivity'" in this concrete and lived context "is the confirmation [or non-confirmation] of a fore-meaning [i.e., a projected prejudice] in its being worked out."[60] In this way, as its "work[ing] out" unfolds, what is required is "neither 'neutrality' in the matter of the object nor the extinction of one's self, but the conscious assimilation of one's own fore-meanings and prejudices."[61] The African philosopher Marcien Towa effectively reproduces this crucial hermeneutical insight when he states that

> rigor and intellectual honesty do not consist, in addressing history [i.e., in the study of history], of eliminating ideological convictions [i.e., prejudices], which is impossible in any case and results in rendering it [i.e., history] that much more inconsistent, more implicit, and thus that much more nebulous, but on the contrary, make them [ideological convictions, i.e., prejudices] explicit, be aware of them the better to defend against their deforming actions [i.e., effects].[62]

And so, what Gadamer is suggesting is an aware reflexive and critical deportment that always already begins by questioning itself. A self-critical stance aware of its lived situatedness.

In this way, "The hermeneutical task becomes automatically a [critical] questioning of things and is always in part determined by this."[63] This "questioning" furthermore, in order to sustain itself, must start from "a process of distinguishing."[64] In other words,

> Whatever is being distinguished must be distinguished from something which, in turn, must be distinguished from it. Thus all distinguishing also *makes visible* that from which it is distinguished. We have described this above as the operation of prejudices. We started by saying that a hermeneutical situation is determined by the prejudices that we [cannot help but] bring with us. They constitute, then, *the horizon of a particular present*, for they represent that beyond which it is impossible to see.[65]

In this "distinguishing," then, what is constantly held in view are one's own prejudices as distinct from that which we encounter in the element(s) of a tradition or a heritage being explored. What one has to critically be alert to, as much as possible, in this situation, is the "tyranny of hidden prejudices that make us deaf to . . . that [which] speaks to us in tradition."[66] In being self-critically aware of our horizon (i.e., in keeping it visible) from within which we engage the horizons of the past; in maintaining this distinction; in "work[ing] out" the sense of what comes to us from our heritage and/or Other traditions; we are engaged in a two-fold "questioning" that is, above all, self-critically aware of itself and questioningly receptive of that which is to be encountered.

In this what is called for is "openness"[67] to that which comes from the text, a willingness to allow it to come forth. This receptiveness, to the extent that it allows itself to be affected by that which the Other—the element(s) of a tradition and/or a heritage as a whole—has to say does so, not in spite of but because of the acuity of the enabling prejudices operative in it, for these "are [the] biases of our openness to the world."[68] This is the tangible function of the "effects of effective-history"[69] which organically—from within—constitute our lived self-awareness of the world. What is central here is not "neutrality"[70] but an engaged active-passivity that is alert to what tradition or aspects of the past, and/or Other traditions, have to say and in this is critically open to and concurrently questioning of its own presuppositions and prejudices.[71]

Thus, the "fusion of . . . horizons" occurs, as noted earlier, when in this two-fold process of "questioning" and "distinguishing" we come to encounter, our heritage (or Other traditions), in and out of a dialogically responsive situation, "as an answer to a question."[72] This, furthermore, is not a methodic postulate but a descriptive rendition of the self-aware facticity of existence, since the "self-awareness of the individual is only a flickering in the closed circuits of historical life."[73] The individual person—and/or community or collective of persons—is not in control of history but *is* only within the bounds of a specific history. A history that internally, and from the outset, constitutes, suffuses, and saturates every fiber of our being. "In truth, history does not belong to us, but we belong to it."[74] In other words, it is not that we inhabit a history but rather that we *are* the history we inhabit. And so, for Gadamer, "Understanding is not . . . thought of so much as an action of one's subjectivity, but as the placing of oneself within a process of tradition, in which past and present are constantly [in a dialogical manner] fused [in and through us]."[75] This conception of understanding is what constitutes the truth of the awareness open to history.

Engaging a text is thus the play of an ongoing and fluid process of anticipating and correlating one's projections to that which shows itself, in the text, in response to these projections. This is an incessant process, through which understanding is possibly attained, in the flowing interaction of "familiarity and strangeness [Vertrautheit und Fremdheit]."[76] It is this "intermediate area," as Gadamer tells us, which "is the true locus [Ort] of hermeneutics."[77] In this fluctuating in between, the projected anticipation of meaning and that which it solicits and encounters, mutually condition, punctuate, and "correct" each other. And so, the gauge, or critical element, in and through which productive prejudices become operative and unproductive, or limiting, prejudices are discarded is thus this very process, of sifting and sieving, tangibly "adapted to the object, a *mensuratio ad rem*."[78] In other words, "The harmony of all the details with the whole is the [sole] criterion of correct understanding."[79] This, in effect and concretely, is what sifts and separates productive from unproductive prejudice, in an ongoing way, constantly tempered and "sharpened by experience."[80] Gadamer wants us to take seriously the innate fluid historicalness of life, which means to comprehend and concretely grasp that in our existing we are—at all times—always already immersed in and determined by a heritage, a history that tacitly choreographs every aspect of our being, and understanding, from within.

Thus, however one looks at it, reason operates—even in its most "scientific" expression—always from within the bounds of specific traditions. And so, Gadamer rhetorically asks,

> Does the fact that one is set within various traditions mean really and primarily that one is subject to prejudices and limited in one's freedom? Is not, rather, all human existence, even the freest, limited and qualified in various ways? If this is true, then the idea of an *absolute reason* is impossible for historical humanity. Reason exists for us only in concrete, historical terms, i.e., it is not its own master, but remains constantly dependent on the given circumstances in which it operates. This is true not only in the sense in which Kant limited the claims of rationalism, under the influence of the skeptical critique of Hume, to the a priori element in the knowledge of nature; it is still truer of historical consciousness and the possibility of historical knowledge.[81]

Now, the question that still needs to be clinched is how we are to differentiate between productive and unproductive prejudice. To be sure, all that I have been meticulously detailing thus far is itself a response to this very question. A response that sees, in full accord with Aristotle, that the question at hand does not lend itself to a concise—"objective"—crisp criterion, but to a critical and concrete comprehension of how actually the event of understanding occurs. This is so because "what distinguishes the human sciences from the natural sciences" is that the "object of the natural sciences can be described *idealiter* as what would be known in the perfect knowledge of nature" whereas "it is senseless [ist es sinnlos]," on the other hand, "to speak of a perfect knowledge of history, and for this reason it is not possible to speak of an object in itself towards which its research is directed."[82] In other words, we are always already and necessarily convolved—in the human sciences—with that which we explore. In keeping with Aristotle then one has to seriously take into account "the nature of the thing one is concerned with."[83]

As Gadamer points out, the "true historical object is not an object at all, but the unity of the one and the other, a relationship in which exist both the reality of history and the reality of historical understanding."[84] The best that can be done is thus to be aware of how the effects of history (i.e., "temporal distance") condition or, more accurately, constitute the acuity of the "biases" (note 68) of our lived understanding by tacitly "distinguishing the true prejudices, by which we understand, from the false ones by which we misunderstand."[85] This "distinguishing" is, for Gadamer, the "power" of tradition—or of an established paradigm, in Kuhnian terms—which the "prejudice against prejudice" undermines and/or disables.[86]

In other words, just as a given scientific paradigm makes it possible for us to "see" in a certain way, in like manner, the enabling prejudices of a tradition "are [the] biases of our openness to the world" (note 68). It is crucial, in order to properly comprehend what Gadamer is saying, to see that this is not an admission of a shortcoming, in hermeneutic understanding, but the concrete specification of the finite character of human reason, in contradistinction to the impossible claim of enlightenment reason. To maintain, or "suspect," that this might be a "flaw" or "shortcoming" in Gadamer's position is, in effect, to confess one's strong attachment to an "idea" of "reason" as "absolute" (note 81). To seek, in effect, a "standpoint that is beyond any standpoint [überstandpunktliche Standpunkt]."[87] Like Odysseus of old we need to "stop our ears," brace ourselves, against this alluring chimera—"a pure illusion [eine reine Illusion]."[88]

Gadamer's position thus arises out of—and is substantiated by—a critical encounter with the heritage of the Enlightenment which constitutes, for him, the general intellectual-historical background/horizon within and out of which he articulates his position. In putting the *prejudice* against *prejudice* in question he challenges, in effect, the hubris of *his* heritage, the tangible inheritance of the West, in its claim to have mastered—via scientific reason—the exigencies of human existence and to have elevated itself above the rest of humankind. His central point, in all of this, is that reason is always, and of necessity, situated in a lived heritage on which it depends. And thus, it can never be "absolute" or "pure" but is necessarily and always already enmeshed and entwined in the concerns of lived-life, suffused with *prejudices* and *prejudgments*.

At this point and in view of our central concern in this chapter—the value of "Gadamer's work," or of philosophical hermeneutics, for contemporary African philosophy—we need to make a quick detour and glance at the work of Lucien Lévy-Bruhl. This is a paradigmatic, or an ideal, example of the kind of enlightenment inspired perspective that Gadamer defrocks.

The famed philosopher and anthropologist Lévy-Bruhl is remembered for his concept of "primitive mentality" which, towards the end of his life, he repudiated. For him, *grosso modo*, Westerners think rationally (i.e., they grasp the "object" in its "objectivity"). They do not admix, or intermingle, in their thinking or reasoning conjectures, emotions, beliefs, and so on, from differing realms of life. On the other hand, the thinking and/or reasoning of "primitives" which, according to Lévy-Bruhl, is subject to the "general laws governing collective representations,"[89] is

> always bound up with preperceptions [sic], preconceptions, preconnections [sic], and we might almost say with *prejudgments* [i.e., prejudices]; and thus it is that primitive mentality, just because it is mystical is also prelogical [sic].[90]

In other words, the mentality of "natives" (i.e., "primitive mentality") is "mystical," "prelogical," precisely because it is "bound up" with "prejudgments," i.e., prejudices. This is an extreme case of the kind of perspective critiqued by Gadamer; in which, the "superiority" of the Western mode of thinking—or, more accurately, of the Western "mind"—is affirmed in view of an impossible idea of reason. An idea that does not recognize, as we saw with Gadamer, that human reason is always situated in, and necessarily entwined with, "prejudgments" (i.e., prejudices).

Indeed, for Gadamer, "What is necessary is a fundamental rehabilitation of the concept of prejudice and a recognition of the fact that there are legitimate prejudices, if we want to do justice to man's finite, historical mode of being."[91] This "rehabilitation," as we have already seen, is the hermeneutic tailor-fitting of reason to human finitude. Or, as Joseph J. Kockelmans puts it, "Every scientific proposition is theory-laden [i.e., suffused with prejudgments] and thus remains fallible in principle. We are [thus] left in science with conjectures and refutations only."[92] Which, in terms of our present discussion, means that

> For humans there is nothing wrong in accepting that to know always means to understand within a context of meaning [i.e., prejudice] that is [always] already given in advance. This acceptance brings indeed an interpretative dimension into the picture. But what is called for here is not skepticism but understanding of, and respect for, the limits of human [finite] understanding.[93]

Indeed, "what is called for" is the recognition and acceptance of the character of human finitude.

To be sure, in the above remarks, I am not trying to valorize Lévy-Bruhl's defunct notion, but to further reinforce Gadamer's view, with which Kockelmans is in complete accord, that reason—and not only that of "primitives"—is always bound up with a lived world(s) in and out of which it articulates itself. That it is always "theory-laden" and necessarily entangled and intermixed with prejudices, prejudgments (i.e., "conjectures"). That it (i.e., reason) always and necessarily articulates itself out of lived situations that supply it with the issues and concerns it reflects on and engages. That it articulates itself in and out of a horizon constituted by concerns that reflexively provoke its reflective undertakings. In this regard, Thomas S. Kuhn, in sync with Gadamer and Kockelmans, in describing the highest level of scientific activity writes,

> Faced with an admittedly fundamental anomaly in theory . . . he [the scientist] will push the rules [and procedures] of normal science harder than ever . . . he will seek for ways of magnifying the breakdown, of making it more striking and perhaps also more suggestive . . . in the latter effort he will, in the first place, often seem [like] a man searching at random, trying experiments just to see what will happen . . . the scientist in crisis will constantly try to generate speculative theories that, if successful, may disclose the road to a new paradigm and, if unsuccessful, can be surrendered with relative ease.[94]

In other words, scientific activity, the kind that can possibly inaugurate "new paradigm[s]," is always a tinkering and a thinking that happens not in the sanitized atmosphere of logic, rigor, and methodic constancy (i.e., "normal science") but always takes place intermingled and entwined in and with the world, "searching at random." This is the realm of "extraordinary science" or science properly speaking.[95] Thus, paradigm inaugurating scientific work (i.e., scientific activity at its highest level) always arises out of a creative state of affairs, a haphazard "searching at random" suffused with "conjectures" and "speculative theories"—"preconceptions, preconnections [sic], and . . . prejudgments" (i.e., prejudices; see note 90).

Engaged, as it is, with "trying experiments just to see what will happen," it requires imagination more than rigor and a willingness to let what shows itself come forth. All of this, necessarily, involves "prejudgments" (i.e., prejudices). Kuhn's account of "extraordinary science" accords nicely with Gadamer's "rehabilitation" of the "concept of prejudice" and—from within the history and philosophy of science—substantially corroborates Gadamer's position. In effect, as Vattimo points out, summing up the contemporary consensus, this accord basically erases "the distinction between *Natur* and *Geisteswissenschaften* since even the so-called hard sciences verify and falsify their statements only within paradigms or preunderstandings [sic]."[96] Thus, scientific thinking is itself internal to and a species of interpretative finite human reason.

In other words, the scientist confronting a "crisis," as Kuhn tells us, "will constantly try to generate speculative theories that, if successful, may disclose the road to a new paradigm." Could it be that s/he is "searching at random," rummaging through her/his heritage, his/her scientific training and general culture (i.e., ideas, beliefs, myths, etc.) for the *right* "biases of our openness to the world"?[97] Strange as it may seem, we have all become "primitives," once again!

V

The originary moment of Gadamer's stance is thus a critical questioning of a received tradition, that of European modernity; in which, " 'through reflection and doubt' "[98] and the "analogy"[99] of "pure reason,"[100] is established an impossible pedestal for rationality. It is important to emphasize this point notably because Gadamer has been accused of espousing, or articulating, a conservative position submissive to tradition.[101] In contradistinction to such charges, Gadamer's point of departure is a critical encounter of a tradition grounded on a narrow and negative conception of prejudgment and the reformulation, following Heidegger's lead, of an enabling conception of prejudice as the grounding source of human understanding.

In articulating his critique, Gadamer explores the theme of temporal distance, utilizes Aristotle's conception of the rationality of ethical conduct as a model for hermeneutics, and details and enunciates a positive/enabling conception of prejudice/prejudgment. He also, as we shall see next, critically appreciates, explores, and appropriates Hegel's dialectical notion of experience. On this point, in reference to Gadamer's own self-assessment regarding Hegel, and the "present day" situation of philosophy, Vattimo writes,

> The point of departure of present day philosophy, says Gadamer, still remains Hegel: a Hegel in whom the dominant concept is not that of *Versöhnung*, of reconciliation and thus of the completed system, of the self-transparency of absolute spirit; but of the concept of objective spirit [il concetto dello spirito oggettivo]. Based on this concept it can be affirmed that Hegel triumphs over all those critiques that had validated against him the scope [la portata] of the objective knowledge of the sciences.[102]

And so, in view of the centrality of Hegel, for Gadamer's thinking, we need now to look at his appreciative reading of Hegel, in some detail, in order to properly grasp, or comprehend, his stance in all of its intricate and nuanced complexity.

Gadamer starts by acknowledging that "Hegel has thought through the historical dimension in which the problem of hermeneutics is rooted."[103] In contrast to the leveled and uniform conception of experience, to be found in the natural sciences and the "historico-critical method,"[104] Hegel retains the "historicality"[105] of experience. Gadamer endorses Hegel's recognition of the concreteness and irreducibility of the negative in human experience. For Hegel, the negative is the central moment through which the movement of consciousness, towards higher levels, is propelled and comes to fruition. The merit of his approach lies in the fact that it does not impute to its object anything external; rather, it closely follows this self-unfolding "from one form of knowing to the next" and develops its actuation "from [within] an immanent necessity"[106] in the concrete thought-object itself.

This movement, moreover, is not conceived as an abstract schematization of experience. It is seen as the dialectical self-unfolding and conceptualization of the particular thought content, as such. After praising and expressing agreement with Hegel, Gadamer goes on to point out that the shortfall in Hegel's position is located in the fact that the "nature of experience is conceived in terms of that which goes beyond it"[107] since experience itself, for Hegel, "can never be science."[108] Experience, as the negative, is merely the fading moment of transition whose flourishing or fulfillment is achieved in a higher mode of consciousness. As Gadamer puts it,

> [For Hegel] . . . the perfection of experience is "science," the *certainty of itself in knowledge*. Hence his criterion of experience is that of self-knowledge. That is why the dialectic of experience must end *with the overcoming of all experience* which is attained in absolute knowledge, i.e., in the complete identity of consciousness and object.[109]

Hegel views experience, or the negative, from the point of view of realized and thus surpassed experience, that is, from the perspective of absolute knowledge which, for him, ends "with the overcoming of all experience." Gadamer, on the other hand, is interested in that which cannot be "overcome," the essential negativity of experience as such, which holds true for all human life. He is concerned with the irreducible structure of finitude, latent in human existence. Hegel to a certain extent retains, in the concreteness of his dialectic, the concreteness of human experience and life, which is what is central for Gadamer. His quarrel with Hegel arises from the latter's impossible claim to a point of view beyond all experience, or finitude, which overlooks its own entrenchment, or rootedness, in mortal existence and purports to legislate for all time.[110]

Hermeneutical experience, if it is to be true to itself, has to incorporate finitude. Experience, says Gadamer, instructs us to recognize "what is." But "what is" and is permanent is not this or that situation. It is "what cannot be done away with" and this is "human finitude." In other words, "true experience is that of one's own historicality."[111] It necessarily follows, then, that hermeneutical experience—which is concerned with understanding that which is preserved and passed down in and through a heritage—in being, itself, within the realm of experience as such, must exhibit its basic structure. It must harbor and tangibly reflect the finite/limited character of human experience. The stance it takes, toward the past and/or Other traditions, is thus an effort not to assimilate but to comprehend that which its own and/or Other traditions harbor and preserve. It does not start from a "certainty of itself in knowledge," but an awareness of its own mortal and specific particularity, as distinct from the past and/or Other traditions.

All of this chimes nicely with Gadamer's critique of the Enlightenment's critique of prejudice; the impossible claim of having attained, a "standpoint . . . beyond any standpoint [überstandpunktliche Standpunkt]" (note 87). As noted in chapter 1, this is the source of the brazenly imperious belief that "the mission of human reason" is to attain "perfect mastery of the world."[112] This is what Gadamer refers to as "the enlightenment's belief in perfection"[113] which "is a pure illusion"[114] analogous to, and the operative sanction of, Hegel's rather extravagant claim that: "logic [i.e., his *Science of Logic*] is . . . the realm of pure thought . . . the exposition of God . . . in his eternal essence, before the creation of nature and a finite mind."[115]

From all that has been said thus far then, it follows that, the hermeneutical effort is the site in which one's own and/or Other traditions are recognized in their finiteness and heard in their distinctive specificity. This is the basic and central claim of Gadamer's "effective-historical consciousness" on which I have staked the possibility of differing traditions encountering each Other in a "self-standing" manner.[116] Up to this point—having preliminarily indicated the concordance of Gadamer and Zär'a Ya'əqob and having seen Gadamer's favorable disposition towards "a Chinese wise person with his disciples"—we have been explicating the substantial core presuppositions and scaffolding of his hermeneutical perspective. We need now to locate and specify its precise sense, by examining Gadamer's direct pronouncements on what he has named the "effective-historical consciousness." We will do so by utilizing examples from the African historical experience and, in this way, we will tangibly validate the assertions made in the opening pages of this chapter.

VI

As Palmer points out, Gadamer "uses typologies of three kinds" of *I-Thou* relations in specifying his conception of the "effective-historical consciousness." These are "(1) the thou as [an] object within a field, (2) the thou as reflexive projection, and (3) the thou as tradition speaking."[117] By exploring these three types of awareness, or lack thereof, of the present in its relation to its own heritage and/or Other traditions, we shall determine the sense and meaning of Gadamer's conception of the "effective-historical consciousness." Our focus in this, as already indicated, will be to highlight how openness to Other traditions is located in the tangible awareness of the finite distinctiveness of one's own historical heritage as a particular human inheritance. This is the claim with which we opened this chapter and must now firmly confirm.[118]

In the first type (the thou as an object "within a field"), the I-Thou relation occurs as the experience of a subject—an abstract "I"—over against an inert object. On the whole, this is the relation and kind of experience in which the human sciences find themselves when they try to replicate the scientific approach of the natural sciences. In this relation the past, and/or Other traditions, are experienced as an object that can be manipulated at will, within a "field" or an arena of concern, in symmetry with established procedures and presuppositions. In this regard, Walt Rostow's *The Stages of Economic Growth: A Non-Communist Manifesto* (1960) and the Soviet distortion of Marx's work that goes by the name *Diamat* (dialectical materialism), typify this stance in being mirror reflections—from opposing political perspectives—of the way the past and/or Other traditions are reduced to the level of manipulability.

In these perspectives, the past or Other traditions have no distinctive specificity of their own and are subordinate to the "five stages of economic growth" (Rostow) or the laws of dialectical materialism. Jean-Paul Sartre makes precisely this point, in criticizing the French Communist Party, when he states that for this kind of Marxism, "[a]nalysis consists solely in getting rid of detail, in forcing the signification of certain events."[119] This kind of thinking is not concerned with the meaning, or sense, of actual unfolding events. Its sole concern is the reigning "truth" of the present: the "party line" and/or the assumptions/prejudices of the "five stages."[120]

The human reality it objectifies is transformed into something static and is never allowed to show itself. It is important to note that this is a kind of formulaic thinking in which lived experience, or that which a heritage discloses, is shunned in favor of an established orthodoxy, be it political and/or "scientific." This is also the outlook of Lévy-Bruhl which, as we noted earlier, in encountering Other traditions affixes on them a label (i.e., "primitive mentality") in symmetry with the prevalent "scientific" presuppositions of ethnographic study. This stance, lacking in any critical sense of its own specificity and human limitation (i.e., that it is a specific and particular finite human perspective among others) elevates itself to the same extent that it downgrades Other traditions and/or its own past.

As we saw in chapter 1, this is the colonizing stance of "la mission civilisatrice" and of Rudyard Kipling's "The White Man's Burden." In this regard, as Basil Davidson points out,

> The whole international [colonial] enterprise was tackled as though the object, to apply the quip of 1886 of a British governor of the Gold Coast, seemed to be to seize on territory and then "as much as possible to rule the country as if there were no inhabitants." Were they not dealing, as the first British high commissioner of East Africa affirmed, "with a *tabula rasa*," a blank and untouched page of humankind where they could write whatever they might wish?[121]

The colonialist attitude instantiates the first type of I–Thou relation precisely because it is not a "relation" but a *reduction* of the Other to an object. In its "scientific" certainty of itself, the first type of I–Thou relation is in sync with the colonial stance in objectifying the Other as a focus of scientific study and/or control. It "encounters" Others, as Vattimo points out, in the rather conceited certainty of itself that, "we Europeans are the best kind of humanity, [and] the whole course of history is ordered so as to realize more or less completely this ideal."[122] The West, in this frame of things, being the *true template* of humanity. This then, is a "self-encounter" of humanity (i.e., of Europe) with less developed, primitive, and/or retarded versions of *itself*.

In the second type (thou as "reflexive projection"), the I–Thou encounter is also experienced inauthentically. The past is recognized in its otherness as a Thou, and yet it is not allowed to come forth or disclose itself. In this situation the present, is basically engaged with itself, as a "reflexive projection," which it takes to be the Other in its proper Otherness. What is at work here is a self-assured and, indeed, a self-absorbed reflection that is blind to, or unaware of, its own distinctive and finite specificity. As Gadamer points out,

> Historical consciousness knows about the otherness of the other . . . It seeks in the otherness of the past [or Other traditions] not the instantiation of a general law [as in the first type], but something historically unique. By *claiming to transcend its own conditionedness* [sic] *completely in its knowing of the other*, it is involved in *a false dialectical appearance*, since it is actually seeking to master, as it were, the past.[123]

In "claiming to transcend its own" finitude, it is victimized by the tacit/lived prejudices latent in the "conditionedness" it claims it has overcome. It falls prey to the "hidden laws"[124] (i.e., the lived prejudices) which lubricate and make possible the normal actuation of its existence. In "claiming to transcend its own conditionedness," it is victimized by "the tyranny of hidden prejudices" that make it "deaf,"[125] be it to its own or Other traditions.

An example, cut-to-order, of this second type of I–Thou relation is missionary paternalism.[126] Conversion is aimed at spiritual mastery. It is focused on saving the native from himself! It presupposes the human deficit of the Other. The revealed truths of Christianity are not subject to dialogue, or discussion, they are obligatory. As V. Y. Mudimbe puts it, "the missionary does not enter into dialogue with the pagans . . . but must impose the law of God that he incarnates . . . God is rightly entitled to the use of all possible means, even violence, to achieve his objective."[127] The missionary projects and sees demons, in the worship traditions of the natives, precisely because he takes himself to be the spokesperson of *the truth*. Indeed, as Gadamer puts it, "A person who does not accept that he is dominated by prejudices will fail to see what is shown by their light."[128] Analogously, Levinas's elevating of the "Bible and the Greeks" above all things human (first section of chapter 2) is a good example of this attitude of being ensnared by "a false dialectical appearance." In "certainty of itself in knowledge" (Hegel), it sees its own specificity (i.e., the "Bible and the Greeks") as constituting the humanity of the human, as such. Thus, in spite of the fact that Levinas rejects and Hegel articulates the totalizing violence of metaphysics, when it comes to the "native" (i.e., the "exotic") they both endorse the silencing effect of this violent effacing (i.e., the totalizing project of "la mission civilisatrice").

This second type of the I–Thou relation is a slightly modified version of the first, in which the Other is totally objectified. This partial objectification, as in the first type, does not risk the standpoint of the present. Missionary work never stakes its own convictions.[129] In both cases, the point of departure is the myopic belief that "we Europeans are the best kind of humanity." In this "encounter," as in the first, the past or Other traditions are rendered mute. The missionary sees the Other, the "natives" as, at best, a lower grade of humanity in need of his/her "elevating redemptive" work (i.e., converting and civilizing). Just as for Levinas, all that which is beyond Europe is merely "exotic" or "dance" and has to be subsumed or "included"[130] within Europe. In all of this, the reigning "truth" of the present—of the Occident vis-à-vis the rest of the globe—is never staked, it is simply assumed and brutally imposed.

After presenting the first two defective types of the I–Thou relation, Gadamer turns to the third type (thou as "tradition speaking"). The basic structure of this dialogical situation is that life encounters life. In other words, the autonomy and independence of tradition, one's own and that of Others—as already noted in the hypothetical example of the "Chinese wise person with his disciples" and of Zär'a Ya'əqob—and the concrete "conditionedness" and /or flaws of one's own situated existence (note 10) are fully acknowledged. In this situated self-awareness the past, or Other traditions, are enabled to speak and the present to listen. In this truly dialogical encounter—Gadamer has the self-deprecating and incessantly self-critical and ironic stance of Socrates in mind[131]—the certainties/convictions of the present are staked and put in question.

It is this willingness on the part of the present (i.e., the interpreter/reader engaged with a text, oral and/or written) to risk its given and established prejudices that makes possible, for the past and/or Other traditions, the auditory space in and out of which they can make themselves heard. This is what is illustrated by the hypothetical example of the "Chinese wise person" and of Zär'a Ya'əqob. And so, as Gadamer puts it,

> [E]ffective-historical consciousness rises above this naïve comparing and assimilating [exemplified in the second type of the I–Thou relation] by letting itself experience tradition [its own and Other traditions] and by keeping itself open to the claim to truth encountered in it. The hermeneutical consciousness has its fulfillment not in its methodological sureness of itself, but in the same readiness for experience that distinguishes the experienced man by comparison with the man captivated by dogma. This is what distinguishes [and concretely constitutes the] effective-historical consciousness.[132]

As indicated earlier, Gadamer holds that experience instructs us to recognize "what is" (i.e., the finitude within which human life unfolds). To gasp what experience has to teach is to recognize one's immersion in history and to function within the bounds of this enabling limit. Only thus and in this way can the past and/or Other traditions be critically understood and heard in that which they transmit and have to say. And this possibility is open to the consciousness which like "the experienced man" is ready to receive what comes forth and risk an open ended encounter without restricting itself to the certitudes and/or convictions of the present.

The hermeneutical consciousness, like the experienced person, knows its past through its practical involvement with the tradition in which it is located. It is ready for experience in recognizing itself as having arisen from within a specific tradition and is thus open, in a critical and released way, for the historicity of its own existence and that of Others. It is receptive, in this way, to that which its historicity and that of Others, may have to offer. In other words, contra Levinas, Gadamer's stance is not grounded on the myopic belief that "humanity consists of the Bible and the Greeks."[133] Nor does he insist that "Europe, that's the Bible and the Greeks" and that

"Everything else in the world must be included in this. I do not have any nostalgia for the exotic. For me Europe is central."[134] Quite to the contrary—as we have seen in our detailed explication in this chapter—Gadamer is concerned with "remain[ing] open to the meaning of the other person or . . . text."[135] For, as Palmer points out, the "effective-historical consciousness" (i.e., the hermeneutical consciousness) is an awareness in which "history is ever at work."[136]

The "work" of "history" shows itself in the historicalness of this awareness in relating to itself and to Others. There is here, it has to be emphasized, a projective seeking that consciously owns up to and starts from *not* the "Bible and the Greeks" but its own finitude, and in this it is fully aware of its specific and distinctive particularity. And so, it is willing to give Others *the benefit of the doubt* and to listen. In this, it is not concerned with the methodic filtering of prejudices, for it is only from within sedimented prejudgments—which constitute the present actuality of a heritage—that the past and what it says can be heard. "Reason," as Gadamer tells us, "exists for us only in concrete, historical terms" and so "it is not its own master, but remains constantly dependent on the given circumstances in which it operates."[137] In this lived awareness of itself, the hermeneutical consciousness is thus open to Otherness. It is this awareness that allows it a certain leeway, a self-critical ironic distance from itself, à la Socrates.

In being aware of its possibilities, it sees itself specified and actuated by the very limits of the heritage that avails it its possibilities. Unlike "the man captivated by dogma," or the scientific Enlightenment, captive to "the mission of human reason" and the "perfect mastery of the world," the "effective-historical consciousness" does not see the past as surpassed and Others as "exotic" (Levinas). Quite to the contrary, in all that has been detailed in this chapter, we have been able to see that such a consciousness is the living incarnation of a stance which, "always sees its own present in such a way that it sees itself, as it sees the historically other."[138] In being alert to and tangibly aware of its own lived situated finitude—in this concrete awareness—"it sees itself," as "historically Other" vis-à-vis "the historically other."

In the face of the Other, as we saw in Gadamer's remarks regarding "a Chinese wise person," this stance grounds itself in the particularity of its heritage (i.e., in the recognition of its specificity, its limits, and/or possible shortcomings). In this it understands that "the historical finiteness of our being" is such that "we are aware that after us others will understand in a different way."[139] Each different understanding being an appropriation of tradition, "a fusion of horizons"[140] from within a specific moment of its self-unfolding. Thus, for Gadamer, there is never a final or terminal understanding of anything. Indeed, as he puts it, "An interpretation that was correct 'in itself' would be *a foolish ideal* that failed to take account of the nature of tradition."[141] What we do have is "a discipline of questioning [eine Disziplin des Fragens] and of research [und des Forschens], a discipline that vouches for the truth [die Wahrheit verbürgt]."[142]

Having now concluded our explication, let us glance back and see what has been achieved. This we will do by reference to the claims made in the first two paragraphs of this chapter. In the words of Plato's Socrates, spoken towards the end of the penultimate book of the *Politeia:* "let us take up again what was said at first, which has led us to this point."[143]

VII

We began this chapter with the claim that Gadamer's stance, in being critically aware of its own situatedness, is open to the past and to Other traditions. In clinching this point it is imperative to note that, for Gadamer, it is "Precisely through our finitude, the particularity of our being, which is evident even in the variety of languages, [that] the infinite dialogue is opened in the direction of the truth that we are."[144] Finitude, for Gadamer, as already noted, is not an insurmountable impasse of human existence, but its very possibility. As we saw in chapter 2, "the truth" of this "infinite dialogue," grounded in our finitude, which "we are," is what Césaire refers to as "a universal rich with all that is particular, rich with all the particulars, the deepening and coexistence of all the particulars."[145] Indeed, "tout le particulier," in all their assorted diversity and in sum, constitute the tangible actuality of "the truth that we are."[146]

Césaire and Gadamer echo each other, out of culturally and historically differing thematic concerns, precisely because each articulates a stance that instantiates, or incarnates, the truth of the "effective-historical consciousness." In recognizing "tout le particulier" as our common human inheritance they inhabit—from within *differing* "particulars"—the realm of "familiarity and strangeness" (note 76) that constitutes our lived postcolonial world. In and out of differing cultural-historical horizons each sees itself, in relation to the Other, within a specific historicity relative to the Other (note 138). This is the stance of openness (Offenheit), in being concretely aware of one's "*being-history*."[147] Or, as Vattimo points out,

> [Our] continuity with the history of humanity [la storia umana]—which we carry with us, in traces [tracce], logical structures, "a priori" forms of experience, in language—is the only possible source [fonte] of criteria, of rules, of rational (better: reasonable) directives which is given to us to possess [che ci sia dato di possedere].[148]

In this image or interpretation of things, the plurality of "particulars" of Césaire and Gadamer are the differing cultures, histories, heritages (i.e., languages) in and through which we maintain our *being*, within the compass of "la storia umana." This is what constitutes, for us all, a lived historically variegated-hybrid and multiple common inheritance of "familiarity and strangeness." This, as Vattimo puts it, is our common "storehouse of treasures,"[149] the originary ground of "the infinite dialogue . . . in the direction of the truth that we are."

And so, the value of "Gadamer's work," for the discourse of contemporary African philosophy, lies in its expository laying out of a perspective attuned to the "familiarity and strangeness" that is our postcolonial world. "Gadamer's work" maps out the inclusive contours and/or parameters of a practice of philosophy focused on the *chiaroscuro* actuality of our contemporary world and thus of Africa's postcolonial condition. Fanon and Cabral—and also Césaire—as I have noted in the introduction to *The Hermeneutics of African Philosophy* (1994), are forerunners of the practice of contemporary African philosophical hermeneutics precisely because each negotiates and articulates—from within the chiaroscuro of Africa's "familiarity and strangeness"—an interpretative stance focused on, and arising from within, the exigencies of this lived situation. Fanon names this in-between "une zone de non-être," and Cabral refers to it as the "frustration complex"[150] of the colonized.

This is the "gap between *actuality* and *ideality*,"[151] "the true locus [Ort] of hermeneutics" (note 77), in and out of which African philosophical hermeneutics actuates itself. To what end? The envisioning and synthesizing of a new world, or, as Césaire puts it, "It is a new society that we must create, with the help of all our brother slaves, a society rich with all the productive power of modern times, warm with all the fraternity of olden days."[152] The next chapter, focusing on Marx, Heidegger, and Césaire, will explore the *negative* source (i.e., the negativity) that will serve as the originary ground of this possibility.

5

Karl Marx, Martin Heidegger, and Postcolonial Africa

> "Brother," he said. "Brother, what are we? What are we blackmen [sic] who are called French?" His voice grew bitter. I had never asked myself that question. I was young then and thoughtless.
>
> —The dying words of Toundi, a houseboy[1]

> Where everyone tolerates and condones scandal, scandal disappears.
>
> —Albert Memmi[2]

> I still believe that the unexamined life is not worth living.
>
> —James Baldwin[3]

I

The concern of Karl Marx's *1844 Manuscripts* is a critique of capitalist relations of production in the way they impact human existence. Enclosed within the confines of European culture and history, it is an assessment of modern society oriented toward the necessity of disclosing a radically different mode of life.[4] It is aimed at thinking the possibility of bypassing a mode of existence which nullifies life in its actualization. The appropriation of life, in work and labor, is experienced as the loss of life. The being of the human being, in relation to all that is, is focused on "having"—possession, property—and yet this "having" is lived as a process of self-negation, mortification, lack.

It is on decoding this paradox, in modern existence, that the *Manuscripts* are focused. In Heideggerian terms, what is at issue, in these texts, is the "being of the inquirer." In other words, what is at issue is the neglect of the "ontic-ontological priority"[5]of human life (i.e., Dasein, there-being) in the context of the capital-labor relation, within which the "average everyday" structure (i.e., the "they self") of modern society is constituted. Looked at in this manner, the *Manuscripts* are in very close proximity to Heidegger's concern with human existence, the "there" of *Sein*.

As Heidegger himself points out, in the last piece of writing that he authored, the aim of his thinking is "to prepare the possibility of a transformed abode of man in the world."[6] As we shall see, in the exposition of the relevant sections of *Being and Time*, Heidegger's discussion of the "they self," (i.e., the *das Man*) of the *Mitsein* (being-with) of modern everyday life, shares with Marx's critique of alienation, the concern with the reduction of human existence to the level of *things* (i.e., the presence-at-hand) that occurs in modern capitalist society. In this regard, as Kostas Axelos puts it,

> Marx and Heidegger do not say in whatever manner the same thing, but their thinking moves within the "same." This unity of the same (*diese Selbigkeit*) embraces them together. Together they are on the un-grounded terrain (*auf dem bodenlosen Boden*) of modern history, in the epoch of subjectivity; together they dare an attempt to overcome philosophy; together they struggle for a new comprehension of being. Marx does not make the distinction between Being and beings [essente]; but maybe Heidegger, on his part, does not take into consideration certain important aspects of the existent [dell'essente].[7]

My purpose, in what follows, is not to explore the various themes outlined by Axelos but to show how, from differing angles, both thinkers focus on the "same." They do so by valuating, focusing on, and making everyday existence, in the modern world, the center of their reflections. They engage this question in terms of the condition of life, in the modern world, and the oblivion of the differentiated totality—the interplay of life in various and diverse spheres—which constitutes the being of human existence.

To be sure, the object of the interpretation is not to level off the differences between Marx and Heidegger. Nor is it to make Marx a questioner of being. Rather, it is to explore the fundamental similitude of these thinkers, on this crucial point. I am not, furthermore, particularly concerned with "understanding a thinker [Marx or Heidegger] in his own terms," but in exploring certain confluences in their thought so as to "pursue it [i.e., their thinking] to the core,"[8] and in so doing bring to the fore that which is in "need of being seen,"[9] in terms of a parallel concern in the situation of postcolonial Africa.

As Hans-Georg Gadamer tells us, when we take account of our human finitude, we become "aware" that we understand always in a "different way," in the way our history and time makes it possible for us to understand. Indeed, before us, "others" have understood the texts to be considered in their own way. Each different understanding or interpretation is, as it were, an appropriation of the text from within a specific moment of a historical horizon and context.[10] In this sense, the reading to be presented here is not an exposition of the "authentic" Marx nor of the "true" Heidegger, whoever they might be, but of those elements—in their respective perspectives—which are pertinent to the African postcolonial condition.[11] Following the example of Antonio Gramsci, in other words, what we hope to do is to mold and/or shape "Our Marx" and "Our Heidegger," so as to press them into service in engaging the contemporary African situation.[12]

And so, in what follows, in looking at Marx (section II) the exposition will orchestrate and layout the analysis of estrangement presented in the *Manuscripts*. Conversely, in looking at Heidegger (section III), the explication will engage the thematic of the "they self" (das Man) in the lived being-with (Mitsein) of modern society and, by utilizing ontic examples, it will to bring to the fore the inherent affinity of Heidegger's *ontological* analysis with Marx's *ontic* critique. In closing (sections IV and V), I will argue that in their respective concerns—with the reduced status of human existence—Marx and Heidegger share an analogous concern with the effort aimed at bypassing what Aimé Césaire refers to as the *chosification* (thingification)[13] of the colonized, which is the enduring effect of colonialism that—still to this day—determines Africa's postcolonial present.

II

The *1844 Manuscripts* are concerned with the concrete existential situation of the modern world.[14] These texts are a detailed critical dialogue with political economy centered on the humanity of the human within the socioeconomic frame constituted by the capitalist mode of production. In the first *Manuscript*, which concludes with the important section on estranged labor, Marx begins by undertaking an extended exploration of the conditions of life, in modern capitalist society, in terms of the abstract categories of political economy. His concern is the conditions of existence that these abstract categories posit and presuppose. He starts by taking political economy at its word and goes on to show, based on an immanent critique, that political economy affirms one thing in theory and does another in practice. It affirms the dignity of labor as the source of wealth in tandem with reducing the laborer, as a human being, to the status of a thing.

> [O]riginally and in theory [in the abstract categories of political economy] the whole produce of labor belongs to the worker. But at the same time he [the political economist] tells us that in actual fact what the worker gets is the smallest and utterly indispensable part of the product—as much, only, as is necessary for his existence, *not as a man*, but as a *worker* and for the propagation, *not of humanity* but of the *slave class of workers*. The political economist tells us that everything is bought with labor [the expenditure of life as activity] and that capital is nothing but accumulated [i.e., objectified, congealed] labor but at the same time he tells us that the worker, far from being able to buy everything, must *sell himself* and his *human identity*.[15]

The discourse of political economy recognizes the worker as the source of wealth and in the same breath forgets the human being. The "human identity" of the worker, which is the originary ground for the possibility of productive labor, is *not* recognized by political economy as the source of wealth. Rather, the human being himself is seen as nothing more than a laboring-thing (i.e., wages or variable capital), an aspect of capital. Within the circuits of capital this is what the "human identity" of the worker is reduced to.

The laborer is the manifestation of life as activity. For Marx, as for Hobbes before him, life is activity. The capitalist on the other hand, in so far as capital is objectified or congealed labor—the result of previous labor (i.e., previous life activity)—is the lived personification of inertia, of a life that does not live its own actuation. "In labor" as life activity, Marx observes "all the natural, spiritual, and social variety of individual activity [i.e., her/his existence] is manifested and is variously rewarded, whilst dead capital always shows the same face and is indifferent to real [i.e., lived] individual activity."[16] The human being, through her/his life, in his/her interaction with the natural and social environment—of which he/she is an integral organic part—shows forth the actuality of what is, in disclosing a world of and for human habitation. The world we live in, in other words, is not merely a "natural" world. It is a world of culture-history constituted in and through the productive self-transformation of nature, which is brought about or actuated through labor (i.e., productive [natural] life activity).

The capitalist (i.e., the rich man) as the embodiment of capital merely subsists as a derivative of lived life. Life as activity, as concretely situated human existence, lives itself. The capitalist simply subsists in a world brought forth by the activity—the life—of the laborer. Indeed, "according to the political economist it is solely through labor that man enhances the value of the products of nature" since labor, or life activity, is "man's active possession."[17] And yet, "according to this same political economy the landowner and the capitalist, who qua landowner and capitalist are merely privileged and idle gods [i.e., inert entities], are everywhere superior to the worker and lay down the law to him."[18] This then is the paradox, the tragic enigma, of modern existence.

In the above passages, the distinctions Marx makes are crucial precisely because it is life in the concrete process of being itself which is being contrasted with the power of inert/lifeless things (i.e., capital). Political economy affirms the first and paradoxically substantiates the second. "The capitalist," says Marx, "possesses this power, not on account of his personal or human qualities but inasmuch as he is an *owner* of capital." He has a juridical relation to it.[19] "His power is the *purchasing* power of his capital."[20] The "power of his capital" is *his* only in so far as he can render service by making his life an instrument (i.e., a thing) useful to the logic of capital. If he fails to do so (e.g., the Wall Street Crash of 1929) in periods of economic depression, the capitalist contemplates suicide. Just as in periods of prosperity his existence is capricious and excessive and constituted by cupidity and conspicuous consumption. His life is service to capital. Capital does not exist for him, rather, he exists for Capital and its ever expanding circuits.

As Marx tells us, "The possessing class and the proletariat class represent one and the same human self-alienation [Selbstentfremdung]."[21] The capitalist "feels satisfied and affirmed in this self-alienation" he lives it and experiences it as "*power*, and possess in it the *appearance* of a human existence."[22] On the other hand, the worker "feels destroyed in this alienation" and experiences life as "impotence" as the "reality of an inhuman existence."[23] Within the circuits of capital the worker and the capitalist occupy inversely related positions, one *positive*, and the other *negative*. In both cases what is lost is the humanity of human existence.

In being the embodiment of the negative pole, in capitalist relations of production, the worker—in struggling to maintain a modicum of human existence—has the possibility of seeing beyond this relation. The capitalist, on the other hand, equates life with the possession of capital. Or, rather, he lives by being possessed by capital! He is "a rational miser."[24] As such he exists only for and insofar as he is an instrument, a *thing*, useful for the constant "expansion of value [i.e., capital]."[25] The worker exists in and as the incarnation of the obverse of this relation. As Marx tells us, capital also produces

> [T]he *human commodity*, man in the role of *commodity*; it produces him in keeping with this role as a *mentally* and physically *dehumanized* being.—Immorality, deformity, and the dulling of the worker and the capitalist.—Its product is the *self-conscious* and *self-acting commodity* . . . the human commodity . . . Great advance of Ricardo, Mill, etc., on Smith and Say, to declare the *existence* of the human being—the greater or lesser human productivity of the commodity—to be indifferent and even harmful. Not how many workers are maintained by a given capital, but . . . how much interest it brings in, the sum-total of the annual *savings*, is said to be the true purpose of production.[26]

In the circuits of capital both the capitalist and the worker are "dehumanized." The misfortune of the latter is that he/she experiences this as suffering and loss. On the other hand the capitalist is benumbed with cupidity. In either case, life, in the form of alienated labor or the cupidity of the capitalist, instead of being a self-actuating manifestation of itself becomes a means (i.e., a tool, an instrument for the aggrandizement of capital).[27]

The more the worker produces the less he/she *is* as a human being. Economic activity is *not* for the sustenance of life but for the expansion of capital (i.e., "how much interest it brings in" is the sole pertinent question). In this frame of things, the humanity of the human (i.e., the capacity to transform the human-natural environment in and through the exertion of life and, concurrently, the capacity of enjoying and being affirmed by this creative transformation) these two aspects of the humanity of the human are held apart, by law, as the condition of existence of the capitalist mode of production. The political struggle of the working class—the class struggle—is aimed at challenging this "artificial" (legal) separation of labor (life activity) from its congealed fruits (capital).

Here we are not concerned with the character of this struggle and how it is to unfold, according to Marxist theory. This is a topic that I have dealt with elsewhere.[28] The only thing that concerns us here is to locate the originary source of this struggle. The reduction of human existence to being an appendage of capital. A laboring and/or an avaricious *thing* whose existence depends solely on this singular aspect (i.e., whether it succeeds in making itself an instrument in the production and reproduction of capital).

What is lost, in this singularizing of life, is the differentiated totality, the richly diverse and inter-implicative aspects of human existence, which come forth in free life activity and constitute the being of human existence. And so, as Marx puts it,

> [T]he man who . . . lives purely by labor, and by a one sided, abstract labor, is considered by political economy only as a *worker*

> [i.e., a laboring-thing]. Political economy can therefore advance the proposition that the proletarian, the same as any horse [i.e. a domesticated beast of burden, a thing], must get as much as will enable him to work. It does not consider him when he is not working, as a *human being* [i.e., a father, mother, spiritual-biological being, needy, etc.] but leaves such considerations to criminal law, to doctors, to religion, to the statistical tables, to politics and to the poorhouse overseer.[29]

What concerns us here is not the soundness of Marx's analysis, as such. It suffices to note that, the validity of his assessment is attested to by the periodic economic crises of capitalism and the growing destitution—in the midst of plenty—of the working poor (i.e., the 99%).[30] Furthermore, the prevailing lack of the sense of life, or "meaning," that pervades and is endemic in modern society—attested to by those who are practitioners of social-work, psychology, and psychoanalysis—is ample evidence for the cogency of his views.[31] In terms of the basic concern of this chapter, as indicated above, what we need now is to see how Heidegger's reflections on das Man parallel Marx's critique.

III

As is well known, Heidegger's question, the question in and out of which his thinking unfolds, is the question of Sein.[32] But because Dasein is the "there" of being, or the lived existence in and through which being shows itself, the human situation and the question of being are intimately intertwined in a privileged manner. For Sein, always and necessarily, is disclosed only in and through the openness (i.e., the lived actuality of human existence) made possible by human involvement in the world of care and concern. As Thomas Sheehan points out, "This is a firm position that Heidegger never renounced [which is that]: "being" is given or appears (*das Sein west*) only in the activities of human beings."[33] And so, Heidegger engages the question of being in and through an analysis of Dasein. He is exclusively focused on human life in its everyday "concrete"[34] actuation. The question of being is thus explored and opened up through a reflection on the lived "average everydayness" of quotidian life.[35]

It is in this regard that the question of the "they self" (das Man), acquires a central position in the problematic of Heidegger's thought, since this question is directed to that which we are, for the most part, in our lived existence.[36] For, if the human being is the gateway, or avenue, for the disclosure of being, then the *authentic* or *inauthentic* possibilities of lived-life necessarily color that which being reveals in and through human existence. Indeed, as Michael E. Zimmerman points out,

> [A]uthenticity is not merely a change in theoretical attitude but instead a transformation of one's [inauthentic] mode of existing. Authenticity means becoming open and committed to one's own possibilities within the limits of one's own historical situation.[37]

If "authenticity" refers to a concrete-ontic modification in human existence, then that which is disclosed in and through this existence—in these two differing modalities—is necessarily colored by the authentic or inauthentic situation in and through which it shows itself. In other words, that which shows itself is necessarily marred, or conversely shows itself and flourishes, as effectuated in and by the way it comes forth.

What has also to be noted and seriously considered, furthermore, is that Heidegger's thinking has an evocative character.[38] He does not propose to prove his point, or win us over, by some kind of conclusive evidence. Rather, through a persistent probing of the issue in question, laced with strenuous and metaphoric expressions, Heidegger "calls" his reader to a different possibility of being/life. In this regard he shares much with Socrates, "the purest thinker of the West."[39] As Romano Guardini correctly points out, Socratic irony is directed solely at transforming the existential demeanor of those engaged in dialogue with him.[40] Analogously, Heidegger's ontological concerns, have an ontic orientation directed toward "the possibility of a transformed abode of man in the world." And so, consequent on an exposition of his basic concern, the question of being, and the privileged status of Dasein in this concern, Heidegger, systematically lays out the method to be utilized and the orientation to be taken. Thus he begins exploring the mode of human existence in the world (i.e., being-in-the-world), as the proper entry to the question of being.

Human existence, for Heidegger, unfolds in and out of its practical pragmatic involvements with entities *present-at-hand* in the context of an always already setup instrumental complex, the *ready-to-hand.* This constitutes the interlinked matrix—the interconnected socio-cultural-technical world—of tools and equipment in and through which modern existence unfolds itself. In this regard, as Karel Kosík has noted,

> The critique that sees in *Being and Time* the patriarchal world of backward Germany has fallen for the mystification of Heidegger's examples. Heidegger, however, is describing problems of the modern twentieth century capitalist world which he exemplifies—quite in the spirit of romantic disguising and concealment—by the blacksmith and forging.[41]

And so, the "there-being" of man, the actuality of human existence, is such that it is always already involved concretely and engaged in and with a world. Humans exist in various worlds concurrently. The world of academia in which I work, the world of the family that I live as a father, that of mechanical work (i.e., car repair) of which I know very little: all of these are differing intersecting environs of existence. We always live in one or another or in some intersecting *pasticcio* thereof, but never without a world.

Thus, the being of Dasein is "care."[42] The pre-reflective world of pragmatic practical circumspective engagement with things which is always already mine. This is the basic mode of the being-in of Dasein. It refers to the "there" of Dasein in the world. This necessarily is a specific world. Unlike entities present-at-hand (things of nature) and those that are ready-to-hand (i.e., instruments, tools), the being of human existence *is* and unfolds out of a world. Its "there" is constituted by its aware tacit and thus lived understanding, of its world. The present and ready-to-hand are merely in-place, fixed in a world.[43] Dasein on the other hand presupposes and is presupposed by the "worldhood of the world," this is that in which "a factical Dasein as such can be said to 'live.'"[44]

Human existence—always situated—unfolds out of the *sense* of the world it is situated in and institutes and which is always, in its very core, a being-with. Being-with is thus a co-primordial structure of Dasein's being-in. As Heidegger puts it, "the world is always already the one that I share with Others."[45] And so,

> The world of Dasein is a with-world [Mitwelt]. Being-in is being-with Others. Their being-in-themselves within-the-world is Dasein-with [Mitdasein].[46]

Circumspective "interhuman"[47] involvement with the ready-to-hand and with entities present-at-hand is the lived actuality of human life. In involvement with entities—things and tools—the purpose, the direction, and the requirement of the work at hand has or harbors within itself the "being-with [of] Others," as that in terms of which and for which involvement with entities is undertaken. The complex of significations in the purpose of involvement thus point to "entities with Dasein's kind of being—entities for which, in their concern, the product becomes ready-to-hand; and together with these we encounter the world in which wearers and users live, which is at the same time ours."[48] The world of the pragmatic instrumental complex, as a whole, is co-primordially the world lived with Others. We experience ourselves—i.e., as teachers, mechanics, tailors, etc.—and Others, also engaged in like activities, intermeshed and intertwined in the daily routine of life made possible by the inlaid maze of gear and equipment; the taken-for-granted environ of our concerns. The inlaid totality of—things and equipment—mediates our interactions, in fulfilling the needs and desires of quotidian life. As Heidegger puts it,

> [W]hen material is put to use, we encounter its producer or "supplier" as one who "serves" *well or badly*. When, for example, we walk along the edge of a field but "outside it," the field shows itself as belonging to such and such a person, and decently kept up by him; the book we have . . . The boat anchored at the shore . . . [are] . . . indicative of Others. The Others who are thus "encountered" in a ready-to-hand, environmental context of equipment, are not somehow added on in thought to some Thing which is proximally just present-at-hand; such "Things" are encountered from out of the world in which they are ready-to-hand for Others—a world which is always mine too in advance.[49]

The Others, as serving "well or badly," are always already there in the network of the instrumental complex. In the book, the boat, the upkeep of the field, and more broadly in the interconnected system of life (i.e., work, travel, communications, leisure, etc.) in and out of which the modern world in all of its complexity unfolds—the Others, as serving or served "well or badly," are always already *there*.

We do not encounter "people," and then what "they do." We experience, ourselves and Others in that which, in doing, actuates our very being/living. This "interhuman" world of everyday concern is radically altered when the regular and thus taken-for-granted fails to occur. When the sociocultural instrumental complex, which mediates the mundane concern with the routine incantations of quotidian life, gets jammed up then the character of the world, out of which it occurs, is disclosed. When, for example, an industrial strike, a power failure, or the uprising of a colonized people in a remote part of the world threatens or dislocates our taken-for-granted comforts and expectations, then the dimensions of existence are fundamentally altered. When,

> something ready-to-hand is found missing . . . this makes a *break* in those referential contexts which circumspections discovers. Our circumspection comes up against emptiness and now sees for the first time *what* the missing article was ready-to-hand *with*, and *what* it was ready-to-hand *for* . . . what is thus lit up is not just one thing ready-to-hand among others; still less is it something *present-at-hand* upon which equipment ready-to-hand is somehow founded: it is in the 'there' before anyone has observed or ascertained it.[50]

What is "lit up" is in the "'there'" and not in the instrumentality of the instrument that is "missing" or the present-at-hand. The "'there'" is the

Da of *Sein* and refers to tangible human existence in the concrete. What is "lit up" is thus the co-being of human Dasein (i.e., the realm in which we relate, "well or badly," to each Other).

The "'there'" of "interhuman" involvement in which being-with unfolds is concerned with entities. In so far as the Dasein-with of Others is understood by reference to the instrumental complex (i.e., as owner, supplier, worker, etc.), it is an element of its functioning. "In that with which we concern ourselves environmentally the Others are encountered as what they are; they are what they do [sie sind das, wae sie betreiben]."[51] Each of us—in our quotidian ordinary interactions—is what s/he does. The Other is not an entity; but the being-with of our sociality which is coterminous with being-in, as involvement and absorption, is mediated and overlaid by the instrumental complex. In this immersion, the Others—who are what "*they do*"—are of necessity "encountered proximally and for the most part in terms of the with-world with which we are environmentally concerned."[52]

And so, "When Dasein is absorbed in the world of its concern—that is, at the same time in its being-with toward Others—it is not itself." And then Heidegger asks, "*Who* is it, then, who has taken over being as everyday being-with-one-another?"[53] To this question Heidegger answers, "The Self of everyday Dasein is the *they-self*."[54] The upshot of all of the above is that Dasein—in its average everyday existence in the modern world—is "the they" (das Man). The amorphous and anonymous quotidian *self*, that each of us is, in the way we are publicly, "each Other like the Other."[55] How then does "the they-self," in its concrete everyday "interhuman" involvement with things and tools, in which we are like all the Others, understand the being that it is?

Having explored, in detail, the thematic of the sociality of the everyday of human existence in the modern world, Heidegger concludes section 27 of *Being and Time* with the following response to the above question:

> From the kind of being which belongs to the "they"—the kind which is closest—everyday Dasein draws its pre-ontological [i.e., ordinary] way of interpreting its being . . . it understands Dasein in terms of the world and comes across it as an entity within-the-world . . . But because the phenomenon of the world itself gets passed over in this absorption in the world, its place gets taken [tritt an seine Stelle] by what is present-at-hand within-the-world, namely, Things. The being of those entities which *are there with us*, gets conceived as presence-at-hand.[56]

It seems then that we have come full circle. Based on a polemically critical exploration of the self-understanding of political economy, the self-consciousness of the modern age, Marx determines that, the circuits of capital reduce human beings to *things*. Heidegger, analogously, based on a descriptive analysis of the lived conditions of the "modern twentieth century capitalist world" (note 41), concludes that the being of human existence in daily interaction, is "conceived as presence-at-hand."

From all that has been said above it should be clear that the world of everyday existence and the world with which the discourse of political economy is concerned are one and the same. Heidegger's analysis of the "they self" parallels Marx's critique of alienation because both focus on the way, the character of lived-life under modern conditions undermines, from within, the very life it actualizes. To be sure, the angle of their respective assessments differ: Marx is concerned with political economy, a discourse focused on economic interactions. And his analysis functions in terms of an underdeveloped ontological notion of the being of human existence. It is in terms of this conception that Marx critiques the alienation of existence—the reduction of human life to the level of a thing—without explicitly laying out its ontological presuppositions.[57]

Heidegger, analogously, is concerned with everyday existence (i.e., the lived work-world of pragmatic instrumental involvement) in co-being with Others. It is here that he locates the *inauthentic* world of the "they self" in which Dasein, in its being, as "being-with," is reduced to the status of a thing (i.e., a present-at-hand entity). This is the analysis whose penetrating negative assessment grounds the evocative character of Heidegger's thought focused, as he tells us, on "the possibility of a transformed abode of man in the world" (note 6). But, just as Marx does not make explicit his ontological underpinnings, Heidegger does not give us an inkling as to how we are to "prepare . . . a transformed abode of man in the world." Indeed, the most that he says is "Only a god can still save us."[58] Which is not saying much.

Thus, as we noted earlier with Axelos, "Marx does not make the distinction between being and beings . . . Heidegger, on his part, does not take into consideration . . . important aspects of the existent." This deficiency in their respective perspectives need not concern us, any further. Our project does not require of us an exploration of what this lack entails, for their respective projects. What it does require of us is to explicitly draw out the results of our explication and show its relation to the conditions of life in postcolonial Africa. The question that still needs to be engaged, in other words, is How does this confluence, in the thinking of Marx and Heidegger—focused on the conditions of modern life—relate to Africa's postcolonial condition, thematized in chapter1?

IV

As we have already seen, Africa's postcolonial condition is not one in which independence has resulted in Africa reclaiming itself. Quite to the contrary, under the rule of a replicant elite/strata, the continent endures as before. And so, Aimé Césaire's rather acerbic formulation regarding colonialism: "My turn to pose an equation: *colonization = thingification*"[59] is still pertinent and applicable. What does this say about the conditions of life in postcolonial Africa? What does it mean to say—under conditions of "formal independence"—that this mordant assessment is still applicable, still valid?

We noted earlier with Ake that, "independence . . . was . . . often a convenience of deradicalization [sic] . . . a mere racial integration of the political elite."[60] In most cases independence replaced "the white man" by an African understudy strata. Having secured power the replicant elite, of this strata, perpetuates colonial conditions as independence. There is a "minimum of readaptation . . . a flag"[61] and, under this alluring façade, the continuation "unchanged . . . of the economy, the thought, and the institutions left by the colonialists."[62] This, however, does not mean that independence was for naught.

In this regard, Basil Davidson has noted that independence was a necessary *étape*, or stage, in Africa's protracted struggle to reclaim itself.

> So, from this standpoint, it does not bother me at all that Africa today is full of trouble. It does not cause me to think that decolonization has been a "failure." Least of all does it make me think that this decolonization was "premature": that everything would have been better if decolonization hadn't begun in the 1950s but decades later, fifty years later, and so on. We thought, and consciously as I recall, that the sooner the better: if only because Africans could not even *begin* to face their [real] problems of unity and progress until they became free to confront these problems. And they could not become free to do this until they were free of the cultural—and therefore political—chains of the colonial period.[63]

Along similar lines, reflecting on the rather tumultuous period—the 1960s—when a great many African territories gained independence, Walter Rodney writes,

> But, all the to-ing and fro-ing from Contonou to Paris and from London to Lusaka and all the lowering and raising of flags cannot be said to have been devoid of meaning. Withdrawal of the directly controlled military and juridical apparatus of the colonizers was essential before any new alternatives could be posed with regard to political organization, social structure, [and] economic development.[64]

In effect, what both these veteran Africanists are telling us is that, to "begin to face their [real] problems," to properly engage the sobering questions of "political organization, social structure, [and] economic development," Africa had to first become sovereign. Instead of French West Africa, British Kenya, Portuguese Angola, with the achievement of independence the formal sovereignty of the people of Angola, Kenya, Senegal, and so on was established. In this formal manner one can say that Africa has indeed reentered the realm of human historical existence. This new status, however, in a tangible way, poses the challenge of giving it substance (i.e., of substantiating it).

Africans had been colonial subjects, today, in principle on a formal level, we are the citizens of sovereign states. It is the lack of substance, of this formal status, which allows us to maintain that Césaire's harsh assessment is still valid. How so? Well, as James Baldwin writing from within the context of segregation, a slightly different context, puts it, the citizen of a state ruled by segregation, analogous to a colonial subject, has a "place," in contradistinction to the free citizen of a non-segregated society, who has a "role."[65] In other words, the segregated is held in his/her "place" by brute force, the unmitigated violence (e.g., lynching) of the segregator. On the other hand, a citizen properly becomes a citizen by claiming and playing his/her "role" in a democratic society, under a republican/democratic organization of public life.[66]

Now, under colonial conditions, as Césaire tells us, the colonizer is awakened to "buried instincts, to covetousness, violence, race hatred."[67] He becomes a brutal "army sergeant, a prison guard, a slave driver,"[68] concurrently the "indigenous man" is reduced to the status of "an instrument of production."[69] In like manner, the officially free citizens of postcolonial Africa, like the segregated—or better still, the colonized—are held in 'place' by the violence of the replicant elite: their submission is the source of its power. Its violence is thus not gratuitous, but the very core of its being. Indeed, as Eqbal Ahmed describes it, the essential character of the *colonial-postcolonial state*—in Africa as in other parts of the "Third World"—is unmitigated violence.

> Scholars have noted that the colonial state was centralized and endowed with a well-organized, modern military, police, and administrative apparatus. The colonial powers gave only minor attention to the growth of representative institutions. Hence it was from its inception a modern despotism in that the quotient of coercion was much greater than that of consensus. More importantly in the colonial state the process of modern state formation was reversed: far from being the creation of an ascendant national bourgeoisie, *it was merely an* extension

> of the metropolitan state. A native class of civil servants and soldiers—the state bourgeoisie of the Third World—was created to serve the colonial state. From the start, then, the creation of the modern [colonial-postcolonial] state in the Third World involved the imposition of a well-developed military bureaucratic superstructure of power over an underdeveloped infrastructure of participation.[70]

This apparatus of coercion: "a well-developed . . . superstructure of power" overlaid on an "underdeveloped infrastructure of participation" constituted, out of the residual remains of "the colonial state," as an "extension of the metropolitan state," holds the *nominal citizens* of postcolonial Africa in check. It cows them into submission as the condition of the possibility of its very existence. An "extension" of a foreign power, it does not have "flexibility" in enforcing its rule. Indeed, as Machiavelli tells us, "nothing is so weak or unstable as a reputation for power that is not based on one's own forces."[71] Tacitly aware of its shaky position, the replicant elite, cannot afford a "democratic" façade. Attempts to claim the 'role' of citizen—no matter how timid—are thus brutally squashed; ferocity is proportionate to feebleness. This is the actuality of independence.

As Davidson tells us, with independence, "Politics came to an end" and the "mere administration" of *things* "took its place, reproducing colonial autocracy as the new 'beneficiaries' took the place of the old governors."[72] In this way, in the words of Fanon, "The party . . . which used to call itself the servant of the people"[73] becomes the enforcer of "obedience and discipline."[74] Instead of facilitating the "role" of citizen and making "Public business . . . the business of the public,"[75] it insist that the only "vocation of the people is to obey, to go on obeying, and to be obedient till the end of time."[76] It forbids the "role" of citizen and insists that "the people," at all times, know their "place."

Opposition is prohibited and "opposition parties . . . by dint of baton charges and prisons [are] condemned first to silence and then to a clandestine existence."[77] As in colonial times, the dialectic of violence is the go-between of those in power and all the rest. Servility reigns. No matter how meekly or hesitantly, if one tries to breach this setup and grasp the 'role' of citizen—the long hoped for status of being a free citizens in a free country—one is violently reminded of his/her "place." Those who were at the forefront of the struggle banish the population, which struggled for and brought about independence, "from history."[78] In this way the formerly colonized are *thingified.*

A thing, like a colonial subject, is something that does not control itself. It has no will of its own. It is utilized and at the disposal of another.

It has no power over itself.[79] The capitalist controls the worker, and reduces him to the status of a laboring thing, by controlling the "cost of existence and reproduction of the worker."[80] In like manner, the replicant elite—which has under its command "the wealth of the country"[81] and the power of the state—controls the resources and the very life of the formerly colonized. In this setup, of the party or movement which led the struggle, "nothing is left but the shell of a party, the name, the emblem."[82] Soon after independence, "being a party militant means that you take the short cut to gain private ends."[83] Without a political voice the population endures in a state of limbo, a perpetual unease.

Want, insecurity, and the fear and disquiet they generate rule the day. The population fragments into an infinite totality of scrounging. Various kinds of criminality and the wholesale prostitution of the female population ensue. If and when an ordinary person acts, or attempts to act, against the confines of this setup—as in colonial times—s/he is advised by the police, but mostly by the army.

One's biological existence requires resigning oneself to being a non-person. This insalubrious context foments duplicity, deceit, "bad faith": the former "militant is turned into an informer."[84] A parvenu lifestyle—owning new cars, colonial villas, etc.—of flashy glitter blooms. The replicant elite moves into what used to be the European "quarter." In all essentials, the colonial past is replicated. This time around, however, the roles of *colonizer* and *colonized* are played by the native—cast on both sides of this antagonistic divide—by reference to the culture of the former colonial power. The replicant strata and its elite and, on the other side, all the rest: reduced to jostling, scheming, scrounging, etc., intent on bare survival and/or getting "ahead."

In this atomized setup, each becomes for the Other a tool, a means of survival (i.e., of "getting by")—a *thing*, an entity present-at-hand. As we saw in chapter 1, the West is directly implicated in this snaring of *life* to *survival*, by the financial-military and political assistance it extends to "our partners."[85] But how did it all come to this?

V

The struggle for independence had been the unproblematic demand of ending direct foreign rule. In true dialectical fashion, once attained, this achievement became the very problem at hand. At the very moment when independence was secured, concurrent with it, commenced the victimization and marginalization of the vast majority. As Vijay Prashad explains, in Africa, as in the "Third World" as a whole, the termination of colonial rule, "came with a built-in flow."

> The fight against the colonial and imperial forces enforced a unity among various political parties and across social classes. Widely popular social movements and political formations won freedom for the new nations, and then took power. Once in power, the unity that had been preserved at all costs became a liability. The working class and the peasantry in many of these movements had acceded to an alliance with the landlords and emergent industrial elites. Once the new nation came into their hands, the people believed, the new state would promote a socialist program. What they got instead was a compromise ideology called Arab Socialism, African Socialism, Sarvodaya or NASAKOM that combined the promise of equality with the maintenance of social hierarchy.[86]

The exhilarating collapse of colonial empires having muddied the political space of independence, as Albert Memmi notes, in this euphoria, it was "often overlooked [that], a decolonized nation is actually only a nation undergoing . . . decolonization" and that "its often highly ambiguous dealings with Europeans [the former colonizers]" is constituted by the obfuscated ambiguity of "its resentment against them . . . while its former admiration for them is being rekindled."[87] In the midst of this "resentment" and "admiration," encouraged by the West,[88] and by their own sense of themselves, those who took power at the end of formal colonial rule, for the most part—in the very act of taking power—terminated the promise of the historic alliances that brought it about. Still, as Rodney points out, "the removal of overt foreign rule actually cleared the way toward a more fundamental appreciation of exploitation and imperialism."[89]

It did so, however, not on a politically neutral terrain. This is the crux of the matter. Africa's reentry into history, once attained, required its consolidation by the systemic *questioning* and undoing of all the multiple and crass deformities—economic, political, cultural, intellectual, etc.—imposed on the colonized. But this *questioning* was itself colonized: formed by the residue of modern Europe's sense of itself which, as we saw in chapter 1, originates in and was constituted by the self-awareness of *The Age of Enlightenment*, and is internalized as the self-awareness of the replicant strata and its elite. And so, as Davidson tells us,

> [T]hey tended to see themselves as the "chosen ones" of history, as those who were to be the instruments of applying the European model [of development] to Africa, and therefore as the saviours of the continent. Being sure of the value of their Western education, they were convinced of their superiority; who but they,

> after all, possessed the keys to the powerhouse of knowledge whence European technology and conquest had flowed? Perhaps they can best be called the "Western-educated few." . . . I tend to call them simply the "few" as opposed to the "many," to the vast majority of Africans, who were neither Western-educated nor contemptuous of their own heritage.[90]

These "few," the replicant strata and its elite, counterpoises itself to the "vast majority," who are "neither Western-educated nor contemptuous of their own heritage." This, then, is the *negativity* that Africa has to overcome so as to give substance to its formal status of sovereignty. Thus, this very process of surpassing this deplorable state of affairs is itself the historic act of reclaiming the "role" of citizen and substantiating our independence.

As Marcien Towa has noted the "greatest actual difference between the Occident and Africa" is the difference between "he who exercises the power of initiative . . . and he who is deprived of this and . . . remains on a natural sub-human level."[91] We have to overcome this *thingification*. We have to reclaim the initiative of history.[92] This is the core exigency of postcolonial Africa. Our impotent *thing-like* inert existence: ensnared between the promise of independence and its deplorable actuality.

As we noted in the last paragraph of chapter 4, this is the "gap between actuality and ideality" which constitutes the hermeneutic in-between of postcolonial Africa. In confronting this limbo, this *negativity*, we can hope for a new Africa. In the words of Césaire: "rich with all the productive power of modern times, warm with all the fraternity of olden days." A possibility that enfolds, concurrently, Marx's critique of estrangement and Heidegger's thinking on "a transformed abode of man in the world."

All we have to rely on, in this daring project, is our hybrid intermixed heritage. "The past opens itself only according to the resoluteness and force of illumination that a present has available to it."[93] In the way we engage it what we hope for may come forth. Resolute questioning—of "tout le particulier," instanced in differing, varied, multiple, and intermingled heritages, which constitute our shared *being*—is thus the task at hand.

Conclusion

Frantz Fanon

Thinking as Openness

> Gobineau defines the Negro as "the being who is most energetically affected by artistic emotion." For what affects the Negro is not so much the appearance of an object as its profound reality, its super-reality; not so much its form as its meaning.
>
> —Léopold Sédar Senghor[1]

> The irrationality of the racist "theories" of a Gobineau or a Lévy-Bruhl neither interest nor convince anyone but racists.
>
> —Amilcar Cabral[2]

I

As Vijay Prashad remarks on the first page of his book *The Darker Nations*, "The Third World was not a place. It was a project. During the seemingly interminable battles against colonialism, the peoples of Africa, Asia and Latin America dreamed of a new world." In concluding his narrative he laments the demise of this project, the "collapse of the Third world."[3] Indeed, much has happened, as Prashad documents, of a catastrophic and tragic nature, in and to the struggles of the formerly colonized and now neo-colonized peoples of the world. What he terms "collapse," however, need not be understood to mean that the "project" of a "new world" is done for and finished.

To be sure, the character of this project—the possibilities it struggled to attain—has taken on a different trajectory. Indeed, its truncation constitutes the actuality of our postcolonial condition. But still, in any truly originary venture, it is seldom possible, if ever, to predict the outcome before the event. And yet, things have really changed!

Nobody today takes the likes of Gobineau, or Senghor, seriously. It has become quite clear that "such invented essences as the Oriental or Englishness, as Frenchness, Africanness [or *Africanité*], or American exceptionalism" all with their own "Platonic idea" that assures their purity "from the beginning to the end of time,"[4] are markers of what was used, at one time, to subjugate and, at a later date and in some cases,[5] to resist subjection. As we move on into the twenty-first century, these *passé* conceptions of ourselves and Others will be left by the wayside as blunt reminders of what is not acceptable anymore, the dead-past.[6] Relics of what we have lived and discarded.

Indeed, Europe's narcissistic narratives of "emancipation and enlightenment" have been surpassed and not only "for entirely European or Western reasons."[7] Long before Jean-François Lyotard's *La Condition postmoderne* (1979), Aimé Césaire's *Lettre à Maurice Thorez* (1956) rejected these grand narratives in reclaiming the historicity of non-European peoples. Césaire reclaimed, for the formerly colonized, the right to narrate themselves into history, in actuating their self-liberation.

The acuity of what he affirms consists in recognizing "tout le particulier"[8] as the heritage we need to project into and as our future. This is what Vattimo has referred to as "a storehouse of treasures"[9] that constitute for us, of the present, a historically variegated multiple inheritance of shared resources. The originative ground of what Gadamer points to as "the infinite dialogue . . . of *the truth that we are*."[10] For, indeed, the formerly subjugated—and now historically and culturally hybridized—have become interlocutors who have to be taken seriously in mutual dialogical interaction.

It is in this context that Fanon, in concluding *Les damnés de la terre*, calls us to invention. We need to keep in mind, as noted earlier with Vattimo, that "in philosophy" as in life in general, "there isn't an objective conducting thread of tradition" and so "it is always possible to rethink history, pulling out [as needed] new things and old things."[11] What we take out and leave behind is thus sifted by a lived and constantly augmented heritage—instantiated in our "effective-historical consciousness"—focused on the reciprocal enhancing of our shared existence. Thus, being open to the possible, in the actuality of the present, we solicit and call forth a new and shared world.

In this, as in the past, we will invent. But this time around tempered by the surpassed pitfalls of what we have come to see as dead ends (Senghor's *Africanité*, for example) and focused on solidarities—nurtured by mutual concerns—which have overcome the delusion of thinking that they possess, or that it is possible to possess, a foolproof system, *metaphysics*, to guard against the risks of inventing.[12] This, then, is the treasured intellectual-political inheritance of humanity.

II

In this volume, I have presented my understanding of this inventive process as a stance of being open to the possible in the texts of philosophy. In the readings presented (chapters 3 to 5) I have tried to "inventively" harness key European thinkers in the service of what I take to be core concerns of postcolonial Africa. I have done this after exploring the paradox of postcolonial Africa (chapter 1) and applauding the promising confluence, in the thematic concerns, of Continental and African philosophy (chapter 2). And all this focused on responding to Fanon's call to "développer une pensée neuve."[13] A new kind of thinking attentive and open to the possible in that which *is*; a thinking engaged with, and directed by, one sole preoccupation: global solidarity in the common concerns that constitute our mutual humanity.

In calling for "une pensée neuve," Fanon is calling us to a more inclusive and more plausible story, a more reasonable story, sensitive to and aware of the differing hues that compose "our worldwide heritage."[14] On this story, and its telling and retelling, hinges the character and substance of our human/inhuman existence. For, as one of the wise elders in Chinua Achebe's *Anthills of the Savannah* tells us,

> It is the story that outlives the sound of war-drums and the exploits of brave fighters. It is the story . . . that saves our progeny from blundering like blind beggars into the spikes of the cactus fence. The story is our escort; without it, we are blind. Does the blind man own his escort? No, neither do we the story; rather it is the story that owns us and directs us. It is the thing that makes us different from cattle.[15]

All this keeping in mind that it is "always possible to rethink"[16] the effort aimed at "inject[ing] the voice of reason into world affairs."[17] To tell and re-tell "the story" within whose narrative, *we*, descendants of former slaves and masters, colonized and colonizers, all of *us*, can be "different from cattle." This telling and re-telling is the measure of our humanity. Thus far, and for the most part, sadly enough, we have been nothing more than *vaqueros* and their domesticated beasts. Brutish ranchers and benumbed brutes, we have indeed made ourselves what we are.[18] But, we can still narrate a different story!

This, then, is the story that *we* cannot afford not to tell and re-tell and, in so doing, explore, embellish, and further fine tune. A story of solidarity, focused on actuating more fully our enduring *effective-history*, the community-of-experience, which is our heritage. In this project of telling and re-telling we would be retrieving, out of the concerns of the present, possibilities enfolded/convolved by our shared community-of-experience. We would thus make ourselves "different from cattle," in reciprocity and interaction, in the visage of the Other (i.e., "tout le particulier"). On this hinge is staked the prospect of a shared and livable future, which is possible. Indeed, "il faut inventer, il faut découvrir."[19]

As James Baldwin tells us, "There is never time in the future in which we will work out our salvation. The challenge is in the moment, the time is always now."[20] This "now," the moment of lived existence, is and unfolds out of our specific and interlaced heritages, our shared inheritances. In this context, and out of it, we engage our respective historicity's and "work out" our exigencies (i.e., the projects for our future). It is in this way that we will spin the stories, which will make us "different from cattle," for it is only this that can be "our salvation" in that which concerns our humanity.

In this circuitous interplay of the past in the future via the concerns of the present, the role of philosophy—African philosophy—is that of transmission. To actuate the task of a reflexive-reflective digging deep into the past, of our shared effective-history, in view of the possibilities that can constitute a desirable, a livable future: a future responsive to and grounded on our community-of-experience. As Aimé Césaire puts it,

> And that is why we must create . . . Yes, in the long run, it is the task of the poets, the artists, the writers, the men of culture [philosophers], by blending, in the daily round of sufferings and denials of justice, both memories and hopes, to create those great reservoirs . . . those great storehouses of strength, from which the people can draw courage . . . to assert themselves and to assault their future.[21]

In all of this what is at stake is the humanity we strive to leave to future generations that will adjoin their own stories (i.e., as continuation, revision, affirmation, negation, and/or some *pasticcio* or other thereof) to the narrations that we leave behind. And so, "if we want humanity to advance . . . to a level different from that which Europe has [thus far] manifested . . . we must invent, we must discover."[22] Since the fifteenth century we have made ourselves into *vaqueros* and their benumbed domesticated brutes—victimizers and victims—straitjacketed into and by the history of imperious Europe. We need now to bypass this residual dead-past, which clings to us like swamp mud.

As Fanon reminds us: "Chaque génération doit dans une relative opacité découvrir sa mission, la remplir ou la trahir."[23] On our openness to this call, *in concreto*, is staked the future of all of us. This, then, is the task of thinking—openness to that which is *possible*—for ultimately, in the stern and harsh words of Heraclitus, the obscure one, "Character for man is destiny."[24]

Notes

All emphasis in the original unless otherwise indicated.

Preface

1. James Baldwin, "Fifth Avenue, Uptown: A Letter from Harlem," *Nobody Knows My Name* (New York: Vintage Books, 1993) 71.

2. This was the impossible dream of Descartes: To establish philosophy on absolutely indubitable grounds, or "What I wish to finish is . . . an absolutely new science enabling one to resolve all questions proposed on any order of continuous or discontinuous quantities." As quoted by F. E. Sutcliffe in the introduction to *Discourse on Method and the Meditations* (New York: Penguin Books, 1977) 8. Having quoted the above, Sutcliffe correctly observes, "The whole of Cartesian philosophy is contained in embryo in this phrase." This also describes, broadly speaking, the metaphysical tradition, as a whole, in its efforts to establish "a transparent language" in and through which to grasp—once and for all—"the truth" (i.e., the *isness* of what is).

3. Gianni Vattimo, *Vocazione e responsabilità del filosofo* (Genova, Italy: Melangolo, 2000) 71. Section 2 of chapter 1 will engage this point more fully.

4. Drew A. Hyland, *The Origins of Philosophy* (Atlantic Highlands, NJ: Humanities Press, 1993) 185.

5. The term *prejudice* is utilized in the way specified by Hans-Georg Gadamer in *Truth and Method* (New York: Crossroad, 1982) 235–74. It does not mean, as in ordinary usage, a biased (in the context of the United States) or bigoted racist view of things. It refers to the totality of culturally-historically saturated pre-judgments, which constitute our sense of the world. Perspectives, *à la* Nietzsche, or as in Heidegger, the average everyday pre-understanding of *Dasein*. This can be either *positive*, *negative*, and/or a variedly interlaced *pasticcio* of both, which concretely orients our lived sense of the world (more on this in chapter 4).

6. Gadamer, *Truth and Method* 235–39.

7. The United States' stance is imperious and aggressive because "regime change" is now an *accepted* part of its political lexicon. Any time the United States administration—Republican or Democrat—encounters a "troublesome" or otherwise difficult adversary, "regime change" is an option that is floated; whether it is utilized or not depends only on its tactical viability at the time and the strength or weakness of the particular "troublesome" adversary. That it is illegal for nations to comport themselves in this way because it goes against all kinds of international accords and conventions established since World War Two (and before) is something that is seldom, if ever, considered or taken account of by United States policy makers. It is as if international law does not apply to the United States any time it is inconvenient or goes counter to the crass—oil, for example—economic interests of this self-proclaimed super power. As Thomas McCarthy has noted, "our anomalous policies on trade, development, energy, environment, 'preemption,' unilateralism, and a host of other things . . . suggest that national false consciousness and self-righteousness have scarcely abated" (*Race, Empire, and the Idea of Human Development* [New York: Cambridge University Press, 2009] 231–32). See also Oona A. Hathaway, "Why We Need International Law," *The Nation* 285.16 (November 16, 2007): 35–37; and Julian E. Zelizer, "It's Obama's White House, but It's Bush's World," *The Washington Post*, August 15, 2010.

8. In other words, "terror" or "terrorism" is a tactic utilized in regular and/or irregular warfare. Is it possible to declare war on a "tactic"? And so, utilizing this rather befuddled and befuddling euphemism, the United States declares war on the Arabs and/or Islam. Indeed, as Edward W. Said has noted, "The United States . . . regards itself as at war with the Arab world, or Islam, or fundamentalism, or something of that sort" (387). And "With regards to the Arabs Europe has always had Islam at its doorstep . . . Islam, don't forget, is the only non-European culture that has never been completely vanquished. It is adjacent to and shares the monotheistic heritage of Judaism and Christianity. So, there is constant friction. And unlike, say, the British in India, the problem has not been settled" (388), both quotations from "Europe and Its Others: An Arab Perspective," in *Power, Politics, and Culture: Interviews with Edward W. Said* (New York: Pantheon Books, 2001). It ought to also be noted that—on the whole—in the language of contemporary Western social-political discourse, "fundamentalism" does not describe the zealots, or fanatics, of any religion; it is reserved exclusively for Islam.

9. Gadamer, *Truth and Method*, 267–68. To Gadamer's formulation I add the view that, at any point in time, "effective-history" always affirms and sustains itself in an ongoing contestations with and against a residual *dead-past* or *dead-history* that threatens to resurface and reassert itself. A good example of this, in today's United States, is the constant effort of Christian conservatives to reverse the progressive gains of secular society by making abortion illegal, or, along similar lines, the constant effort of the right-wing political establishment to undermine the gains of African Americans, and minorities in general, secured by the civil rights movement. I utilize the terms *dead-past* and *dead-history* to emphasize that the effectiveness of "effective-history" sustains itself not passively but by actively affirming its effectiveness against a *dead-history* or a *dead-past* that—in an ongoing manner—constantly

threatens to revive, resurface, and reestablish itself (more on this in chapter 4). In *The Ethics of Ambiguity* (Secaucus, NJ: The Citadel Press, 1948), Simone de Beauvoir utilizes the term *the dead past* (28), once and in passing, to refer to the discarded possibilities in the life of individuals. As indicated above, my use is wider and it is meant to function in conjunction with, and by way of supplementing/strengthening, Gadamer's conception of "effective-history," which suggests as much without ever explicitly affirming it.

10. Vattimo, *Vocazione* 73. As we shall see in chapter 2, Vattimo, a prominent contemporary Italian philosopher in the Continental tradition, is unequivocally sympathetic to the emancipatory efforts of non-European peoples. His stance originates in his appreciation of the favorable circumstance that has resulted from the demise of direct colonial rule (i.e., the curbing of Western hubris). What I am proposing in this study is to explore the consequences of this situation from the Other side—the side of the formerly colonized.

11. Okanda Okolo, *Pour une Philosophie de la Culture et du Developpement* (Kinshasa, Zaire: Presses Universitaires du Zaire, 1986) 45. As is the case with German and French thinkers, Okolo—who is a product of French education—uses the term *scientifique* to refer to any systematic study without restricting himself to the natural sciences.

12. Okolo 45.

13. Martin Heidegger, *Sein und Zeit* (Tübingen: Max Niemeyer Verlag, 1979) 315; *Being and Time*, trans. J. Macquarrie and E. Robinson (New York: Harper & Row, 1962) 363.

14. By Europe I mean Europe and the various parts of the globe that have been settled by a predominantly European population. J. M. Blaut, *The Colonizers Model of the World* (New York: Guilford Press, 1993) note 1, 43. Latin America does not fit this profile because even if Spanish and Portuguese dominate its culture, it is more *mestizo* than European and its anticolonial struggles have more in common with the struggles of Asia and Africa than with the displacement of one power elite by another, within the confines of established and shared Western traditions, which is emblematic of predominantly European-settled territories.

15. In 1973, Paul M. Sweezy, commenting on subsequent developments in the Vietnamese resistance against United States imperialism—the imperial power that replaced the French—wrote, "What has happened in Vietnam is quite simply that the last and greatest of the capitalist empires has suffered a stunning defeat from which it can never fully recover. Things will never be the same again. The great majority of the human race living in Asia, Africa, and Latin America, who have been slaughtered, enslaved, and mercilessly exploited for some four centuries, now know that they can stand up to the mightiest technological and military power the world has ever seen." Paul M. Sweezy, "On Discovering Marxism," *Monthly Review* 24.10 (March 1973): 55.

16. On this point, in "*Anch'io Per La Tua Bandiera*," *Africus, Periodico Dell'Associazione Onlus Italia Eritrea* II.6 (Settembre 2003): 7, Gian Carlo Stella writes, "There were numerous episodes of *ascari* rebellions and desertions (an endemic condition of any military structure) and also, but very rarely, rebellions of entire sections (almost always caused by the nonobservance of the rules of engagement, as

we would say today)." In a publication celebrating the *ascari* in their contribution to the "greatness" of Italy, it is "understandable" that Stella would try to emphasize the nonpolitical nature of these "rebellions and desertions," that is, "the nonobservance of the rules of engagement." In Eritrean folklore, however, the explicitly political/anticolonial nature of these rebellions is well documented. On this point see, Aba Gebreyesus Hailu's novel *The Conscript* written in Tigrinya in 1927, trans. Ghirmai Negash (Athens: Ohio University Press, 2013).

17. I came across this phrase in Bernard-Henri Levy's *Barbarism with a Human Face* (New York: Harper Colophon Books, 1980) 84. In hyphenating it I mean to use it as a technical term to descriptively designate the lived experiences that, in a general and amorphous way, form the backdrop—or structuring ground—of the ideas and beliefs that constitute a heritage, or tradition, at any given moment in time. This is not something static but a dynamic, fluid—and always changing—totality that is augmented by an internal process of self-calibration and filtering, in reference to core values-concerns and the exigencies of the time (i.e., the lived moment).

18. For an example of what I am suggesting, see International Jewish Anti-Zionist Network, "From Warsaw to Gaza: International Holocaust Remembrance Day" (January 27, 2009).

19. Amilcar Cabral, *Revolution in Guinea* (New York: Monthly Review Press, 1969) 52.

20. Immanuel Kant, *Perpetual Peace*, trans. Lewis White Beck (Indianapolis, IN: Bobbs-Merrill, 1957) 19. This text will be explored in chapter 3.

21. Frantz Fanon, "Vérités premiéres à propos du problème colonial," *Pour la revolution africaine* (Paris, France: François Maspero, 1964) 141.

22. Lewis R. Gordon, *Disciplinary Decadence* (Boulder, CO: Paradigm, 2006) endnote 28, 140.

23. "New U.S. Embassy in Iraq cloaked in Mystery," *Associated Press*, April 14, 2006.

24. The aim, in other words, is not merely to replace one set of restrictive prejudices with another but to cultivate and nurture the *enabling prejudices* that arise out of our shared world (see endnotes 5 and 9 above). In all of this, what needs to be kept in mind, as Edward W. Said reminds us, is that "The whole effort to deconsecrate Eurocentrism" for example "cannot be interpreted, least of all by those who participate in the enterprise, as an effort to supplant Eurocentrism with, for instance, Afrocentric or Islamocentric approaches." *Reflections on Exile and Other Essays* (Cambridge, MA: Harvard University Press, 2000) 380. On this point, see also the preface to my book *Contested Memory: The Icons of the Occidental Tradition* (Trenton, NJ: Africa World Press, 2007).

25. For the way I utilize this term, please see endnote 9 above.

26. On this point, see the insightful distinction Cornelius Castoriadis makes between Socrates "the philosopher-citizen" and Plato "the philosopher who wants to be above the city." Cornelius Castoriadis, "Intellectuals and History," *Philosophy, Politics, Autonomy, ed. D. A. Curtis* (New York: Oxford University Press, 1991) 5–6.

27. Heidegger, *Sein und Zeit* 5, the first two sentences in the second paragraph.

28. Tsenay Serequeberhan, *The Hermeneutics of African Philosophy: Horizon and Discourse* (New York: Routledge, 1994) 28.

Introduction

1. Omar Khyyám, *Rubáiyát of Omar Khyyám*, trans. Edward Fitzgerald (New York: Random House, 1947) quatrain no. 31, 23.

2. As Plato tells us, early on in the *Republic*, philosophy is concerned with "the manner of one's life" *Plato's Republic*, trans. G. M. A. Grube (Indianapolis, IN: Hackett, 1974) #329d, 4.

3. Quentin Lauer, *The Nature of Philosophical Inquiry* (Milwaukee, Ill: Marquette University Press, 1989) 6.

4. As Heidegger puts it, "Such standing in the clearing of Being I call the ek-sistence of man. This way of being is proper only to man. Ek-sistence so understood is not only the ground of the possibility of reason, *ratio*, but is also that in which the essence of man preserves the source that determines him." *Martin Heidegger*, "Letter on Humanism" in *Martin Heidegger Basic Writings*, ed. David Farrell Krell (New York: Routledge, 1993) 228. The *existence* of a society-culture is the actuality that comprises the *ek-sistence* of those who constitute, in the totality of their various life projects—their "standing in the clearing of Being"—the lived historicity or actuality of said society. The terms *ek-sistence* and *existence* here function—roughly—as the "subjective" and "objective" poles of our lived being-in-the-world.

5. As Heidegger makes clear, in *An Introduction to Metaphysics*, the disclosure, or clearing, in and through which Being shows forth (the *Dasein* or there-being of human existence) is co-terminus and co-primordial with the ontic cultural-historical actuality—the *polis*, for example—of specific historical formations. *Martin Heidegger, An Introduction to Metaphysics*, trans. Ralph Manheim (New Haven and London: Yale University Press, 1977) 152.

6. This term is the central category of Hegel's *Philosophy of Right* and his most important contribution to modern ethical and political philosophy. As Hegel points out in the *remarks* to paragraph four, the *will* is the road traversed, by Spirit, in its advance from its given (natural or elemental) condition as intelligence to "thinking proper." G. W. F. Hegel, *Hegel's Philosophy of Right*, trans. T. M. Knox (New York: Oxford University Press, 1967) 21. He further stipulates that the will is nothing other than the *capacity* of any person "to posit any content in himself by his own effort." This empty capacity, the immediacy of an abstract undifferentiated will and how this is formed into an ethical life (i.e., a community) and made the substance of formally equal citizens, this is what Hegel shows in the *Philosophy of Right*. Each society, or ethical life, forms the abstract capacity born into its midst (babies, i.e., the elemental substrate of the next generation) into members of specific historical totalities. Each member of such a totality, in relation to other members of Other such totalities, and differing totalities, relative to each Other are, each to the other, a *radical Otherness*. Along similar lines, Aristotle tells us that nature provides us with the empty "potencies" for the "virtues of character" (or of vice, for that matter), and we "produce the being-at-work [*energeia*] of them" or we complete them "by means of habit" or habituation. Aristotle, *Nicomachean Ethics*, trans. Joe Sachs (Newburyport, MA: Focus, 2002) 1103a, lines 19 to 30. We are, in our human substance—our culture-history—products not of nature but of the habituation-formation (*Bildung*) that we each owe to our respective societies in which we were born and raised. In our

lived formation/upbringing we thus become the embodiments of concrete histories-cultures and so to each other—as members or incarnations of different societies—a *radical Otherness* (for specific examples of what this means, see note 9 below).

7. As Karl Marx puts it, "To be radical is to grasp things by the root. But for man the root is man himself." Karl Marx, *Early Writings*, trans. Rodney Livingstone and Gregor Benton (New York: Vintage Books, 1975) 251. It should be noted that Heidegger's etymologizing (see note 4 above) is akin to and serves the same purpose, in his thinking, as Marx's insistence on reclaiming the originary sense of words.

8. The generosity—the welcoming and open hospitality—of the Arawak Indians, for example, who warmly greeted Columbus's ships, is partly explained by this openness to the risky, a core component of our humanness. In contrast to the Arawak Indians, Columbus, as he himself tells us, was lacking in this regard. Of his first encounter (of the natives of the world he stumbled upon) he writes, "They . . . brought us parrots and balls of cotton and spears and many other things . . . They would make fine servants . . . With fifty men we could subjugate them all and make them do whatever we want" (quoted in Howard Zinn, *A People's History of the United States* (New York: HarperCollins, 2003) 1. Guided by the expansionist energies of his day, Columbus is a fine specimen of the "they-self" (i.e., the *das Man*) mindset of Christian Europe in the age of ascending capitalism—the dawn of modernity. In this regard, Luce Irigaray writes, "Western man has above all failed to recognize and has neglected that which, it seems to me, should characterize his species: the ability to enter into relations with the other without reducing this relation to the satisfaction of instincts, of needs." Luce Irigaray, *Between East and West*, trans. Stephen Pluháček (New York: Columbia University Press, 2002) ix. Columbus's remarks confirm Irigaray's observations *not*, however, for "Western man" as such, but for the *das Man* instituted by modern capitalist civilization.

9. In Marco Polo's travels to ancient Cathay or in the periods of history that are variously described as the "Age of Discovery" or adventure or in the encounter of Columbus and the inhabitants of the "new world" (see note 8 above) on both sides, these were perilous encounters. Encounters of humans which were, each to the other, "polarities of radical Otherness," or as Basil Davidson put it, "A profound mutual ignorance accompanied all this: another fact, even a structural fact, which needs to be remembered. Profound ignorance: but also a pervasive contempt on one side and bewilderment on the other. The Europeans knew a little geography by the time they launched their colonial invasions, but almost nothing of the peoples who inhabited that geography. The whole international enterprise was tackled as though the object, to apply the quip of 1886 of a British governor of the Gold Coast, seemed to be to seize on territory and then 'as much as possible to rule the country as if there were no inhabitants.' Were they not dealing, as the British high commissioner of east Africa affirmed, 'with a *tabula rasa*,' a blank and untouched page of humankind where they could write whatever they might wish?" Basil Davidson, *Africa in Modern History* (New York: Penguin Books, 1985) 32.

10. As Serge Latouche points out, the "West has destroyed 'cultural solipsism' . . . Never again . . . will 'a single human group be able to call itself 'men,' 'true men' [excluding of all others]." Serge Latouche, *The Westernization of the World* (Cambridge, UK: Polity Press, 1996) 121. This ending of isolation dialectically cre-

ates a propitious situation in which radical Otherness—or seclusion—is not, any more, a human historical possibility.

11. What I am proposing is to explore the fruitful consequences that follow from this situation, in which my work is also situated.

12. On this, see Immanuel Wallerstein, *European Universalism* (New York: The New Press, 2006). As Nietzsche puts it, "But I . . . think that today we are . . . far from the ridiculous immodesty that would be involved in decreeing from our corner that perspectives are permitted only from this corner. Rather has the world become "infinite" for us all over again, inasmuch as we cannot reject the possibility that *it may include infinite interpretations*." Friedrich Nietzsche, *The Gay Science*, trans. Walter Kaufmann (New York: Vintage Books, 1974) no. 374, lines 16–21, 336.) It is interesting to note that when Nietzsche expressed the above view, this "ridiculous immodesty" which he scorns was the order of the day in the West's relation to the rest of the world.

13. George McTurnan Kahin, *The Asian-African Conference* (New York: Kennikat Press, 1972) 45. For a more recent discussion of this conference, see Vijay Prashad, *The Darker Nations* (New York: The New Press, 2007) 31–50.

14. Okolo 46.

15. Our present world is thoroughly hybridized and suffused with mixture and thus constitutes a hybridized totality. Any talk of "purity," or complete distinctness, in our present situation is nothing more than the expression of an unreflective essentialist naïveté.

16. Aimé Césaire, *Discours sur le Colonialisme* (Paris, France: Présence Africaine, 1955) 19. This neologism, coined by Césaire, refers to the reduction of the colonized to the level of things.

17. On an "outsider perspective" see my book, *Contested Memory: The Icons of the Occidental Tradition* (Trenton, NJ: Africa World Press, 2007) xx–xxi. See also Ramin Jahanbegloo, "Edward Said's Conception of the Public Intellectual as 'Outsider'" in *Radical Philosophy Review*, 8.1 (2005): 29–34.

18. For the use I make of this Gadamerian term, see the preface to this study.

19. On this point, see also the preface to *Contested Memory*.

20. On this point, see my concise discussion of Charles Taylor, Hans-Georg Gadamer, and Gianni Vattimo in Tsenay Serequeberhan, "Africana Philosophy: Prospects and Possibilities," *The Oxford Handbook of World Philosophy*, ed. Jay L. Garfield and William Edelglass (New York: Oxford University Press, 2011) 468–71.

21. On this point, see Aimé Césaire, "The Man of Culture and his Responsibilities," *Présence Africaine*, 24–25 (February–May, 1959).

22. Frantz Fanon, *Les damnés de la terre* (Paris: François Maspero, 1974) 229–33. Fanon's enduring relevance, in my view, goes without saying. On this point, see Lewis R. Gordon, *Introduction to Africana Philosophy* (New York: Cambridge University Press, 2008) 220–21.

23. Lauer 33.

24. Gianni Vattimo, *Credere di Credere* (Milano: Garzanti, 1996) 14–15.

25. On this point, to quote Heidegger, "*Sein—nicht Seiendes—'gibt es' nur, sofern Wahrheit ist. Und sie ist nur, sofern und solange Dasein ist*. [Being—not beings—is there, inasmuch as truth is. And truth *is* only, inasmuch as and so long as Dasein is]." *Sein und Zeit* 230.

26. Chinua Achebe, *Hopes and Impediments* (New York: Anchor Books, 1989) 151.

27. Fanon, *Les damnés de la terre* 17.

28. See the extensive remarks on this point in endnote 6 of chapter 1.

29. This is the source of the ontic-ontological privilege of *Dasein* (i.e., human existence) in its relation to Being (see Heidegger's remarks quoted in endnote 25 and endnote 4 above).

30. Ludwig Wittgenstein, *Philosophical Investigations*, 3rd ed., trans. G. E. M. Anscombe (New York: Macmillan, 1958) paragraph 309, 103.

31. *Plato's Republic* 514a. In this regard, utilizing the image of a labyrinth, Cornelius Castoriadis writes, "To think is not to get out of the cave; it is not to replace the uncertainty of the shadows by the clear-cut outlines of things themselves, the flame's flickering glow by the light of the true Sun. To think is to enter the Labyrinth; more exactly, it is to make be and appear a Labyrinth when we might have stayed 'lying among the flowers, facing the sky.' It is to lose oneself amidst galleries which exist only because we never tire of digging them; to turn round and round at the end of a cul-de-sac whose entrance has been shut off behind us–until, inexplicably, this spinning round opens up in the surrounding walls cracks which offer passage." Cornelius Castoriadis, *Crossroads in the Labyrinth* (Cambridge, MA: The MIT Press, 1984) ix–x. But where are the "cracks which offer passage" to lead us to? It seems that this "offer" is a *ruse* of metaphysics if it offers to lead us to "the true Sun," or somewhere yonder, beyond Wittgenstein's "bottle" or Plato's "cave." Not to fall prey to this ploy, these "cracks" can only be conceptualized as leading us deeper and deeper into the "Labyrinth" and that which "opens up" can only be one more disclosure in the labyrinthine network of existence. As I have argued elsewhere (*Contested Memory: The Icons of the Occidental Tradition*, 6–7), Castoriadis's stance, in its fixation on Europe, is susceptible to the effects of this *ruse*. It is as if " 'lying among the flowers, facing the sky' " is a surrogate for, or akin to, what Kant says of the supposed idleness of "the South Sea islanders" which is not compatible "with what is called duty." Immanuel Kant, *Fundamental Principles of the Metaphysics of Morals* (New York: The Liberal Arts Press, 1955) 40. Is, then, to "never tire of digging" the Western *duty* to civilize? In contradistinction to Castoriadis, as persuasively argued by Gianni Vattimo, it has become quite clear that, what Castoriadis refers to as "To think," the task of philosophy, "should not and cannot teach where we are to be directed to, but to live in the condition of one who is not directed in any direction." Gianni Vattimo, *Al di là del soggetto* (Milan, Italy: Feltrinelli Editore, 1984) 12. Among other things, in this study and in various ways, we will explore, work out, and expand further the implications of this perspective articulated by Vattimo, in terms of the contemporary concerns of African philosophy.

32. I borrow this image from Vattimo's splendid book, *Al di là del soggetto* 11.

33. Karel Kosík, *Dialectics of the Concrete* (Hingham, MA: D. Reidel, 1976) 44–45 and Antonio Gramsci, "*Indifferenti*," in *Scritti Giovanili* (Turin, Italy: Einaudi, 1958) 78–80.

34. David Guterson, *Snow Falling on Cedars* (New York: Vintage Books, 1995) 418. The character Nels Gudmundsson—an old experienced defense lawyer—bril-

liantly brought to life in the cinematic rendition of the story by Max Von Sydow, makes this point in the following manner: "'I am an old man' Nels Gudmundsson continued 'I do not walk so well anymore, and one of my eyes is useless. I suffer from headaches and from arthritis in my knees . . . I nearly froze to death last night . . . And so, like you, I hope for warmth tonight and . . . I would wish for my life to continue pleasantly for many years . . . This final wish . . . is not something I can readily count on, for if I do not pass on in the next ten years I will certainly do so in the next twenty. My life is drawing to a close. 'Why do I say this?' Nels Gudmundsson asked, moving nearer to the jurors now and leaning towards them, too. 'I say this because as an older man I am prone *to ponder matters in the light of death* in a way that you are not'" (418, emphasis added). Aristotle makes this same point when he writes, "So one ought to pay attention to the undemonstrated statements and opinions of people who are experienced or old, or of people with practical judgment, no less than to the things they demonstrate, for by having an eye sharpened by experience, they see rightly" (1143b, lines 10–14). This is the same kind of reasoning that, in indigenous African traditions, recognizes age as a secure source of finite human wisdom.

35. This resolute and engaged stance toward the mortality of human existence, as Heidegger tells us on the unnumbered first page of *Being and Time*, is a sensibility of thought inaugurated, in twentieth-century philosophy, by him, in an effort to engage in a concrete (*konkrete*) and situated thinking of "the question of Being." And yet Heidegger's thinking, in *Being and Time*, the cornerstone of his work, suffers from an ontic-ontological ambiguity, for *Sein* is thought from within a specific historicity (i.e., that of the Occident) and yet it is presented, in such a way that it seems to occur or show itself—as if its showing occurred or could occur—in a non-situated, and thus non-localized manner, empty or divested of any ontic-historical specificity. As if it could show itself naked of history! It seems to me that this is the reason why, in sections 11 and 17 of *Being and Time*, Heidegger makes reference to "*einer primitiven Daseinsstufe*" and "*primitiven Welt*" as if the linear totalizing conception(s) of history which these terms presuppose—in order to make any kind of sense—had not been rendered obsolete by his own work. And, in a slightly different context, he makes the rather obscene racist remark: "[It is said:] Nature, too, has its history. But then Negroes may be said to have history. Or then does nature not have history?" (quoted in Richard Wolin, *Heidegger's Children* [Princeton, NJ: Princeton University Press, 2001] 183). This racist statement and the linear totalizing notion of history implicit in section 11 and 17 (unessential sections of *Being and Time*, in my view) do not detract an iota from the achievement of *Being and Time* which, among other things, puts in question the metaphysics of a singular linear history and refocuses thinking on the concrete lived character (i.e., the happening) of actual lived-life or human *ek-sistence*. These minor sections, and Heidegger's racism, betray a personal failure to measure up to what his own work has made possible. Regarding Heidegger's politics, I am in complete accord with Gianni Vattimo when he says, "the problem is not that of establishing up to what point Heidegger might have been a Nazi sympathizer, but to demonstrate something that up to now nobody has been able to do convincingly, his political choice as a consequence of his thought." Diego Fusaro and Italo Rebecchi, *Gianni Vattimo* (n.d.) par. 1.

Chapter 1

1. Fanon, *Les damnés de la terre* 58.

2. As quoted by Gérard Chaliand in the exordium to *Revolution in the Third World* (New York: The Viking Press, 1977).

3. The contemporary discourse of African philosophy is itself a theoretic offshoot of decolonization. On this point, see Theophilus Okere, *African Philosophy: A Historico-Hermeneutical Investigation of the Conditions of its Possibility* (Lanham, MD: University Press of America, 1983) vii; and Marcien Towa, "Consciencisme," *Présence Africaine*, 85.1 (1973): 148–149.

4. Vattimo, *Vocazione* 71.

5. Vattimo, *Vocazione* 71.

6. As Vattimo puts it: "I try to persuade you citing authors that I know you have also read and experienced, who were not in their turn demonstrating that 2 + 2 is 4 [*i quali a loro volta non dimonstravano propriamente che 2 + 2 fa 4*], but were seeking for *an interpretation of the common situation*" (Vattimo, *Vocazione* 71). In a slightly different context, Vattimo makes the same point in *The Future of Religion* when he states, "the distinction between *Natur* and *Geisteswissenschaften*" is erased "since even the so-called hard sciences verify and falsify their statements only within paradigms or preunderstandings [*sic*]. If 'facts' thus appear to be nothing but interpretations, interpretation, on the other hand, presents itself as (the) fact: hermeneutics is [thus] not a philosophy but the enunciation of historical existence itself in the age of the end of metaphysics." Gianni Vattimo, *The Future of Religion* (New York: Columbia University Press, 2005) 45. What is in question, in all of the above, are not conceptions and ideas internal to an accepted tradition—a "normal science" exchange of ideas focused on rigor—but a situation of "extraordinary science" in which ideas between traditions, or in a tradition in crisis, are being assessed in an effort to sift out possible avenues of exist, from a crisis, that can possibly lead to a new paradigm. This is the basic idea that Vattimo is asserting holds true in all realms of human existence, a view that Thomas S. Kuhn in *The Structure of Scientific Revolutions* (Chicago: The University of Chicago Press, 1970) articulated systematically from within the confines of the history and philosophy of science. It is important to note that this is the regular state of affairs in philosophic discourse that has not been reduced to an ideological profession of faith (i.e., a worldview). As Drew A. Hyland points out in *The Virtue of Philosophy* (Athens: Ohio University Press, 1981), the proper vocation of philosophy is to cultivate this openness to possibilities by an ongoing questioning in full recognition of our finitude, our lived horizon. In this perspective, "the facts" (i.e., the established knowledge in any area, or field, of study) are nothing more than the accepted interpretations, or understandings, of what "is" that has sedimented, as such, in or as a heritage or tradition of knowledge. Interesting discussions, in philosophy as in other fields, occur only when these "facts" (i.e., the recognized interpretations of the *is-ness* of what is) become worthy of questioning (3–17). In other words, it is not a question of ascertaining the "facts" but of exploring interpretations in view of common concerns and a shared situation. It ought to be noted, in passing, that the standard meaning of the word "fact," derived from the "Latin *factum*, from neuter of *factus*, past participle of *facere*,

to do or make," means something done or made and accepted as such. It does not mean immutable or unchanging.

7. Vattimo, *Vocazione* 71.

8. This is how Socrates puts it, in the *Phaedo*: "I am in danger at this moment of not having a philosophical attitude about this, but like those who are quite uneducated, I am eager to get the better of you in argument, for the uneducated, when they engage in argument about anything, give no thought to the truth about the subject of discussion but are only eager that those present will accept the position they have set forth. I differ from them only to this extent: I shall not be eager to get the agreement of those present that what I say is true, except incidentally, but I shall be very eager that I should myself be thoroughly convinced that things are so." Plato, *Plato: Five Dialogues*, trans. G. M. A. Grube (Indianapolis, IN: Hackett, 1981) #91a–b, 129.

9. Vattimo, *Vocazione* 72.

10. Vattimo, *Vocazione* 72.

11. On the way I utilize this term, please see endnote 5 in the preface to this study.

12. Vattimo, *Vocazione* 52. This is akin to Antonio Gramsci's conception of philosophy as an exploration of the traces that constitute our existence and have collected/sedimented without the benefit of an inventory. Antonio Gramsci, *Quaderni Del Carcere*, vol. 2 (Turin, Italy: Giulio Einaudi, 1975) 1375–78.

13. In full, this is what Socrates says in *Crito*: "Or was that well-spoken before the necessity to die came upon me, but now it is clear that this was said in vain for the sake of argument, that it was in truth play and nonsense?" Plato, *Plato: Five Dialogues* #46d, 48.

14. This is what Antonio Gramsci means when he states that philosophy and history form a block. It should be noted, in passing, that much of what Gramsci says regarding the relation of philosophy to history, in the *Quaderni Del Carcere*, implicitly anticipates many of the critical insights of philosophical hermeneutics (i.e., Hans-Georg Gadamer's work) on tradition and the positive role of prejudice in understanding.

15. On this point, see Marcien Towa's "Conditions for the Affirmation of a Modern African Philosophical Thought," in *African Philosophy: The Essential Readings*, ed. Tsenay Serequeberhan (New York: Paragon House, 1991) 194–98.

16. Hans-Georg Gadamer, *Truth and Method* (New York: Crossroad, 1982) 266.

17. *Hegel, Hegel's Philosophy of Right* 11.

18. Immanuel Kant, *Critique of Pure Reason*, trans. N. K. Smith (New York: St. Martin's Press, 1965) 9.

19. Nietzsche, #3, 35.

20. Martin Heidegger, in the "voice" of the Teacher, gives a detailed and lucid exposition of this point in *Discourse on Thinking* (New York: Harper & Row, 1966) 81–90.

21. Towa, "Conditions for the Affirmation of a Modern African Philosophical Thought" 195.

22. In *Contested Memory: The Icons of the Occidental Tradition* (Trenton, NJ: Africa World Press, 2007) I have—focusing on Kant, Hegel, and Marx—presented a de-structive reading and documented, in detail, how this service is rendered.

23. Anne Hugon, *The Exploration of Africa* (New York: Harry N. Abrams, 1993) 19.

24. Hugon 19.

25. Hugon 19–20, emphasis added.

26. The circularity of this self-validation is a beguiling and beguiled vicious circle precisely because it is unaware of its prejudgments or prejudices and how they "load" the "objective" descriptions it purports to present, in contrast to the "non-vicious circularity of . . . our human situation," noted earlier (see the text related to endnote 13 in the preface). The circularity of colonial description consists in pasting, re-pasting, and perpetuating conceptions and prejudices it takes to be "objective" precisely because it is blind to the partiality out of which it operates. In contrast to this, the circularity of the "hermeneutical circle" is not vicious, precisely because it consciously—to the extent that this is humanly possible—engages in an ongoing exploring of, and critically focusing on, the *prejudices* of the partial/finite human situation in and out of which it necessarily operates. In this it is constantly immersed in a self-critical attitude, tied to and anchored in the recognition of its historicity—its finitude—which effectively guards against the vicious circularity of a self-assured "objectivist" stance. This and related issues will be dealt with extensively in chapter 4 of this study. On this point, see also my book, *The Hermeneutics of African Philosophy* (New York: Routledge, 1994) note 67, 135.

27. Sir Isaiah Berlin, *The Age of Enlightenment* (New York: A Mentor Book, 1956) 14. As Berlin puts it in full, "The eighteenth century is perhaps the last period in the history of Western Europe when human omniscience was thought to be an attainable goal." This unattainable hope (i.e., "human omniscience") transmuted into various forms of scientism has strongly influenced the scientific, philosophical, social-political, and popular imagination of the nineteenth and twentieth century and endures to this day. For a concise exposition of this scientistic stance, see William Barrett's "Positivism," which is the introduction to the third volume of *Philosophy in the Twentieth Century* (New York: Random House, 1962).

28. Romano Guardini, *The End of the Modern World* (Chicago: Henry Regenery, 1968) 51.

29. Amilcar Cabral, "Identity and Dignity in the Context of the National Liberation Struggle," in *Return to the Source: Selected Speeches* (New York: Monthly Review Press, 1973) 59.

30. Immanuel Kant, *Kant on History*, ed. Lewis White Beck (Indianapolis, IN: Bobbs-Merrill, 1963) 3. As Gadamer shows in *Truth and Method* (245), this audacity of reason is based on the impossible claim/supposition that human reason is capable of complete detachment from its mortal moorings (more on this in chapter 4).

31. Alan Ryan, "Professor Hegel Goes to Washington," in *The New York Review of Books*, 39.6 (March 26, 1992): 10.

32. Heinz Kimmerle, "The Intercultural Dimension in the Dialogue between African and Western Philosophy," in *Perspectives in African Philosophy: An Anthology on "Problematics of an African Philosophy: Twenty Years After (1976–1996)*, ed. Claude Sumner and Samuel Wolde Yohannes (Ethiopia, Addis Ababa: Addis Ababa University Press, 2002) 252.

33. Edward W. Said, "Representing the Colonized: Anthropology's Interlocutors," in *Reflections on Exile and Other Essays* (Cambridge, MA: Harvard University Press, 2000) 295.

34. The reader ought not to be surprised by my use of the word "ethnic." The greatness of the Anglo-Saxon race ("The White Man's Burden") or the duty of the French to civilize ("*la mission civilisatrice*") are, properly speaking, ethnic-political myths which were articulated in and out of the atmosphere of learning and knowledge that spurred on expansion and conquest. On this point, see Kwame Anthony Appiah, *In My Father's House* (New York: Oxford University Press, 1992) 47 (remarks on Martin Farquhar Tupper); and Thomas McCarthy 167–68 (remarks on James Mill and John Stuart Mill, and specifically on J. S. Mill, 171–77).

35. For example, in Kant, it is the Providence-sanctioned "unsocial sociability" of human nature that brings it about, something inlaid/innate in the very being of the nature of human existence.

36. Richard H. Popkin, "Hume's Racism," *The Philosophical Forum*, 9.2–3 (Winter–Spring 1977–1978): 213.

37. McCarthy 166–67. See also Robert Bernasconi and Anika Maaza Mann, "The Contradictions of Racism: Locke, Slavery, and the Two Treatises," in *Race and Racism in Modern Philosophy*, ed. Andrew Valls (New York: Cornell University Press, 2005).

38. Serequeberhan, *Contested Memory*, chapter 2.

39. McCarthy 64.

40. Serequeberhan, *Contested Memory*, chapter 3.

41. Serequeberhan, *Contested Memory*, chapter 4.

42. On this point, see Kant's "Reviews of Herder's Ideas for a Philosophy of the History of Mankind" in *Kant on History* 47.

43. Jean-Jacques Rousseau, *The First and Second Discourses together with the Replies to Critics and Essay on the Origin of Languages*, trans. and ed. Victor Gourevitch (New York: Harper & Row, 1986) 220.

44. Jean-Jacques Rousseau, *On the Social Contract Discourse on the Origin of Inequality Discourse on Political Economy*, trans. Donald A. Cress (Indianapolis, IN: Hackett, 1983) 27.

45. Here, I am relying on Cornelius Castoriadis's conception—that societies, and individuals in societies, institute themselves in and through a grounding social imaginary. As he puts it, "Society poses itself as being something . . . re-presented by 'attributes,' which are the currency of imaginary significations. . . . 'To itself' society is never a collection of perishable and substitutable individuals living in a particular territory, speaking a particular language, 'externally' practicing certain customs. On the contrary, these individuals 'belong' to this society *because* they participate in its social imaginary significations—in its 'norms,' 'values,' 'myths,' 'ideas,' 'projects,' 'traditions,' etc.—and *because* (whether they know it or not) they share the will to belong to this society and to make it continue to exist [i.e., reproduce itself]." Cornelius Castoriadis, "The Crisis of Western Societies," *Telos* 53 (Fall 1982): 24.

46. Castoriadis, *Philosophy, Politics, Autonomy* 200.

47. It ought never to be forgotten that the success of Europe's global expansion was made possible by systematic and unmitigated acts of brutality.

48. Hugon 68.

49. Philippe Nemo, *What is the West?* (Pittsburgh, PA: Duquesne University Press, 2006) 40.

50. Nemo 53.

51. Nemo 45.

52. Nemo 54.

53. Guardini bypasses this Christian input to the colonialist penchant of "the new man of the modern age," endnote 28 above.

54. Karl Marx and Frederick Engels, *On Colonialism: Articles from the New York Tribune and Other Writings* (New York: International, 1972) 41.

55. Marx and Engels 41.

56. J. H. Parry, *The Age of Reconnaissance* (New York: A Mentor Book, 1963) 33.

57. James Baldwin, "Nationalism, Colonialism, and the United States: One Minute to Twelve—A Forum," *The Cross of Redemption*, ed. Randall Kenan (New York: Vintage Books, 2011) 11, emphasis added.

58. A. J. Baker, *The Rape of Ethiopia* (New York: Ballantine Books, 1971) 23.

59. Baker 22–23. If one listens to the words of *Faccetta Nera* (i.e., the 1935 Fascist hymn written by Giuseppe Micheli, music by Mario Ruccione) it is a song aimed at Abyssinian women, "Moretta che sei schiava fra gli schiavi," and which lauds "Gli eroi caduti liberando te!" The song, focused on "Facceta nera, bell'abissina," proclaims that "il nostro motto é Libertà e Dovere" and—all told—the betterment and liberation of enslaved Abyssinia (for the lyrics, in the original and translation, see Wikipedia entry "Faccetta Nera").

60. Placide Tempels, *Bantu Philosophy* (Paris: Présence Africaine, 1969) 171–72.

61. Jean-Paul Sartre, *Being and Nothingness* (New York: Gramercy Books, 1956) 67–70.

62. D. K. Fieldhouse, "The Myth of Economic Exploitation," *The Colonial Empires* (New York: Delta Books, 1966) 380–94.

63. Fieldhouse 382.

64. Chinua Achebe, *Home and Exile* (New York: Anchor Books, 2001) 19. For a recent assessment of the colonial experience that tacitly and not so tacitly clings to the *idea* that it benefited the colonized see, Claude Askolovitch, "*La vérité sur la colonization*," *Le Nouvel Observateur* 2144 (December 8–14, 2005): 12–14.

65. Edward W. Said, *The Pen and the Sword: Conversations with David Barsamian* (Monroe, ME: Common Courage Press, 1994) 66, emphasis added.

66. The only African territory that escaped this fate was Abyssinia and the adjacent territories directly to its south, southwest, and southeast. The King of Showa, Menelik II, who had established himself as the *Neguse Negest* ("King of Kings") of Abyssinia, managed to escape subjugation by, on the one hand, defeating the Italians at the battle of Adwa in 1896 and simultaneously conniving with Italy, Britain, and France to secure weapons and recognition for his own colonizing ventures in the adjacent territories to the south, southwest, and southeast of Abyssinia proper. This was how the boundaries of present-day Ethiopia (i.e., Abyssinia plus the

territories it subjugated) came into existence. On this, see Harold G. Marcus, *The Life and Times of Menelik II: Ethiopia 1844–1913* (Trenton, NJ: Red Sea Press, 1995); Bonnie K. Holcomb and Sisai Ibssa, *The Invention of Ethiopia* (Trenton, NJ: Red Sea Press, 1990); and Addis Hiwet, *Ethiopia:, From Autocracy to Revolution* (London, UK: Occasional Publication No. 1, Review of African Political Economy, 1975).

67. Rudyard Kipling, "The White Man's Burden (1899)," in T. S. Eliot, *A Choice of Kipling's Verse* (New York: Anchor Books, 1962) 143–45.

68. Said, *The Pen and the Sword* 68, emphasis added.

69. Cheikh Hamidou Kane's *L'aventure ambiguë* (Paris, France: Julliard, 1961), a work of historical fiction, is an excellent illustration of the castrating effects of this pedagogy. See also Çağri Tuğrul Mart, "British Colonial Education Policy in Africa," *Internal Journal of English and Literature* (December 2011): 190–94.

70. For more on this, see my discussion of "Europeanized" and "non-Europeanized" in *African Philosophy: The Essential Readings*, 8–9.

71. As John P. Mckay, Bennett D. Hill, and John Buckler tell us, in their textbook rendition of European global conquest: "Violent antiforeign [sic] reactions exploded . . . again and again, but the superior military technology of the industrialized West almost invariably prevailed. Beaten in battle, many Africans and Asians concentrated on preserving their cultural traditions . . . Others found themselves forced to reconsider their initial hostility. Some (like Ismail of Egypt) concluded that the West was indeed superior in some ways and that it was therefore necessary to . . . copy European achievements." John P. Mckay, Bennett D. Hill, and John Buckler, *A History of Western Society Vol. II: From Absolutism to the Present, 3rd ed.* (Boston: Houghton Mifflin, 1987) 849. The legitimacy of the "antiforeign reactions" is *not* commented on; it is merely noted as futile periodic "explosions" which had to be quelled, and were indeed quelled, and resulted in the more *reasonable* attitude of preserving cultures, at the expense of political sovereignty, which further led to the *reasonable* acceptance of Western superiority. In this manner the subjugation of the world is presented as the violent, but necessary, course of how things had to develop. Tacitly the reader is carried along and made to accept and implicitly endorse the view that European global violence, imposed by "superior military technology," even if deplorable, was the necessary and *reasonable* course of how things human and historical developed and indeed had to develop. As J. M. Blaut points out, "Textbooks are an important window into a culture; more than just books, they are semiofficial statements of exactly what the opinion-forming elite of the culture want the educated youth of that culture to believe to be true about the past and present world." J. M. Blaut, *The Colonizer's Model of the World* (New York: The Guilford Press, 1993) 6. In other words, textbooks, in a tacit and so much more effective manner, serve a *normalizing* function of establishing that which is seen as acceptable and legitimate. It ought to be noted—and I make this observation based on my own elementary and high school education in "Ethiopian Eritrea" and Ethiopia—that, to this day, most African countries utilize Western textbooks, in most subjects, to "cultivate" and "nurture" the minds of their young.

72. Basil Davidson, *Africa in Modern History* (New York: Penguin Books, 1985) 82–83.

73. Davidson, *Africa in Modern History* 43.

74. Davidson, *Africa in Modern History* 43.

75. Tempels, *Bantu Philosophy* 66, see also page 178, emphasis added.

76. Ngugi Wa Thiong'o, *Homecoming* (Chicago: Lawrence Hill Books, 1983) 31–32. Needless to say, in this quote, Ngugi is not advocating circumcision but critiquing the grounds for its critique. For a critique and rejection of this heinous practice (i.e., female genital mutilation) in the African traditional culture, see Paulin J. Hountondji, "Reason and Tradition," *Philosophy and Cultures*, ed. H. Odera Oruka and D. A. Masolo (Nairobi, Kenya: Bookwise, 1983) 144–45.

77. The South African film *Tsotsi* (2005, directed by Gavin Hood)—in the way it portrays the lifestyle of the family whose baby is abducted and the gangster "lifestyle" of the abductors—presents an accurate depiction of what I mean by the term *replicant*. In like manner, the character "Coleman Silk," as depicted by Philip Roth in his novel *The Human Stain* (New York: Vintage Books, 2001) and brought to life by Anthony Hopkins in its cinematic rendition (2003, directed by Robert Benton), is an excellent example of the self-negating "bad faith" that constitutes the being of the *évolué* or *assimilado*, that I have named *replicant*. Such a person is constituted by tacitly internalized sedimented layers of mimicked affectations that constitute his/her person as "naturally" alien and thus hostile to the indigenous African culture-history in which s/he was born. Franz Kafka's "A Report to an Academy" in *Selected Stories of Franz Kafka* (New York: Random House, 1952) is also a lucid illustration of this point. On the extroversion of contemporary Africa, see Paulin J. Hountondji, "Daily Life in Black Africa: Elements of a Critique," *The Surreptitious Speech*, ed. V. Y. Mudimbe (Chicago: The University of Chicago Press, 1992); for the servility that grounds this extroversion, see Aimé Césaire, *Discourse on Colonialism* (New York: Monthly Review Press, 1972) 22. See also what Albert Memmi says of the colonized who accepts assimilation in *The Colonizer and the Colonized* (Boston: Beacon Press, 1967) 120–28. I coined the neologism "replicant" in order use it as a convenient shorthand for all of this.

78. Jean-François Lyotard, *Peregrinations* (New York: Columbia University Press, 1988) 18.

79. Said, *The Pen and the Sword* 67.

80. It is imperative to note that there is nothing pacific about "pacification." It is the systematic destruction of an indigenous society. It took the French forty years (1830 to 1870) to "pacify" Algeria. By "intellectual-cultural subjection" I mean to suggest a similar kind of eradication, on the level of reflection and thought, of the indigenous society.

81. For an example of this, see Yambo Ouologuem, *Bound to Violence* (London, UK: Heinemann Educational Books, 1968) and Chinua Achebe's remarks on Ouologuem and his Western reviewers in *Hopes and Impediments* (New York: Anchor Books, 1989) 77–82.

82. Frantz Fanon, *Les damnés de la terre* (Paris: Maspero, 1974) 12.

83. For an example of this, see Buchi Emecheta's self-deprecating views regarding her "diluted" "Africanness" and Achebe's insightfully acerbic remarks on these views in Achebe, *Home and Exile* 71–72, 81.

84. See what Fanon says on this point in "*Racisme et culture*," *Pour la Révolution Africaine* (Paris: François Maspero, 1964) 41.

85. For the term *ek-sistence*, see endnote 4 in the introduction to this study.

86. Fanon, *Les damnés de la terre* 14.

87. Léopold Sédar Senghor, *On African Socialism*, trans. Mercer Cook (New York: Praeger, 1964) 80, 81.

88. Senghor 82.

89. Julius K. Nyerere, "Africa: The Current Situation," *African Philosophy*, 11.1 (June 1998): 8. The African political scene being what it is—rather sordid—on reading this quote, the reader might be tempted to think, "People who live in glass houses should not throw stones." Nyerere, however, is one of the few African leaders who have never inhabited a "glass house." This, for example, is what Chinua Achebe says of him: "One shining act of bold, selfless leadership at the top, such as unambiguous refusal to be corrupt or tolerate corruption . . . will radiate powerful sensations of well-being and pride through every nerve and artery of national life. I saw such a phenomenon on two occasions in Tanzania in the 1960s. The first was when news got around (not from the Ministry of Information but on street corners) that President Nyerere after paying his children's school fees had begged his bank to give him a few months' grace on the repayment of the mortgage on his personal house. The other occasion was when he insisted that anyone in his cabinet or party hierarchy who had any kind of business interests must either relinquish them or leave his official or party position. This was no mere technicality of putting the business interests in escrow but giving it up entirely. And many powerful ministers including the formidable leader of TANU Women were forced to leave the cabinet." Chinua Achebe, *The Trouble With Nigeria* (Enugu, Nigeria: Fourth Dimension, 1983) 17.

90. Albert Memmi, *The Colonizer and the Colonized* 118.

91. See endnote 1 above.

92. Edward W. Said, "The Politics of Knowledge," in *Reflections on Exile and Other Essays* (Cambridge, MA: Harvard University Press, 2000) 376.

93. Chinua Achebe, *Home and Exile* 26–27. As Gore Vidal tells us, for example, in the introduction to Edgar Rice Burroughs's *Tarzan of the Apes* (New York: Signet Classic, 1990), originally published in 1914 and which "sold over twenty-five million copies in fifty-six languages," the author, Burroughs, never set foot in Africa. It is such fiction that—to this day—serves as the setting for most Westerner attitudes toward Africa and Africans.

94. Bethwell A. Ogot, "Rereading the History and Historiography of Epistemic Domination and Resistance in Africa," *African Studies Review* 52.1 (April 2009): 10.

95. In other words, "normal science" utilizes a discourse rooted in the paradigm inaugurating work of "extraordinary science" (on this, see endnote 6). Analogously, tales of travel reinforced and warranted by metaphysical speculations (i.e., "extraordinary science") are the grounding source of commonsensical notions, ideas, and taken for granted beliefs (i.e., "normal science") about African and Africans that constitute, in part, the self-awareness of the Westernized African.

96. Kwasi Wiredu, *Cultural Universals and Particulars* (Bloomington, IN: Indiana University Press, 1996) 137.

97. Hans-Georg Gadamer, *The Enigma of Health* (Stanford, CA: Stanford University Press, 1996) 139.

98. I say "Portuguese-NATO colonialism" because the fascist colonial administration of Salazar was able to sustain its struggle against African independence for so long only because of the active political-military assistance it was able to secure from NATO and the various United States administration of the time.

99. It should be noted that the Eritrean National Independence Armed Struggle (1961–1991) was directed against U.S. imperialism and Soviet hegemony, fought by proxy. To view it as merely an inter-African "squabble" is to betray ones naïveté regarding the machinations of power politics.

100. Gerald Caplan, *The Betrayal of Africa* (Toronto, Canada: Groundwood Books, 2008) 34.

101. Claude Ake, *Democracy and Development in Africa* (Washington, DC: The Brookings Institution, 1996) 3–4.

102. Edward W. Said, "Never Just a Blind Supporter," interview, *Palestine Report* 24 (November, 1995): 8.

103. Sembène Ousmane, *Xala* (Chicago: Lawrence Hill Books, 1976) 84, emphasis added.

104. Cornelius Castoriadis, "Reflections on 'Rationality' and 'Development,'" *Philosophy, Politics, Autonomy* (New York: Oxford University Press, 1991) 181–82.

105. Castoriadis, "Reflections on 'Rationality'" 200–201.

106. Not only in the way it governs does this strata imitate colonial rule, but also in its daily life and comportment, in the way it rears its children and in the things it aspires to; its life is an imitative sustaining of the colonial lifestyles it once envied. Much like house servants, the replicant elite emulates its former colonial masters.

107. Frantz Fanon, *Les damnés de la terre*, 94. On Fanon's prophetic insight, see Olufemi Taiwo, "On the Misadventures of National Consciousness: A Retrospect on Frantz Fanon's Gift of Prophecy," *Fanon: A Critical Reader*, ed. Lewis R. Gordon (Cambridge, MA: Blackwell, 1996).

108. On how the continent "testifies against itself" please see Sean Carey, "Africa: What Aid Does to a Continent," *New Africa* 498 (September, 2010): 94–96.

109. Donald G. McNeil, Jr., "Kamuzu Banda Dies; 'Big Man' Among Anticolonialists [sic]," *The New York Times*, November 27, 1997, A50. I focus on Senghor and Banda because they are "ideal" replicant "types," at two extremes: refined and mediocre. To get a sense of what African "independence" has been, especially in the economic sector, under the likes of Senghor and Banda, see Michel Leclercq's interview of René Dumont titled "You only listen to Cassandra when Troy is on fire," *New Africa* 500 (November, 2010): 46–49.

110. Fanon, *Les damnés de la terre* 117.

111. Eqbal Ahmed, "The Postcolonial System of Power," *The Selected Writings of Eqbal Ahmed*, ed. Carollee Bengelsdorf, Margaret Cerullo, and Yogesh Chandrani (New York: Columbia University Press, 2006) 139.

112. Ahmed 138–39.

113. Martin Plaut, "The UN's All-Pervasive Role in Africa," *BBC News*, July 18, 2007, 2.

114. As Kwame Nkrumah points out, "Although apparently strong because of their support from neocolonialists and imperialists, they are extremely vulnerable. Their survival depends on foreign support. Once this vital link is broken, they

become powerless to maintain their positions and privileges." Kwame Nkrumah, *Class Struggle in Africa* (New York: International, 1975) 12. A case in point is Mengistu Hailemariam's Ethiopia. When the Carter Administration made it difficult for Mengistu to secure arms to squash domestic opposition, and more urgently, to prosecute the colonial war in Eritrea, he became, overnight, a Marxist-Leninist and realigned Ethiopia with the USSR, in the then-raging Cold War. Soon thereafter, with the demise of the USSR—lacking a foreign prop to protect it from the wrath of the *Eritrean Independence Movement* (i.e., The Eritrean People's Liberation Front [EPLF] and the armed domestic opposition)—Mengistu's military dictatorship, "a house of cards," collapsed.

115. Elizabeth Blunt, "Corruption 'Costs Africa Billions,'" *BBC News*, September 18, 2002, 1.

116. I borrow this formulation from the title of chapter 7 of Kwame Gyekye's *Tradition and Modernity* (New York: Oxford University Press, 1997) but disagree with him regarding the "moral" revolution or "rearmament" required to rid ourselves of this abysmal situation. What needs to be called into question is the neocolonial setup, or frame, in which we are ensnared and made to live within the confines of the heritage of our defeats.

117. The "*thingification*" imposed on the vast majority of the citizens of postcolonial Africa will be explore in chapter 5.

118. Karen Allen, "South Africa Leaders Ignore Marikana Lessons at Their Own Peril," *BBC News Africa*, September 7, 2012.

119. Allen.

120. Patrick Bond, "From Racial to Class Apartheid," *Monthly Review*55.10 (March, 2004): 52. The film *Tsotsi* (2005), directed by Gavin Hood, is an accurate rendition of the character of daily life—for the vast majority—in post-apartheid South Africa.

121. Caplan, *The Betrayal of Africa*, chapters 4 and 5. See also John Bellamy Foster, "A Warning to Africa: The New U.S. Imperial Grand Strategy," *Monthly Review* 58.2 (June 2006).

122. Vice Admiral Robert Moeller, "The Truth about Africom," *Foreign Policy*, July 21, 2010. The quote is from the first page of the article in paragraph 4, emphasis added.

123. Daniel Volman, "Africom and the Obama Administration," *Africa Security Research Project* (April 2009) par. 9.

124. Gianni Vattimo. "Preface," *L'Europa A Sud, Le speranze congiunte di Africa ed Europa* (Turin, Italy: Edizioni Trauben, 2003) 7–8. I would like to thank Professor Lidia Procesi for sending me a copy of this book, which I was not able to secure in the United States.

125. Barack Obama, *The Audacity of Hope* (New York: Vintage Books, 2006) chapter 8.

126. For a fine display of this duplicity, see President Obama's speech in Ghana, July 11, 2009. (http://www.america.gov/st/texttrans-english/2009/July/20090711110050.html).

127. Aimé Césaire, *Discourse on Colonialism*, trans. Joan Pinkham (New York: Monthly Review Press, 1972) 9, translation slightly modified; Aimé Césaire, *Discours sur le Colonialisme* (Paris: Présence Africaine, 1955) 7.

128. Rick Rozoff, "The Pentagon's Last Frontier: Battle-Hardened Troops Headed to Africa," *Global Research* (June 13, 2012). See also Glen Ford, "Where Will the U.S. Strike Next in Africa?" Message posted to http://www.democraticunderground.com/10021096708 (Aug 8, 2012).

129. Just as colonialism institutes the material-cultural conditions conducive to its existence, independence has to create the counter-material-cultural conditions conducive to its concrete consolidation. For the term *pre-phase*, see the text cited in endnote 57 above. On this point, see also Peter Clottey, "Eritrea Favors Investment Partnership Over Aid" *Voice of America* (June 10, 2012) and Celia W. Dugger, "Charity Finds That U.S. Food Aid for Africa Hurts Instead of Helps," *New York Times* (August 14, 2007).

130. Ralph Waldo Emerson, "Self-Reliance," *Selected Essays*, ed. Larzer Ziff (New York: Penguin Books, 1982) 176.

131. Claude Ake, *Democracy and Development in Africa*, chapter 5.

132. McCarthy 233.

133. See endnote 101 above for the full citation.

134. Aimé Césaire, *A Season in the Congo* (New York: Grove Press, 1968) 13.

135. Naomi Klein, "Latin America's Shock Resistance," *The Nation*, 285.17 (November 26, 2007), 28.

136. The best example of this, presently, is the hostility toward Venezuela's Bolivarian attempt at democratic-socialist transformation that emanates from the United States.

137. For a recent example of such a "formal" and futile undertaking, please see Portia Walker "Libyan Voters Prepare for New Political Freedom," *USA Today* (July 6, 2012) 4A.

138. The example that readily comes to mind is the tragic devastation visited on democratic Chile, the Chile of Salvador Allende. It is necessary, therefore, to conceptualize ways of defending against imperialist intervention. Like Allende, Nkrumah was overthrown by a coup engineered from the centers of Western power. As Bethwell A. Ogot points out, "Nkrumah was overthrown in . . . 1966 not because he had ignored the homefront [sic], but because the neocolonial forces had vested interests in keeping African countries underdeveloped." Bethwell A. Ogot, "Rereading the History and Historiography of Epistemic Domination and Resistance in Africa," *African Studies Review*, 52.1 (April 2009) 17.

139. Said, *Reflections on Exile* 379.

140. Amilcar Cabral, *Return to the Source* (New York: Monthly Review Press, 1973) 52. For a complete misunderstanding of what African efforts at self-transformation are aimed at, see Philippe Nemo, *What is the West?* (Pittsburgh, PA: Duquesne University Press, 2004) 95–96.

141. Afonso M. Ucuassapi, *Dalle Indipendenze Alle Libertà* (Milan, Italy: Mimesis Edizioni, 2013) 32.

142. Kuhn, *The Structure of Scientific Revolutions* 34.

143. In the service of these "code-words" the United Nations is used as a convenient cover. For a recent example, please see Mary Beth Sheridan and Scott Wilson, "U.S. Actions in Libya May Speak Louder than Words," *The Washington Post* (March 19, 2011).

144. For an interesting attempt along these lines, see Kwasi Wiredu, "Democracy and Consensus in African Traditional Politics: A Plea for a Non-party Polity," *Postcolonial African Philosophy*, ed. E. C. Eze (Cambridge, MA: Blackwell, 1997).

145. Césaire, *Discours sur le Colonialisme* 19.

146. Karl Marx, "Letter to Arnold Ruge (September 1843)," *Early Writings*, trans. Rodney Livingstone and Gregor Benton (New York: Vintage Books, 1975) 207.

147. On this point, see also Marcien Towa, *L'idee d'une philosophie négro-africaine* (Yaoundé, Cameroun: Editions Cle, 1979) chapter 3.

148. Herbert Marcuse, "The Individual in the Great Society," *The Essential Marcuse*, ed, Andrew Feenberg and William Leiss (Boston, MA: Beacon Press, 2007) 10.

149. This term was the designation, in the 1970s, for the USSR and its East European satellites, a designation that perpetually falsified what it claimed to name.

150. Towa, *L'idée d'une philosophie négro-africaine* 50.

Chapter 2

1. Antonio Gramsci, "Oppressed and Oppressors," in *History, Philosophy and Culture in the Young Gramsci* (a school essay written in 1910), edited by Pedro Cavalcanti and Paul Piccone (Saint Louis, MI: Telos Press, 1975), 156.

2. Chinua Achebe, "The Truth of Fiction," in *Hopes and Impediments* (New York: Anchor Books, 1989), 145. Achebe explains the sense of this proverb thus: "We can learn from the battered corpse by the roadside; not simply by observing it but by creating the chastening fiction *that we are it*, that the corpse of another man is *not*, as the Igbo proverb would have it, a log of wood, but ourselves. (Except that on further reflection that proverb is not in fact the outrageous thing I have just said. Another man's corpse *seems to us* like a log of wood, is what it says—a rather different matter and a very sad reflection on our impaired imagination, on our malfunctioning powers of identification with the plight of our fellows.)."

3. Emmanuel Levinas, "Lévy-Bruhl and Contemporary Philosophy" (originally in *Revue philosophique de la France et de l'étranger* [No. 4, October-December 1957] page. 147) in *Entre Nous Thinking-Of-The-Other* (New York: Columbia University Press, 1998), 39. As is well known, Lucien Lévy-Bruhl's notion of a "pre-logical mentality" was the basic idea that determined European conceptions and attitudes towards the humanity of Africa into the late 1950s. Levinas does not critique Lévy-Bruhl's ideas regarding the humanity of the people whose thinking he purportedly describes; ideas that Lévy-Bruhl himself later on repudiated, as evinced by his posthumously published notebooks. In fact Levinas regrets this change of heart! His only concern is to highlight the view that Lévy-Bruhl undermines the notion of an abstract subjectivity then prevalent in philosophy. It is further necessary to note that Levinas's text, originally published in 1957, was included in *Entre Nous: Essais sur le penser-à-l'autre* (Editions Grasset & Fasquelle, 1991), published four years prior to his death. In view of the fact that authors are consulted when texts are republished, it is clear that Levinas did not feel the need to add, or subtract, anything from this text. Commenting on a similar attitude to that of Levinas, Aimé Césaire wrote in 1955: "A waste of time! M. Caillois considers the rectification to be null and void.

For M. Caillois, the true Lévy-Bruhl can only be the Lévy-Bruhl who says that primitive man talks raving nonsense." *Discourse on Colonialism* translated by Joan Pinkham (New York: Monthly Review Press, 2000), 52.

4. Under the leadership of Kwame Nkrumah Ghana was the first African country south of the Sahara to gain independence and is credited with catalyzing the whole process of African de-colonization. One year earlier Sudan had also secured its independence—this event, however, did not have the same kind of catalytic effect on the Continent as a whole associated with the name of Nkrumah and Ghana.

5. Raoul Mortley, *French Philosophers in Conversation* (New York: Routledge, 1991), 18.

6. Emmanuel Levinas, *Totality and Infinity* ((Pittsburgh, PA: Duquesne University Press, 1969), 73–74. Here I cannot explore the intricacies of Levinas's perspective; all I can do is to highlight what he himself sees as the source of his thinking.

7. This is Aimé Césaire basic thesis in, *Discours sur le Colonialisme* (Paris, France: Présence Africaine, 1955).

8. Ibid. 12.

9. Emmanuel Levinas, *Ethics and Infinity* (Pittsburgh, PA: Duquesne University Press, 1985), 117, emphasis added. This text is a translation of, *Ethique et infini, Librairie Arthème Fayard et Radio France*, 1982.

10. Richard Kearney, "Dialogue with Emmanuel Levinas," in *Face to Face with Levinas*, edited by Richard A. Cohen (New York: SUNY Press, 1986), 20.

11. Emmanuel Levinas, "The Word I, the Word You, the Word God," in *Alterity and Transcendence* (New York: Columbia University Press, 1999), 95–96.

12. Césaire, *Discours sur le Colonialisme*, 9–11. On this point see also Albert Memmi's description of the negative and mutually conditioning relation of *The Colonizer and the Colonized* (Boston, MA: Beacon Press, 1967).

13. Florian Rötzer, *Conversations with French Philosophers* (New Jersey: Humanities Press, 1995), 63.

14. Ibid. 63, emphasis added. Regarding views, expressed by Levinas, similar to the one cited here and in endnotes 5 and 13, Robert Bernasconi writes: "[I]n spite of such statements of Levinas's personal attitudes, his philosophy can, after some modification, still provide a basis for cross-cultural encounter[s]" ("African Philosophy's Challenge to Continental Philosophy," in *Postcolonial African Philosophy*, edited by E. C. Eze [Cambridge, MA: Blackwell, 1997], endnote 8, page 193). Needless to say I respectfully disagree. For critical observations on Levinas, similar to my own, see Nelson Maldonado-Torres, "Decolonization and the New Identitarian Logics after September 11: Eurocentrism and Americanism against the New Barbarian Threats" (*Radical Philosophy Review*, vol. 8, no. 1 [2005] page 45). It should also be noted, in this regard, that Levinas's callous remarks on the tragic events that transpired in Sabra and Shatila—the 1982 massacre of Palestinian refugees by Phalangist soldiers actively aided by the Israel Defense Force—are not worthy of a philosopher whose very name is supposed to be synonymous with concern for "the Other." For Levinas's uncaring comments see, "Ethics and Politics," in *The Levinas Reader* ([Cambridge, MA: Blackwell, 1994], 294).

15. Commenting on this arrogant stance, as expressed in Hegel's *Philosophy of History* (1830), which Levinas—in effect if not in intent—endorses, Marcien Towa

writes: "Western imperialism finds one of its most elaborate ideological justifications in the Hegelian philosophy of history, according to which the modern civilization of Europe constitutes the universal synthesis of all the values produced by humanity in the course of its long history. . . . The other civilizations have nothing of value to offer Europe, universal heritage of humanity, which it does not already posses, as a surpassed moment of the historic development of Spirit, integrated in it under the title of a particular determination." Marcien Towa, "*Propositions sur l'identité culturelle*," *Présence Africaine*, no. 109, (1st Quarterly 1979), 84.

16. The colonial era is basically between "about 1880 and 1960." To be sure, there were earlier incursions, and settlements, and European colonies and white minority regimes lasted into the early 1990s. The above dates indicate only the period of the "high tide" of colonialism. On this point see, Basil Davidson, *Cross Roads in Africa* (Nottingham, England: Spokesman, Bertrand Russell House, 1980), 14.

17. See endnote 60 in chapter 1 for the full citation.

18. Loren Eiseley, *Darwin's Century* (New York: Anchor Books, 1961), 263.

19. Ibid.

20. Ibid. 264.

21. In other words, as Eiseley informs us, this is the "knowledge" of the Europe of the 1850s, of the 19th century (chapter 10 of Eiseley's already cited book). As such, it is the "knowledge" that justifies the colonial project and serves as the buttress of Temples's views. But it is also what must inform Levinas's thinking. How else can one understand his clichéd stale remarks regarding the exotic and dance?

22. James Baldwin, "Princes and Powers," (first published in 1959), in *Nobody Knows My Name* (New York: Vintage Books, 1993), 16.

23. As Plato tells us in the *Phaedo* the body is "a kind of prison" (62b) of the soul. And as St. Augustine of Hippo informs us, in the first chapter of the first Book of his *Confessions* the human soul cannot rest until it rests in God. It is this "sample of humanity" (*Bantu Philosophy*, 169), imprisoned in the inferior African-native culture, that Temples wants to save and mold and sees as the main objective of the colonial project (*Bantu Philosophy*, chapter seven, specifically page 172). This dualism, which is still with us today, is what I refer to as a "defunct metaphysics."

24. Emmanuel Levinas, "Reflections on the Philosophy of Hitlerism," *Critical Inquiry*, vol. 17, no. 1, (autumn 1990), 71. As Albert Memmi has noted: "In the racist way of thinking, *difference is evil*." (*Dominated Man* [Boston, MA; Beacon Press, 1968], 188). Isn't this, in effect, what Levinas is saying in labeling the world beyond Europe exotic? In being labeled exotic (i.e., strange, foreign, alien) aren't the cultural-historical formations that constitute the totality of the world other than "the Bible and the Greeks," being placed beyond the pale of humanity proper? Isn't the logic of what Levinas affirms analogous to the discriminatory and racist stance of the Nazis which led to the ultimate horror of horrors?

25. I say "recommenced" because, appearances not withstanding, the colonized—whose struggles might ebb and wane—never cease from contesting, in open and/or hidden ways, the suppression of their humanity. On this point see the sections titled "background," in the first six chapters, of Richard Gibson's, *African Liberation Movements* (New York: Oxford University Press, 1973).

26. Basil Davidson, *Africa in Modern History* (New York: Penguin Books, 1985), 199.

27. Regarding the "idea" of European superiority and African inferiority, Basil Davidson, speaking from his own and his generation's experience, writes: "We have it very clearly indeed in our own academic tradition, and right up to most recent years. I [am] think[ing] of a statement by the Regis Professor of History at Oxford who said textually, in a series of much publicized lectures given *ex cathedra* in 1963 (November 20th): 'Perhaps in the future there will be some African history to teach, but at present there is none; there is only the history of the Europeans in Africa.' 'So far as the Africans are concerned,' he went on, 'there are only the unrewarding gyrations of barbarous tribes in picturesque but irrelevant corners of the globe.' This was the standard point of view throughout the colonial period in Britain and, so far as my reading has gone, in Italy, in France and elsewhere as well." *Cross Roads in Africa*, 15. Along similar lines, Gerald Caplan points out that: "Renowned Oxford historian Hugh Trevor-Roper excluded Africa from his course on world history on the grounds that 'there is only [in Africa] the unrewarding gyrations of barbarous tribes in picturesque but irrelevant corners of the globe.' For him, African history was nothing more than the history of whites in Africa." *The Betrayal of Africa* (Berkeley, CA: Groundwood Books, 2008), 13–14.

28. Jean-Paul Sartre's preface to Frantz Fanon's, *Les damnés de la terre* (Paris, France: Éditions La Découverte & Syros, 2002), 17. *The Wretched of the Earth* (New York: Grove Press, 1968), 7, the translation has been slightly modified.

29. This is the basic aim of missionary work, to de-culture or destroy the attire of native cultural-historical existence and, out of this destruction, extract the "human essence" to be invested with, or molded in the image of Christian Europe, i.e., the truth of human existence as such. It is interesting to note that in all essentials the structure of this undertaking is identical to Hegel's notion of *Aufhebung*.

30. For various pioneering expressions of this rejection see, *Présence Africaine*, nos. 8-9-10, June-November 1956, specifically "Modern culture and our destiny," 3–6 and Alioune Diop's "Opening address" 9–18.

31. What has to be emphasized about this deracinating experience is that it implicates the one "assimilated" in the deprecation—the active denial and negation of the humanity, the history, the culture, etc.—of the society from which he/she originates. The reader ought to note that there is here at work a kind of cultural-historical alienation and/or suicide.

32. James Baldwin, "East River, Downtown: Postscript to a Letter from Harlem," (1961), in *Nobody Knows My Name*, 77.

33. Ibid. 79. Here it should be noted that, the promising developments in Africa affected not only the radical elements in the African-American community—the Panthers and Malcolm X—but the civil-rights movement as a whole.

34. On this point see sections 3 to 5 of chapter 1 of this study. Even before the advent of independence, the formerly colonized, articulated their stance *vis-à-vis* the colonial adversary in terms of concretely reclaiming their mangled humanity, i.e., the historicity, or *visage*, of their being. On this point see, James Baldwin, "Princes and Powers," (1960) in *Nobody Knows My Name* (New York: Vintage Books, 1993); Alioune Diop, "Modern Culture and Our Destiny," *Prsénce Africaine*, no. 8, 9, & 10,

June-November 1956; and Aimé Césaire, "*Lettre à Maurice Thorez*," (Paris, France: Prsénce Africaine, 1956).

35. In other words: "There is a preconception held by many people, even on the left, that imperialism [i.e., colonialism] made us enter history at the moment when it began its adventure in our countries . . . Our opinion is exactly the contrary. We consider that . . . imperialism . . . made us leave history—our history." Amilcar Cabral, "Brief Analysis of the Social Structure in Guinea," in *Revolution in Guinea: Selected Texts* (New York: Monthly Review Press, 1969), 68. The obverse of colonialism/imperialism, the anti-colonial struggle, is thus a process aimed at re-entering history.

36. That Apartheid, Jim Crow, colonial rule, and in general segregation, are odious forms of rule imposed by terror is a point that—today—does not need much argument.

37. For a suggestive article regarding this dialogue see Robert Bernasconi's, "African Philosophy's Challenge to Continental Philosophy," in *Postcolonial African Philosophy*, edited by E. C. Eze (Cambridge, MA: Blackwell, 1997).

38. Charles Taylor, "Understanding the Other: A Gadamerian View on Conceptual Schemes," in *Gadamer's Century*, edited by J. Malpas, U. Arnswald, and J. Kertscher (Cambridge, MA: The MIT Press, 2002), 279.

39. Hans-Georg Gadamer, *Gadamer in Conversation*, edited and translated by R. E. Palmer (New Haven and London: Yale University Press, 2001), 54.

40. Aimé Césaire, *Lettre à Maurice Thorez*, 11. Césaire's is one of the earliest rejections of such a perspective.

41. Gianni Vattimo, *Credere di Credere* (Milan: Garzanti, 1996), 22.

42. For what is meant by "a hermeneutically self-aware and self-critical reason" see, Gianni Vattimo, "The Reconstruction of Rationality," in *Beyond Interpretation* (Stanford, CA: Stanford University Press, 1997), 97–111.

43. Jacques Derrida, *Learning to Live Finally*, an interview with Jean Birnbaum (Hoboken, NJ: Melville House Publishing, 2007), 40. For a perspective in African philosophy that utilizes Derrida's notion of "deconstruction" see, Lucius Outlaw, "African 'philosophy': deconstructive and reconstructive challenges," in *Contemporary Philosophy: A New Survey, vol. 5, African Philosophy*, edited by Guttorm Floistad (Martinus Nijhoff Publishers: Dordrecht, 1987).

44. In other words, Taylor, Gadamer, and Vattimo are critical of *Enlightenment Reason*, the heritage of modern and contemporary philosophy (Habermas, for example), and articulate the stance of a less pretentious critically self-aware reason (Vattimo's, *pensiero debole*, for example).

45. Gianni Vattimo, *Nihilism and Emancipation* (New York: Columbia University Press, 2004), 35.

46. For the distinction between *productive* and *unproductive* prejudice see Hans-Georg Gadamer, *Truth and Method* (New York: Crossroad Pub., Co., 1982), 245–253. This distinction will be properly explored in chapter 4.

47. Ibid. 246. To be sure, Gadamer expresses this view rhetorically: "What distinguishes legitimate prejudices from all the countless ones which it is the undeniable task of critical reason to overcome?" In other words there are legitimate and non-legitimate "prejudices" and the task of "critical reason" is to "overcome" the

latter while nurturing the former. The interrogative stance of the above sentence, as should be clear, is not really asking anything, it is merely affirming, in a dramatic manner, the view that it is indeed the task of critical reason to "overcome" or expunge negative prejudice.

48. Ibid. 247.

49. Or as Nietzsche puts it: "But I should think that today we are at least far from the ridiculous immodesty that would be involved in decreeing from our corner that perspectives are permitted only from this corner. Rather has the world become 'infinite' for us all over again, inasmuch as we cannot reject the possibility that it may include infinite interpretations" (#374, 336).

50. In the prologue to his "Idea for a Universal History from a Cosmopolitan Point of View" (1784), Kant describes, in more or less this manner, his venture into the realm of history. Kant, *Kant on History* 11–12.

51. Ibid. 24. In a long footnote, on this same page, Kant writes: "Only a learned public, which has lasted from its beginning to our day, can certify ancient history. Outside it, everything else is *terra incognita*; and the history of peoples outside it can only be begun when they come into contact with it. This happened with the Jews in the time of the Ptolemies through the translation of the Bible into Greek, without which we would give little credence to their isolated narratives. From this point, when once properly fixed, we can retrace their history. And so with all other peoples. The first page of Thucydides, says Hume, is the only beginning of all real history." It seems that Levinas's views—with which we started this chapter—merely echo, or paraphrase, Kant's considered opinion regarding Europe's superior position in the world.

52. Immanuel Kant, *Education* (Ann Arbor, MI: University of Michigan Press, 1964), 4. This text on pedagogy was originally published by Kant in 1803, one year before his death, and can thus be taken as Kant's final word on "savage nations."

53. Hans-Georg Gadamer, "Greek Philosophy and Modern Thought" (1978) in, *The Beginning of Knowledge* (New York: Continuum, 2002), 123.

54. Vattimo, *Vocazione* 52.

55. For Gadamer's lucid exposition of this point please see, "*Logos* and *Ergon* in Plato's *Lysis*," in *Dialogue and Dialectic* (New Haven and London: Yale University Press, 1980), 1–20.

56. I say "minimally alienated" because, thus far in world history, the encounters of different peoples, the influence and counter-influence of differing cultures, and the intersecting of various histories has occurred—in most cases than not—in and through violent conflict. Residues of this are bound to be with us for quite some time. In the present context, what we can realistically hope for are "minimally alienated" relations which, over time and progressively, could become non-alienated. In this regard Lewis R. Gordon writes: "For it is the case that the natives have transcended the status of informants and now offer an opportunity to co-invent a new relationship . . . the achievement of which would be . . . a genuinely new world." *An Introduction to Africana Philosophy* (New York: Cambridge University Press, 2008), 220. Analogously, I am arguing that converging developments in Continental and African philosophy, arising out of a *de facto* shared heritage, need to be cultivated and further enhanced.

57. Gianni Vattimo, *La società trasparente* (Milano, Italia: Garzanti Editore, 1989), 11.

58. On the ontic-cultural level, our *ek-sistence* always shows itself as multifaceted and diverse while, on the level of ontology, we share a common human condition—an openness to possibilities—that can be clogged, or partially so, by the ontic-political forms imposed on it. On this point see my book, *The Hermeneutics of African Philosophy* (New York: Routledge, 1994), 20–21 and 75–78.

59. Tsenay Serequeberhan, "Africanity at the End of the 20th Century," *African Philosophy*, vol. 11, no. 1 (June 1998), 20.

60. Martin Heidegger, *What is Philosophy?* (New Haven, CT: College and University Press, 1956), 97.

61. Gianni Vattimo, *Nihilism and Emancipation* (New York: Colombia University Press, 2004), 52.

62. Amilcar Cabral, *Return to the Source* (New York: Monthly Review, 1973), 58–59.

63. This openness to dialogue is a stance that has been advocated by the formerly colonized world since before the earliest days of political independence. As Patrice Lumumba emphatically noted in 1959: "We do not want to cut ourselves off from the West, for we are . . . altogether in favor of friendship between races, but the West must respond to our appeal. Westerners must understand that friendship is not possible when the relationship between us is one of subjugation and subordination." *Lumumba Speaks*, the speeches and writings of Patrice Lumumba (1958–1961), edited by Jean Van Lierde, translated from the French by Helen R. Lane, and introduced by Jean-Paul Sartre (Boston, MA: Little Brown and Co., 1963), 72 and 73. More recently, the popular president of Bolivia, Evo Morales, on the question of dialogue and democracy, echoes Lumumba when he affirms: "We will never break off relations with the U.S. We're coming from a culture of dialogue, but dialogue without strong-arm pressures. We've met Señorita Condoleezza—a very nice woman—and they say they want to be partners with Bolivia. But I think we still need to understand each other's definition of democracy." "A Voice on the Left," *Time*, vol. 167, no. 23 (June 5, 2006), 37.

64. Edward W. Said, *Culture and Imperialism* (New York: Vintage Books, 1994), 221.

65. Baldwin, "Fifth Avenue, Uptown: A Letter from Harlem," in *Nobody Knows My Name*, 71.

66. Derrida, *Learning to Live Finally*, 45.

67. Frantz Fanon, *Les damnés de la terre* (Paris, France: François Maspero, 1974), 62.

68. Ibid.

69. For such a nervous attitude see chapter 6 of Karl Jaspers, *The Future of Mankind* (Chicago, IL: The University of Chicago Press, 1961).

70. Fanon, *Les damnés de la terre*, 62.

71. Philippe Nemo, *What is the West?* (Pittsburgh, PA: Duquesne University Press, 2004), see especially chapter 6 for Nemo's deplorable "bunker" mentality.

72. Here I am thinking of Arab-Moorish Spain and the prolific dissemination of knowledge, into Europe, that emanated from it until 1492 and the final demise

of Granada, the last surviving center of Moorish power and culture on the Iberian Peninsula.

73. Aimé Césaire, *Lettre á Maurice Thorez*, 15.

74. On this point see my book, *Contested Memory: The Icons of the Occidental Tradition* (Trenton, NJ: Africa World Press, 2007), xxii–xxiii.

75. On this point see Marcien Towa, "*Propisitions sur l'identite culturelle*," *Présence Africaine*, 89–90. See also Kwame Gyekye, "Philosophy, Culture, and Technology in the Postcolonial," in *Postcolonial African Philosophy*, edited by E.C. Eze (Cambridge, MA: Blackwell, 1997).

76. I have touched on this point in the last two paragraphs of section 7 in chapter 1. Chapter 5 will present a more ample exploration of this theme.

77. On this term, see endnote 9 and 10 of the introduction.

78. This is the title of one of the last pieces (1960) that Fanon authored as an Algerian militant ("*Cette Afrique à venire*," in *Pour la revolution africaine* [Paris, France: François Maspero, 1964], 203–216). As we have already seen in chapter 1, the hopes Fanon (and others of his generation) had for a truly independent Africa were not realized. In invoking these hopes, after having explored their failure, what I am suggesting is that such "hopes" are never lost—once and for all—so long as those who inherit their patrimony find ways of articulating their possibility.

79. Towa, "*Propositions sur l'identité culturelle*," 87.

80. If one examines the various documents—programs, poems, pamphlets, songs, etc.—that, in their totality, constitute "the voice" of the African Liberation Movement, as a whole, one finds that these documents all start from a recognition and radicalized appropriation of the social-democratic heritage of the modern world.

81. Fanon, *Les damnés de la terre*, 232.

82. Gianni Vattimo, *La vita dell'altro* (Cosenza, Italy: Marco Editore, 2006), vii.

83. "Narcissistic" because as Vattimo points out: "Enlighteners, Hegel, Marx, positivists, historicists of every kind thought, more or less, all in the same manner that the meaning of history is the actualization of civilization, *that is* of the type of modern European man." *La societa trasparente*, 10.

84. Derrida, *Learning to live Finally*, 44–45, emphasis added.

85. Hans-Georg Gadamer, "The Problem of Historical Consciousness," in *Interpretative Social Science, A Second Look*, edited and introduced by Paul Rabinow and William M. Sullivan (Berkeley and Los Angeles, CA: University of California Press, 1987), 86.

86. Hans-Georg Gadamer, "The Universality of the Hermeneutical Problem," in *Philosophical Hermeneutics*, translated and edited by David Linge (Berkeley, CA: University of California Press, 1976), 16, emphasis added.

87. See endnote 73 for the full citation.

88. See endnote 81 for full citation.

89. For efforts in this direction see my book, *Contested Memory: The Icons of the Occidental Tradition* (Trenton, NJ: Africa World Press, 2007).

90. Taylor, "Understanding the Other: A Gadamerian View of Conceptual Schemes," in *Gadamer's Century*, 296.

91. See endnote 2 for the full citation.

Chapter 3

1. An earlier version of this chapter was an invited paper presented at the African philosophy conference, "*Reason, Culture, and Humanism: The Philosophy of Kwasi Wiredu*" organized by the Department of Philosophy, University of Louisville, Louisville Kentucky, October 31–November 1, 2008.

2. *A Century of Philosophy*, Hans-Georg Gadamer in conversation with Riccarod Dottori (New York: Continuum, 2004), 141.

3. Allen W. Wood, introduction to *Basic Writings of Kant* (New York: The Modern Library, 2001), pp. xxii–xxiii. Wood expresses, verbatim, this same view in his book *Kant* (Malden, MA: Blackwell, 2005), 21. In Wood's view, Kant's *Perpetual Peace*, enables us to see beyond the contemporary quagmire of international politics. What I intend to do, in this chapter, is to question this view which Wood seems to think is incontestable.

4. In his last speech to the people of Chile President Salvador Allende stated, among other things, the following: "In this definitive moment, the last thing which I can say to you is that you learn this lesson: foreign capital, imperialism, united with reaction, created the climate for the armed forces to break with their tradition . . ." in *For Neruda, For Chile*, edited by Walter Lowenfels ([Boston, MA: Beacon Press, 1975], 45). For an eyewitness account of the brutal manner in which Victor Jara and thousands of Chileans (*circa* three thousand five-hundred) lost their lives on this tragic day see pages 79–80, in this same text. The documentary film *Salvador Allende* (2004) by Patricio Guzman documents, in great detail, the tragedy that befell the Chilean people. The film *Missing* (1982), by Costa-Garvas, is a fictional rendition of these same events focused on an American family affected by these tragic events.

5. For a sampling of such views please see, *Perpetual Peace, Essays on Kant's Cosmopolitan Ideal*, edited by James Bohman and Matthias Lutz-Bachmann (Cambridge, MA: MIT Press, 1997).

6. By this I mean that, most everybody today is outraged—as well they should—by September 11, 2001 but not too many people even remember September 11, 1973. This amnesia, in this as in most other things that have to do with the West's relation to the rest of the world, betrays an ingrained two-facedness that continues to define the West's political stance in relation to the rest of the globe. As I hope my reader will see part of my argument, in this chapter, is that implicitly and inadvertently Kant's views endorse and facilitate, this "amnesia." Kant—in effect—gives moral and philosophic sanction to the duplicity of the West.

7. The span of time in question is the period of world history just before World War II which is marked by the initial beginnings of the end of direct/overt Western dominance (i.e., colonialism) and the initiation of protracted—armed and political—struggles focused on reclaiming the sovereignty of the formerly colonized world. This period of history, to the present, is the segment of time I have in mind.

8. Kant, *Kant on History* 9.

9. Kant, *Kant on History* 98.

10. Kant, *Kant on History* 98.

11. Ibid. 100.
12. Ibid. 99, emphasis added.
13. Ibid.
14. This, of course, is a purely intuitive conjecture on Kant's part. For this "homage" to "the concept of law" (i.e., this "lip service") could also be taken as evidence of the inherently malevolent and deceitful/cunning disposition of humanity as such.
15. Kant, *Kant on History* 100.
16. Kant, *Kant on History* 100.
17. Kant, *Kant on History* 100.
18. Kant, *Kant on History* 100.
19. Kant, *Kant on History* 100.
20. Kant, *Kant on History* 100–101, emphasis added.
21. Aristotle, 1099b, line 26, 15.
22. Niccolò Machiavelli, *The Prince*, edited by Quentin Skinner (New York: Cambridge University Press, 1990), 85.
23. Heraclitus fragment no. 119 in, Kathleen Freeman, *Ancilla to the Pre-Socratic Philosophers* (Cambridge, MA: Harvard University Press, 1983), 32.
24. Machiavelli, *The Prince*, 85.
25. Ibid. 87.
26. *Kant on History*, 101, emphasis added.
27. On this point see Wood's remarks in the introduction to, *Basic Writings of Kant*, xxii.
28. See the prologue to, "Perpetual Peace," in *Kant on History*, 85.
29. As quoted by Jonathan Schell, "The Case Against the War," in *The Nation*, vol. 276, no. 8 (March 3, 2003), emphasis added, 17.
30. Barack Obama, *The Audacity of Hope* (New York: Vintage Books, 2008), chapter 8.
31. *Kant on History*, 98. A beggar, or a homeless person, for example, does not have any rights to the contents of my wallet. If I feel pity and/or compassion for him or her, I can be merciful and benevolent towards her or him and sacrifice a dollar or two, for his or her benefit. She or he, however, cannot demand money from me as a right. In like manner, in inter-state relations, good will and rights do not mix; they are like *water* and *oil*. Rights end where good will begins.
32. *Hegel's Philosophy of Right* (Oxford, UK: Oxford University Press, 1973), translated by T. M. Knox, paragraph 36.
33. For Hegel, this reciprocal recognition, among states, is held in place by the mutual tension and hostility that constitutes the workings of world history and is resolved by the most powerful as the expression of *Weltgeist*.
34. Claude Lefort, *Writing The Political Test*, translated and edited by David Ames Curtis (Durham and London: Duke University Press, 2000), p. 157.
35. To get a good sense of what it means to say that the "powerful" will act "in the manner in which the powerful act," see Deborah Solomon's interview with Robert Kagan entitled, "Europeans Are Sissies," *The New York Times Magazine* February 16, 2003, page 11. In this interview Kagan—a neo-conservative author of the recently published book, *Of Paradise and Power: America and Europe in the New*

World Order—relishes the idea that the United States of America is a military might, a "powerful" state, and thus willing and ready to go to war in Iraq. The Europeans, on the other hand, are weak and are thus good only at maintaining peace, as Kagan puts it: "And what are you going to do when the civilized comes up against the primitive?" To be sure, Kagan is of no account, but we are told that he has become "the toast of the foreign-policy set," as he acknowledges with gusto, "a pop star" of the present foreign-policy establishment. Is it far fetched then to think that nothing has changed? Indeed, old style imperialism is alive and well!

36. *Kant on History*, emphasis added, 101.

37. Ibid. 101, emphasis added.

38. Ibid. 98.

39. Ibid. 101–102.

40. Ibid. 102, footnote number 8.

41. Florin Rötzer, *Conversation with French Thinkers*, forward by Rainer Rochlitz, translated by Gary E. Aylesworth (Atlantic Highlands, NJ: Humanities Press, 1995), p. 69.

42. See endnote 26 for full citation.

43. *Kant on History*, 101.

44. One need only consult chapter 8 of *The Audacity of Hope* (endnote 30) to confirm the validity of this judgment.

45. On this point see Marcien Towa's interesting remarks, in "*Propositions sur l'identité culturelle*," *Présence Africaine*, no. 109 (1st Quarterly 1979), 82–91, specifically proposition number six. It ought to be kept in mind that "weak" and "small" are relative terms and do not mean feeble or completely inconsequential states.

46. Amilcar Cabral, "Anonymous Soldiers for the United Nations," in *Revolution in Guinea: Selected Texts*, translated and edited by Richard Handyside (New York: Monthly Review Press, 1969), pp. 51–52.

47. As quoted by Bereket H. Selassie, *Conflict and Intervention in the Horn of Africa* (New York: Monthly Review Press, 1980), 58.

48. *Kant on History*, 99–100.

49. A. J. Baker, *The Rape of Ethiopia* (New York: Ballantine Books, 1971). 8–23.

50. Michael Ignatieff, "The Burden," *The New York Time Magazine* (January 5 2003), 53. The cover page, of the above cited magazine advertises Ignatieff's article by re-titling it, "The American Empire (Get Used to It.)." This title better describes the jingoistic stance of the article. On Ignatiff's piece please see, William D. Hartung, "The New Imperialism," *The Nation*, (February 17, 2003), vol. 276, no. 6, 5–6.

51. See endnote 13 in the introduction to this study for the relevant remarks.

52. The paradigmatic example of this is the case of Eritrea *vis-à-vis* Ethiopia. Eritrea placed its trust in the United Nations and even after it won its freedom after 30 years of struggle—and as many years of UN neglect—it legalized its status as a sovereign state by conducting a UN supervised referendum that ratified its hard won freedom, *secured by force of arms*.

53. John King, "Bush: Join 'coalition of the willing'" November 20, 2002 Posted: 6:13 PM EST (2313 GMT) http://edition.cnn.com/2002/WORLD/europe/11/20/prague.bush.nato/. For the way humanitarian concerns are utilized for imperial ends

see, Ellen Brun and Jacques Hersh, "Faux Internationalism and Really Existing Imperialism," *Monthly Review* vol. 63, no. 11, April 2012.

54. For an example of how this is done see, Stephen Kinzer, *All the Shah's Men* (Hoboken, NJ: John Wiley & Sons, 2003); see also Edwidge Danticat and Ariel Dorfman, "The Torture Debate" subtitled "President Bush says harsh interrogation tactics are a key tool in the War on Terror: Two authors consider the painful dilemma posed by this claim: Does It Work?" in *The Washington Post*, Sunday, September 24, 2006, pages B1 and B5.

55. *Plato's Republic*, translated by G. M. A. Grube (Indianapolis, IN: Hackett, 1974), #358e–359a-c, page. 31, emphasis added.

56. Frantz Fanon, *Les damnés de la terre* (Paris: Maspero, 1974), 174.

57. Ibid.

58. UN News Centre, "New General Assembly President calls for democratization of the United Nations," http://www.un.org/apps/news/story.asp?NewsID=28080&Cr=general+assembly&Cr1. See also, President Isaias Afwerki's address to, the 66th session of the United Nations General Assembly, September 23, 2011, http://www.tesfanews.net/archives/3979. As far back as 1947, two years after the formation of the United Nations, Albert Einstein had called for such democratizing measures, focused on strengthening the General Assembly and weakening the Security Council ("Open letter to the General Assembly of the United Nations," in *Essays in Humanism* [New York: Philosophical Library, 1950] 30).

59. For the full citation see endnote 39 in chapter 2.

60. *Lumumba Speaks*, the speeches and writings of Patrice Lumumba, 1958–1961, edited by Jean Van Lierde, translated from the French by Helen R. Lane, and introduced by Jean-Paul Sartre (Boston, MA: Little Brown & Co., 1963), 74.

61. Lefort, *Writing The Political Text*, 157.

62. Einstein, "Towards a World Government (1946)," in *Essays in Humanism*, 15.

63. See endnote 13 of the introduction for the full citation.

64. Martin Heidegger, *Sein und Zeit* (Tübingen: Max Niemeyer Verlag, 1979), 38; *Being and Time*, translated by J. Macquarrie and E. Robinson (New York: Harper & Row, 1962), 63.

Chapter 4

1. Portions of this chapter are composed of modified, re-thought, and extensively reworked extracts (and associated notes) from a paper I did for Father W. J. Richardson's class *Hermeneutics* (1st semester 1982–83, Boston College), a version of which, "Heidegger and Gadamer: Thinking as 'Meditative' and as 'Effective-Historical Consciousness,'" was published in *Man and World* 20: 41–64 (1987). At the time Professor Hans-Georg Gadamer graced us with his presence, as a guest speaker, and shared with us his views on Heidegger's later work. As these lines materialize on my screen I can still remember the palpable excitement of that class and the wonderful experience of Father Richardson's teaching. More recently, this chapter has also benefitted from the critical remarks of Jay L. Garfield which were expressed on the occasion of my presentation of a shorter and earlier version, as an invited talk, at Smith College on November 4, 2010, "Gadamer and Other Traditions: The

Case of Africa." The Talk was presented under the general theme, "*How to do Things with Texts: Interpretation, Translation and Hermeneutic Theory*."

2. Chinua Achebe, *Anthills of the Savannah* (New York: Anchor Books, 1989), 117–118. For an interesting assessment of Achebe's work see Bob Thompson, "Things Fall into Place," *The Washington Post* (March 9, 2008), *Style & Arts* section, M1–M6.

3. Frantz Fanon, *Les damnés de la terre* (Paris: François Maspero, 1974), 141; *The Wretched of the Earth* (New York: Grove Press, 1968), 206–207.

4. Gianni Vattimo, "Gadamer and the Problem of Ontology," in *Gadamer's Century*, edited by J. Malpas, U. Arnswald and J. Kertscher (Cambridge, MA: MIT Press, 2002), 299.

5. Richard E. Palmer, *Hermeneutics* (Evanston, Ill: Northwestern University Press, 1969), 197.

6. The phrase *consciousness saturated with history* is my rendition of Gadamer's "*wirkungsgeschichtliche Bewusstsein*" (*Wahrheit und Methode* [Tübingen: J. C. B. Mohr, 1965], 324), which I first utilized in my already cited article (see endnote 1). The translation I am utilizing (*Truth and Method* [New York: Crossroad, 1982]) renders this term "effective-historical consciousness" (Ibid. 305). While on the whole relying on this translation, in order stick as closely as possible to what Gadamer actually says—as needed—in my explication I will cite the German original and also utilize Gianni Vattimo's Italian translation which is presented "face to face" with the German original (*Hans-Georg Gadamer, Verità e Metodo, Testo tedesco a fronte, traduzione e apparati di Gianni Vattimo* [Milano, Italia: Bompiani, 2005]).

7. As Jeff Malpas puts it, on the first page of his entry on Gadamer, in *The Stanford Encyclopedia of Philosophy*: "Hans-Georg Gadamer is the decisive figure in the development of twentieth century hermeneutics—almost certainly eclipsing, in terms of influence and reputation, the other leading figures, including Paul Ricoeur, and also Gianni Vattimo (Vattimo was himself one of Gadamer's students)" and yet he "is perhaps less well known, and . . . less well-appreciated, in philosophical circles outside Europe than are some of his near-contemporaries." *The Stanford Encyclopedia of Philosophy* (Summer 2013 Edition), Edward N. Zalta (ed.), URL = (http://plato.stanford.edu/archives/sum2013/entries/gadamer/). It is my hope that this chapter will contribute toward ameliorating this unfortunate state of affairs. On Gadamer's life and work see also, James Risser, "In Memoriam: Hans-Georg Gadamer (1900–2002)," in *Continental Philosophy Review*, vol. 35, no. 3, July 2002.

8. Regarding hermeneutics Lewis R. Gordon writes: "A problem with hermeneutical approaches . . . is the kind of suspension they have on questions of truth" (*Disciplinary Decadence* [Boulder, CO: Paradigm Publishers, 2006], 81). One of the things this chapter hopes to do is to respond *grosso modo* to this concern from within the thematic of finitude and throwness—the lived worldliness of human *ek-sistence*—in and out of which questions of truth can and do arise.

9. Hans-Georg Gadamer, *Gadamer in Conversation: Reflections and Commentary*, edited and translated by Richard E. Palmer (New Haven & London: Yale University Press, 2001), 99–100, emphasis added.

10. Ibid. Palmer renders *denaturiert* as *disfigured*, but it seems to me that *denaturalized* would be a better rendition since it does not lose the reference to nature in the original.

11. Immanuel Kant, *Observations on the Feeling of the Beautiful and Sublime*, translated and introduced by John T. Goldthwait (Berkeley, Los Angeles, Oxford: University of California Press, 1960), 110.

12. Gadamer, *Truth and Method*, 238; *Wahrheit und Methode*, 253.

13. Ibid.

14. I say "read generously" precisely because, such a reading is suggested by the open demeanor of the responses that Gadamer gives throughout the book of interviews. In this context "a Chinese wise person with his disciples" can serve as a placeholder for a "wise person" or Sage from any other culture. It is also important to note, furthermore, that Gadamer refers to a lived dialogical practice of thinking (i.e., "a Chinese wise person with his disciples") and not to pre-established ideas, "belief systems," and/or conceptions.

15. Gadamer, *Gadamer in Conversation*, 54. Regarding these remarks see also the discussion in chapter 2 section 2.

16. On this point see chapter 1 section 3.

17. This is a heritage that derogates Otherness. On this point see the second chapter of my book *Contested Memory: The Icons of the Occidental Tradition* (Trenton, NJ: Africa World Press, 2007) and my article "Eurocentrism in Philosophy: The Case of Immanuel Kant" in *The Philosophical Forum*, vol. 27, no. 4 (Summer 1996), in which I utilize Heidegger's notion of "destruction" ([*Destruktion*] *Being and Time*, pt.1, sec. 6) to systematically present a de-structive unpacking of the Eurocentric metaphysics on which, Kant's politico-historical reflections, are grounded. See also chapter 6 of my book *Our Heritage* (Lanham, MD: Rowman & Littlefield, 2000) where I explore Plato's remarks on Greeks and on non-Greeks in book 5 of the *Politeia*.

18. Gadamer, *Truth and Method*, 305.

19. Zär'a Ya'əqob, "The Treatise [*Hatäta*] of Zär'a Ya'əqob," in Claude Sumner, *Classical Ethiopian Philosophy* (Addis Ababa, Ethiopia: Commercial Printing Press, 1985), 235. I have inserted square brackets [ ] because as Sumner himself points out, in his sectional introduction to Zär'a Ya'əqob's text, "the title in the *ge'ez* [i.e., in the original] is . . . *hatäta*" (Ibid. 225).

20. Ibid. 235.

21. See chapter 5 of my book, *Our Heritage*.

22. Gadamer, *Truth and Method*, 158–159.

23. Ibid. 272.

24. Ibid. 210.

25. Aristotle, 1094b, lines 23–25, 2.

26. Hans-Georg Gadamer, "The Problem of Historical Consciousness," in *Interpretative Social Science*, edited by Paul Rabinow and William M. Sullivan (Berkeley and Los Angeles, CA: University of California Press, 1979), 86, and 115–125.

27. Gadamer, *Truth and Method*, 289.

28. Ibid. 214.

29. Ibid. 230.

30. Ibid.

31. Palmer, *Hermeneutics*, 163–164.

32. Gadamer, *Truth and Method*, 235.

33. Ibid.

34. Dermont Moran, *Introduction to Phenomenology* (New York: Routledge, 2000), 282.

35. As Palmer puts it, "The . . . basic Heideggerian conceptions of thinking, language, history, and human experience are carried over into Gadamer" and a little further, "For Heidegger and Gadamer, language, history, and being are not only interrelated but interfused." *Hermeneutics*, pages 166 and 177 respectively.

36. Gadamer, *Truth and Method*, 239–240, emphasis added.

37. Ibid. 242; *Wahrheit und Methode*, 258. In section 3 of chapter 1 we have already seen how this was at the *core* of the imperious mindset that sustained Europe's penchant for global expansion.

38. Ibid. 239.

39. Ibid. 244.

40. Ibid.

41. Ibid. 339; *Wahrheit und Methode*, 358.

42. Ibid. 244; Ibid. 260.

43. Hans-Georg Gadamer, "The Universality of the Hermeneutical Problem (1966)," in *Philosophical Hermeneutics*, translated and edited by David E. Linge (Berkeley, CA: University Press of California, 1976), 9. The quoted text has "linquistic" instead of "linguistic," clearly a printing error.

44. Gadamer, *Truth and Method*, 324.

45. Palmer, *Hermeneutics*, 166.

46. Nietzsche, #374, 336. For Gadamer, it is not Dilthey or Husserl but Nietzsche who is the "true predecessor of Heidegger in raising the question of being" (*Truth and Method*, 228).

47. Gadamer, "The Universality of the Hermeneutical Problem (1966)," 9. José Ortega y Gasset makes a similar point–articulating an analogues perspective–when he states: "Hence we say that we *hold* such and such ideas, whereas rather than holding our beliefs we are them." *History as a System* (New York: W.W. Norton & Co., 1961), 174.

48. Gadamer, *Truth and Method*, 265.

49. Ibid. 263. The very title *Truth and Method* is, as some commentators have suggested, a kind of challenge to the idea that it is only "method" that gives us access to "truth." On this point see Vattimo's lecture on *YouTube* (http://www.youtube.com/watch?v=I1aNsAAImZU) and Palmer, *Hermeneutics*, 163.

50. Gadamer, *Truth and Method*, 267.

51. Ibid. 267.

52. Ibid. 273.

53. Ibid. 252.

54. Ibid. 267.

55. Ibid. 252, *Wahrheit und Methode*, 268. The original reads: "*Was unser geschichtliches Bewußtsein erfüllt, ist immer eine Vielzahl von Stimmen, in denen die Vergangenheit widerklingt.*" The sense one gets from this sentence is that our self-awareness is internal to and always in flux; composed, as it is, of "*eine Vielzahl von*

Stimmen (a variety of voices)" that resounds in it and constitutes it, in an ongoing way, which never quite comes to term.

56. At this point a concrete example, from recent history, might be helpful. James Baldwin, commenting on William Faulkner—an anti-racist white liberal writer who has difficulty breaking with his Southern heritage, the heritage of Mississippi, i.e., of the Confederacy—states the following. "The difficulty . . . is that the Southerner clings to two entirely antithetical doctrines, two legends, two histories. Like all other Americans, he must subscribe, and is to some extent controlled by the beliefs and principles expressed in the Constitution [i.e., the cornerstone of the effective-history of the United States]; at the same time, these beliefs and principles seem determined to destroy the South [i.e., the dead-history of the Confederacy]. He is, on the one hand, the proud citizen of a free society [i.e., a specific/individual incarnation of the effective-history of the United States] and, on the other, is [still] committed to a society which has not yet dared to free itself of the necessity of naked and brutal oppression [i.e., the Confederacy, part of the dead-past or dead-history of the United States]. He is part of a country which boasts that it has never lost a war [i.e., United States]; but he is also the representative of a conquered nation [i.e., the South]." "Faulkner and Desegregation" (1956) in *Nobody Knows My Name* (New York: Vintage Books, 1993). pp. 122–123. The source of the schizoid racial attitude of a person like Faulkner is his conflicted allegiance to contradictory histories. The effectiveness of effective-history [*gewesen* history] affirms itself by pushing against a *dead-past* or *dead-history* [*vergangen* history]. And so, beneath the surface, held in check by the effectiveness of effective-history is to be found the undercurrent of a cadaverous/retrograde *dead-past* or *dead-history* which always threatens to come to the fore, whenever the effectiveness of effective-history faces a fork in the road of its convictions. Faulkner, and others like him, must "filter-out" and affirm or "hear" and make a decision for one or the other of these two conflicting histories. To a large extent, this will depend on which "effective-history,"—that of the United States or the Confederacy—holds more sway over their allegiance, or controls their being, i.e., their lived existence. Now, in his formulation of "effective-history" Gadamer strongly suggests this disposition of the individual person, as decisive, within the flow of the effects of "effective history" without ever explicitly affirming it. As noted in endnote 10 of the preface, this is my way of remedying or reinforcing/supplementing Gadamer's conception of "effective-history." On the terms *gewesen* and *vergangen* see, Vattimo, "Gadamer and the Problem of Ontology," in *Gadamer's Century*, 303 and *Vocazione* 74.

57. Gadamer, "The Problem of Historical Consciousness," 88, emphasis added. I hope the reader sees how the citation just given validates the remarks made in the previous endnote (no. 56).

58. Gadamer, *Truth and Method*, 271.

59. Ibid. 250.

60. Ibid. 237.

61. Ibid. 238.

62. Marcien Towa, "*Consciencisme*," *Présence Africaine*, no. 83, 1st Quarterly (1973), 156.

63. Gadamer, *Truth and Method*, 238.
64. Ibid. 272.
65. Ibid. emphasis added.
66. Ibid. 239.
67. Ibid. 238. See also the text, above, associated with endnotes 12 and 13.
68. Gadamer, "The Universality of the Hermeneutical Problem," 9. It is interesting to note in this regard that a baby for *circa* the first 3 months of its life (as the professionals who work with newborns tells us) is incapable of "making sense"—any kind of sense—of that which it encounters through the *sensory-mechanical* apparatus of its body. Its *visage* is "bland," "open," "smooth," and "innocent"—in like manner its *sensory-mechanical* relation to "its world" is *empty*. It is as it develops markings (i.e., character) and its visage gets progressively "marked," in an ongoing way and shaped/molded/tempered by its lived experiences that it begins acquiring a personality, "a perspective" i.e., *prejudgments* or *prejudices*, on its lived existence, and in this process is constituted—as a human being—by the "biases" of its "openness to the world."
69. Gadamer, *Truth and Method*, 267.
70. Ibid. 238; *Wahrheit und Methode*, 253.
71. In this regard the Enlightenment's "prejudice against prejudice" in its scientistic certainty of itself is a "hidden prejudice"—in plain view—cloaked by the "tyranny" (endnote 66) of its own self-assuredness.
72. Gadamer, *Truth and Method*, 333; *Wahrheit und Methode*, 352.
73. Ibid. 245.
74. Gadamer, *Wahrheit und Methode*, 261; *Truth and Method*, 245.
75. Gadamer, *Truth and Method*, 258.
76. Gadamer, *Truth and Method*, 262; *Wahrheit und Methode*, 279.
77. *Wahrheit und Methode*, 279 (The original reads: "*In diesem Zwischen ist der wahre Ort der Hermeneutik*"). *Truth and Method*, 263.
78. Ibid. 231–232.
79. Ibid. 259.
80. Aristotle, 1143b, line 14, 115.
81. Gadamer, *Truth and Method*, 245, emphasis added.
82. Ibid. 253; *Wahrheit und Methode*, 269.
83. See endnote 25 above.
84. Gadamer, *Truth and Method*, 267.
85. Ibid. 266.
86. See endnote 36.
87. Gadamer, *Truth and Method*, 339; *Wahrheit und Methode*, 358.
88. Ibid. The original from which the cited texts in endnote 87 and in the present endnote are taken is the following. "*Der überstandpunktliche Standpunkt, von dem aus seine wahre Identität gedacht würde, ist eine reine Illusion.*"
89. Lucien Lévy-Bruhl, "How Natives Think," in *African Philosophy: Selected Readings*, edited by Albert G. Mosley (Englewood Cliffs, NJ: Prentice Hall, 1995), 41. As we saw in the first section of chapter 2, Levinas praises Lévy-Bruhl precisely on this point.
90. Ibid. 55, emphasis added.

91. Gadamer, *Truth and Method*, 246.

92. Joseph J. Kockelmans, "On the Problem of Truth in the Sciences," in *Proceedings and Addresses of the American Philosophical Association* (APA), supplement to vol. 61, no. 1, (September 1987) 14.

93. Ibid. 16.

94. Thomas S. Kuhn, *The Structure of Scientific Revolutions, 2nd edition* (Chicago, Ill: University of Chicago Press, 1970), 86–87. See also Kuhn, "Scientists and Their World Views," in *The Truth about The Truth*, edited by Walter Truett Anderson (New York: A Jeremy P. G. P. Tracher/Putnam Book, 1995), 198.

95. On this see, Thomas S. Kuhn, "Logic of Discovery or Psychology of Research?" in *Philosophy of Science, 2nd edition*, edited by M. Curd, J. A. Cover, and C. Pincock (New York: W.W. Norton & Co., 2013). This also, long before Kuhn, is what Heidegger affirms in 1954 when he writes "science itself ['normal science'] does not think, and cannot think" and this is "the assurance of its appointed course." *What Is Called Thinking?* (New York: Harper & Row Pub., 1968), 7–8, see also, on this point, Heidegger's exposition of the relation of grounding work, to "positive research," in the realm of scientific activity in *Being and Time* (1927) section 3.

96. Gianni Vattimo, "The Age of Interpretation," in Richard Rorty and Gianni Vattimo *The Future of Religion*, edited by Santiago Zabala (New York: Columbia University Press, 2005), 45.

97. See endnote 68.

98. Gadamer, *Truth and Method*, 210.

99. Ibid. 194.

100. Ibid.

101. On this point see, Holly L. Wilson, "Gadamer's Alleged Conservatism," in *Phenomenology, Interpretation, and Community*, edited by Lenore Langsdorf and Stephen H. Watson with E. Marya Bower (New York: State University of New York Press, 1996).

102. Gianni Vattimo, "*L'ontologia Ermeneutica Nella Filosofia Contemporanea*" which is the introduction Vattimo attaches to his translation of Gadamer's *mangum opus* (*Verità e Metodo* [Milano, Italia: Bompiani, 2005], xxix). In effect, what Gadamer and Vattimo are telling us is that, minus the extravagant claims of "absolute spirit," Hegel still defines the contemporary philosophic horizon.

103. Gadamer, *Truth and Method*, 310.

104. Ibid. 311.

105. Ibid. 317.

106. Hans-Georg Gadamer, *Hegel's Dialectic* (New Haven, CT: Yale University Press, 1976), 83.

107. Gadamer, *Truth and Method*, 319.

108. Ibid.

109. Ibid. 318–319, emphasis added.

110. For Hegel: "Accordingly, logic [i.e., his *Science of Logic*] is to be understood as the system of pure reason, as the realm of pure thought. This realm is truth as it is without veil and in its own absolute nature. It can therefore be said that this content is the exposition of God as he is in his eternal essence before the creation

of nature and a finite mind." *Hegel's Science of Logic*, translated by A.V. Miller (New York: Humanities Press, 1976), 50.

111. Ibid. 321.

112. See endnote 25 in chapter 1 for the full citation.

113. See endnote 37 above.

114. See endnote 88 above.

115. See endnote 110 above for the full citation.

116. See the first paragraph of the present chapter.

117. Palmer, *Hermeneutics*, 191–92.

118. See section 2 above.

119. Jean-Paul Sartre, *Search for a Method* (New York: Random House, 1968), 27.

120. The model, or paradigm, that readily comes to mind for such thinking, is Auguste Comte's "*philosophie positive*" (1842) in which everything is determined by "a great fundamental law, to which the mind [i.e., the human mind as such] is subjected by an invariable necessity" such that "by its very nature" it develops in three sequential stages "the theological method . . . the metaphysical method . . . and the positive [i.e., scientific] method." *Introduction to Positive Philosophy* edited and introduced by Frederick Ferré (Indianapolis, IN: Bobbs-Merrill Co., 1970), 1–2.

121. Basil Davidson, *Africa in Modern History* (New York: Penguin Books, 1985), 32.

122. Gainni Vattimo, *La società trasparente* (Milan, Italy: Garzanti, 1989), 10.

123. Gadamer, *Truth and Method*, 323, emphasis added.

124. James Baldwin, "The Discovery of What it Means to Be an American" (1959), *Nobody Knows My Name* (New York: Vintage Books, 1993), 11.

125. See endnote 66 for the full citation.

126. This is the "paternalism" which Aimé Césaire refers to as "'*fraternalisme*,'" and points out is the common attitude of all European political tendencies, in their relations to the non-European world, which he categorically rejects in his, *Lettre á Maurice Thorez* (Paris, France: Présence Africaine, 1956), 11.

127. V. Y. Mudimbe, *The Invention of Africa* (Bloomington, IN: Indiana University Press, 1988), 47–48.

128. Gadamer, *Truth and Method*, 324.

129. Placide Temples, *Bantu Philosophy* (Paris, France: Présence Africaine, 1959), specifically chapter 7. For an illustration of this *I–Thou* relation, in its missionary instantiation, see Chinua Achebe's fictional recreation of such an "encounter" in chapter 21 of *Things Fall Apart*.

130. See endnote 14 in chapter 2.

131. Socrates describes this stance in the *Phaedo* thus: "I am in danger at this moment of not having a philosophical attitude about this, but like those who are quite uneducated, I am eager to get the better of you in argument, for the uneducated, when they engage in argument about anything, give no thought to the truth about the subject of discussion but are only eager that those present will accept the position they have set forth. I differ from them only to this extent: I shall not be eager to get the agreement of those present that what I say is true, except incidentally,

but I shall be very eager that I should myself be thoroughly convinced that things are so." *Plato Five Dialogues*, translated by G.M.A. Grube (Indianapolis, IN: Hackett, 1981), no. 91a-b, p. 129.

132. Gadamer, *Truth and Method*, 325.

133. See endnote 5 in chapter 2.

134. See endnote 14 in chapter 2.

135. Gadamer, *Truth and Method*, 238.

136. Palmer, *Hermeneutics*, 191. See also the remarks in endnote 6.

137. Gadamer, *Truth and Method*, 245.

138. Ibid. 272.

139. Ibid. 336.

140. Ibid. 337.

141. Ibid. 358, emphasize added.

142. Ibid. 447; *Wahrheit und Methode*, 465. I hope that this can serve as a response to the concern voiced by Gordon (see endnote 8). Responding to a similar kind of concern Vattimo writes: "The novelty of the thinking of the 20th century, and above all of Heidegger, consists in having seen that these structures, which Kant believed to be the same for reason in all times and places are, themselves, historico-destinal [*storico-destinali*] events. This, more or less, is what I intended earlier speaking of the fact that we are 'caught' and 'given to ourselves' in a web . . . the web of tradition, of that which in language is trans-mitted [*tra-mandato*] to us and which conditions and makes possible every one of our experiences of the world. Philosophy, as a way of reflecting, of' 'returning to' these transcendental conditions—but historically changeable, like language and culture—of experience, is not a science: it does not 'demonstrate' enunciations, it does not solve problems in order to move on, cumulatively, to the solution of others; it is rather an exercise in mortality, and therefore also, to a certain extent, it is an 'edifying' or 'aesthetic' discourse, to the extent that it does not conclude, but intensifies and enriches, complicates with broad and 'bottomless' references, our experience of things. We cannot therefore say: the truth (in an originary philosophic sense [*nel senso filosofico, originario*]) is this or that. To this question we respond instead with a lengthy discourse, and we intend by this that the term *truth* alludes to this complex situation, to our being-thrown (as Heidegger says) in a horizon of understanding the world which is inscribed [*scritto*] in our language and in our cultural tra-dition [*tra-dizione*], without however meaning by this that stable structures can be singled out, given once and for all." *Al di la del soggeto* (Milan, Italy: Giangiacomo Feltrinelli Editore, 1984), 20–21.

143. *Plato's Republic*, trans., G. M. A. Grube (Indianapolis, IN: Hackett, 1974), #588b, page 235.

144. Gadamer, "The Universality of the Hermeneutical Problem (1966)," in *Philosophical Hermeneutics*, 16.

145. See endnote 73 in chapter 2.

146. On this point see my book, *Contested Memory: In Icons of the Occidental Tradition*, 95–96.

147. Tsenay Serequeberhan, "Africanity at the End of the 20th Century," *African Philosophy*, vol. 11, no. 1 (June 1998), 13.

148. Gianni Vattimo, *Al di la del soggeto* (Milan, Italy: Idee/Feltrinelli, 1984), 13. This is the sense of Gadamer's remark: "Being that can be understood is language [*Sein, das verstanden warden kann, ist Sprache.*]," *Truth and Method*, 432; *Wahrheit und Methode*, 450. In other words, all "*che ci sia dato di possedere*" is only in and through language and thus this makes it the actuating placenta of being, i.e., existence.

149. Ibid. 12.

150. Frantz Fanon, *Peau noire masques blancs* (Paris, France: Éditions du Seuil, 1952), 8 and

Amilcar Cabral, "Identity and Dignity in the Context of the National Liberation Struggle," in *Return to the Source: Selected Speeches* (New York: Monthly Review Press, 1973), 62.

151. Tsenay Serequeberhan, *The Hermeneutics of African Philosophy: Horizon and Discourse* (New York: Routledge, 1994), 9.

152. Aimé Césaire, *Discourse on Colonialism*, translated by Joan Pinkham (New York: Monthly Review Press, 1972), 31.

Chapter 5

1. Ferdinand Oyono, *Houseboy* (Portsmouth, NH: Heinemann, 1990), 4.

2. Albert Memmi *Dominated Man* (Boston, MA: Beacon Press, 1969), 193.

3. James Baldwin, *Nobody Knows My Name* (New York: Vintage Books, 1993), xii.

4. In the first endnote of chapter 4 of *Contested Memory: The Icons of the Occidental Tradition* (Trenton, NJ: Africa World Press, 2007), I have noted that the *1844 Manuscripts* had to be assessed differently than "the materialist conception of history." The *Manuscripts* are not structured by a metaphysics of history. They are not focused, as "the materialist conception of history" is, on the metaphysical straitjacketing of human existence into the, thus far, already established forms of Western history.

5. Martin Heidegger, *Being and Time* (New York: Harper & Row Publishers, 1962), 34. I utilize the standard translation of *Being and Time* by John Macquirrie and Edward Robinson and, as needed, I consult the German text *Sein und Zeit* (Tübingen: Max Niemeyer, 1979).

6. Martin Heidegger, "Modern Natural Science and Technology," in *Radical Phenomenology*, ed., by John Sallis (Atlantic Highlands, NJ: Humanities Press, 1978), 4. Regarding the importance of this text Sallis writes: "This text was addressed to the participants in the tenth annual meeting of the Heidegger Conference . . . at DePaul University . . . two weeks before Heidegger's death, and . . . is reported to have been the last composed by him" (Ibid. 1). This then can be taken as Heidegger's "will and testament" regarding the character and intent of his work.

7. Kostas Axelos, *Marx e Heidegger* (Naples, Italy: Guida Editori, 1977), 99.

8. Martin Heidegger, *What is Called Thinking*, (New York: Harper & Row, 1968), 185.

9. Martin Heidegger, *An Introduction to Metaphysics* (New Haven, CT: Yale University Press, 1977), 176.

10. Hans Georg-Gadamer, *Truth and Method* (New York: Crossroads Pub., 1982), 336. This, as we saw in chapter 4, is the truth of the "effective-historical consciousness."

11. This was the "condition" systematically explored in chapter 1.

12. Antonio Gramsci, "*Il nostro Marx*," in *Scritti Giovanili* (Italia, Torino: Giulio Einaudi, 1972), 217–221.

13. Aimé Césaire, *Discours sur le Colonialisme* (Paris, France : Présence Africaine, 1955), 19.

14. Herbert Marcuse, *Studies in Critical Philosophy* (Boston, MA: Beacon Press, 1973), 10.

15. Karl Marx, *The Economic and Philosophic Manuscripts* (New York: International Pub., 1972), 70, emphasis added.

16. Ibid. 66–67.

17. Ibid. 70.

18. Ibid.

19. Ibid. 78.

20. Ibid.

21. Karl Marx, "Alienation and Social Classes," in *The Marx-Engels Reader, 2nd Edition*, edited by Robert C. Tucker (New York: W.W. Norton & Company Inc., 1978), 133.

22. Ibid.

23. Ibid.

24. Karl Marx, *Capital Vol. 1*, edited by Frederick Engels (New York: International Pub., 1967), 153.

25. Ibid.

26. Marx, *The Economic and Philosophical Manuscripts*, 121.

27. Ibid. 120.

28. On this see the remarks in endnote 4.

29. Marx, *The Economic and Philosophical Manuscripts*, 71–72.

30. The reference to "the 99%" comes from the recent populist "occupy movement." For the relevance of Marx's work see, Stuart Hall's presentation "Karl Marx and Marxism" in the series, *Films for the Humanities & the Sciences*, Published, July 12, 2013 (http://www.youtube.com/watch?v=m8bdndigRA8).

31. On this point see, Charles Guignon, *The Good Life* (Indianapolis, IN: Hackett Pub., Co., 1999), xi–xii and 271–272.

32. For a shift, regarding this view, see Thomas Sheehan, "A Paradigm Shift in Heidegger Research," *Continental Philosophy Review*, vol. 34, no. 2 (June 2001), 187–192. In keeping with this "shift" I drop the capitalization of the word 'being' and focus on the *Sache selbst* of what is in question.

33. Ibid. 191. In full: "This is a firm position that Heidegger never renounced: "being" is given or appears (*das Sein west*) only in the activities of human beings, which are always discursive, synthetic-differential activities. Before *homo sapiens* evolved, there was no "being" on earth: it did not lurk within things, waiting to be discovered; it was not hiding in the wings, waiting for a *Dasein* to come along so that it could reveal itself. Likewise before creation there was no "being" in God's heaven, because "being" for Heidegger does not mean "in existence." The status

of "out-there-ness" (i.e., "existence" whether in this universe or in God's heaven) is not what constitutes "being" for Heidegger. If anything, "in-here-ness" does, the condition of *Innerweltlichkeit*, of "having sense."

34. On the first unnumbered page of *Being and Time* we read: "Die konkrete Ausarbeitung der Frage nach dem Sinn von "Sein" ist die Absicht der folgenden Abhandlung." ["The concrete elaboration of the question based on the sense of "*being*" is the purpose of the following treatise."]

35. Heidegger, *Being and Time*, 69.

36. On this point see the last three sentences of Theodore Kisiel's, "Towards a Topology of Dasein" in *Heidegger: The Man and the Thinker* edited by, Thomas Sheehan (Chicago, Ill: Precedent Pub., Inc., 1981), 105.

37. Michael E. Zimmerman, "Karel Kosik's Heideggerian Marxism," in *The Philosophical Forum*, vol. 15, no. 3 (Spring 1984), 220.

38. As noted in endnote 6, Heidegger's focus is on "a transformed abode of man in the world." This is what orients the evocative character of his thinking.

39. Martin Heidegger, *What is Called Thinking* (New York: Harper& Row Pub., 1968), 17.

40. Romano Guardini, *The Death of Socrates* (New York: Meridian Books, 1965), 6.

41. Karel Kosik, *Dialectics of the Concrete* (Dordrecht, Holland/Boston, MA: D. Reidel Publishing Co., 1976), 86. Confirming Kosik, on this crucial point, Hugh J. Silverman writes, in the introduction to *Postmodernism and Continental Philosophy* (edited by Hugh J. Silverman and Donn Welton [New York: SUNY Press, 1988], 3–4), that the:

> "Transcendental view of things, where all could be put in order, where rules could replace human existence, where a plan could resolve all confusion and disharmony was exceptionally dangerous and horrifying. . . . The Charlie Chaplin *Modern Times* film (. . .) depicts with humor the stultifying effects of over-technologization without thought and mechanization without humanization. . . . The philosophical response [i.e., critique] of a Heidegger was to reject the transcendental overview and to replace it with an account of our being-in-the-world as a relation of beings to being. Interpretation, understanding, and authenticity were called for. To hear the call of being was to situate oneself in a context in which despair and related emotions could be meaningful but not oppressive."

42. Heidegger, *Being and Time*, 157.

43. Ibid. 93.

44. Ibid.

45. Ibid. 155.

46. Ibid.

47. I borrow this term from Emmanuel Levinas ("Dialogue with Emmanuel Levinas," conducted by Richard Kearney in, *Face to Face with Levinas*, edited by Richard A. Cohen [New York: SUNY Press, 1986], 20). I utilize it to indicate the

absorbed involvement of various persons with a task such that the activity, of each, melts into the joint effort of all.

48. Heidegger, *Being and Time*, 100.

49. Ibid. 153–154, emphasis added.

50. Ibid. 105.

51. Ibid. 163.

52. Ibid.

53. Ibid.

54. Ibid. 167.

55. Ibid. 164, *Sein und Zeit*, 127. The German reads: "*In der Benutzung öffentlicher Verkehrsmittel, in der Verwendung des Nachrichtenwesens (Zeitung) ist jeder Andere wie der Andere.*" And so, the phrase, "each Other is like the Other," renders the German, "*ist jeder Andere wie der Andere.*"

56. Ibid. 168. The last and crucial sentence in the original reads: "*Das Sein des Seienden, das mit-da-ist, wird als Vorhandenheit begriffen.*" *Sein und Zeit*, 130 (emphasis added).

57. The 70s of the last century saw the heyday, in Marxist literature, focused on extracting the implicit ontology that structures the *1844 Manuscripts*. Among the most interesting of such efforts, Bertell Ollman, *Alienation: Marx's Conception of Man in Capitalist Society* (New York: Cambridge University Press, 1973) and Kostas Axelos, *Alienation, Praxis, and Techne in the Thought of Karl Marx* (Austin, TX: University of Texas Press, 1976).

58. "*Nur noch ein Gott Kann uns retten,*" *Der Spiegel* 31st May, 1976 (pp. 193–219). Interview conducted by R. Augustein and G. Wolff, on the 23rd of September 1966. The quoted sentence is on page 11 of the internet version, in Heidegger's third answer. Retrived from http://web.ics.purdue.edu/~other1/Heidegger%20Der%20 Spiegel.pdf.

59. Aimé Césaire, *Discourse on Colonialism*, translated by Joan Pinkham (New York: Monthly Review Press, 1972), 21, translation slightly modified. Pinkham puts double quotation marks on Césaire neologism *chosification* which is rendered by *thingification*, but Césaire does not.

60. See endnote 101, chapter 1.

61. See endnote 107, chapter 1.

62. See endnote 110, chapter 1.

63. Basil Davidson and Antonio Bronda, *Cross Roads in Africa* (Nottingham, England: Spokesman Press, 1980), 25.

64. Walter Rodney, *How Europe Underdeveloped Africa* (Washington, DC: Howard University Press, 1974), 280.

65. James Baldwin, "The Discovery of What it means to be an American" (1959), in *Nobody Knows My Name* (New York: Vintage books, 1989), 5.

66. Because of the lack of public control and accountability Baldwin in, "Faulkner and Desegregation," published in 1956 (*Nobody Knows My Name*), refers to the period of history from the end of slavery unto his time as "years of quasi-freedom" (Ibid. 118). American society, during this period, officially sanctioned racism and segregation and thus abridged the 'role' of citizen. The life of citizens of color, during this time, was analogous to that of the colonized and to the *nominal* citizens of postcolonial Africa.

67. Césaire, *Discourse on Colonialism*, 13.

68. Ibid, 21.

69. Ibid.

70. Eqbal Ahmed, "The Postcolonial System of Power," in *The Selected Writings of Eqbal Ahmed*, forward by Noam Chomsky, edited by Carollee Bengelsdorf, Margaret Cerullo, and Yogesh Chandrani (New York: Columbia University Press, 2006), 138–139.

71. Niccolò Machiavelli, *The Prince*, edited by Quentin Skinner (New York: Cambridge University Press, 1990), 51.

72. Basil Davidson, *Africa in Modern History* (New York: Penguin Books, 1985), 298.

73. Frantz Fanon, *The Wretched of the Earth* (New York: Grove Press, 1968), 183.

74. Ibid. 182.

75. Ibid. 194.

76. Ibid. 168.

77. Ibid. 182.

78. Ibid. 169.

79. On this see also, Achille Mbembe, *On the Postcolony* (Berkeley, CA: University of California Press, 2001), 235–243.

80. Karl Marx, "Wage Labour and Capital," in *The Marx-Engels Reader, 2nd edition*, ed., Robert C. Tucker (New York: W.W. Norton, 1978), 206.

81. Fanon, *The Wretched of the Earth*, 167.

82. Ibid. 169.

83. Ibid. 186.

84. Ibid. 182.

85. See endnote 122 in chapter 1.

86. Vijay Prashad, *The Darker Nations* (New York: The New Press, 2007), xvii.

87. Memmi, *Dominated Man*, 8.

88. See section 6 of chapter 1.

89. Rodney, *How Europe Underdeveloped Africa*, 280.

90. Davidson, *Africa in Modern History*, 148–149. As Frederick Douglass tells us, in their dehumanized condition, slaves "seem to think that the greatness of their masters was transferable to themselves" (*Narrative of a Slave* [New York: A Signet Book, 1968], 37). This is akin to the thinking of the replicant strata.

91. Marcien Towa, "Propositions sur l'identité culturelle," *Présence Africaine*, no. 109, 1st Quarterly (1979), 86–87.

92. Ibid. 85.

93. Martin Heidegger, "Indication of the Hermeneutical Situation," in *The Heidegger Reader*, edited and introduced by Günter Figal (Bloomington, IN: Indiana University Press, 2009), 39.

Conclusion

1. Léopold Sédar Senghor, "The Spirit of Civilization or the Laws of African Negro Culture," *Présence Africaine*, no. 8/9/10 (June–November, 1956), 52.

2. Amilcar Cabral, *Return to the Source: Selected Speeches* edited by the Africa Information Service (New York: Monthly Review Press, 1973), 49.

3. Vijay Prashad, *The Darker Nations* (New York: The New Press, 2007), 279.

4. Edward W. Said, "Representing the Colonized" in *Reflections on Exile and Other Essays* (Cambridge, MA: Harvard University Press, 2000), 376. As Said has noted, "What interests me in the politics of identity that informed imperialism in its global phase is that just as natives were considered to belong to a different category–racial or geographical–from that of the Western white man, it also became true that in the great anti-imperialist revolt represented by decolonization this same category was mobilized around, and formed the resisting identity of, the revolutionaries" (Ibid. 377).

5. In other words, "Englishness . . . Frenchness . . . or American exceptionalism" have never been used for purposes of resistance. On the other hand "Africanness," or *Négritude*, as Fanon points out in *Les damnés de la terre*, at one time–in the initial phases of resistance–served as a psychological prop for those engaged in the dire and arduous project of revolt ([Paris: François Maspero, 1974], 143–144).

6. Dr. Martin Luther King Jr., points out that, at the inception of the modern civil rights movement, many African-Americans were held back and psychologically victimized by such conceptions. As he puts it: "Many of the Negroes who joined the protest did not expect it to succeed. When asked why, they usually gave one of these answers: 'I didn't expect Negroes to stick with it,' or, 'I never thought we Negroes had the nerve,' or, 'I thought the pressure from the white folks would kill it before it got started.' In other word, our nonviolent protest in Montgomery is important because it is demonstrating to the Negro, North and South, that the many stereotypes he has held about himself and other Negroes are not valid. Montgomery has broken the spell and is ushering in concrete manifestations of the thinking and action of the New Negro.'" *I Have a Dream*, writings and speeches that changed the world, edited by James M. Washington (New York: HarperCollins Pub., 1992), 6. In other words, as in Hegel's *Phenomenology of Spirit*, consciousness comes to know itself in the process of overcoming itself. Overcoming previous manifestations of itself which, in its later actuation/incarnation, are manifested as inadequate/truncated (i.e., dead-past) forms of itself that needed to be bypassed.

7. Said, "Representing the Colonized," 312.

8. See endnote 73 in chapter 2 for the full citation.

9. Gianni Vattimo, *Al di la del soggeto* (Milan, Italy: Idee/Feltrinelli, 1984), 12.

10. See endnote 86 in chapter 2 for the full citation.

11. This passage, which was also cited and commented on in the preface (endnote 10), is descriptive of what I believe I have done throughout this study. In returning to it, I hope my reader agrees that the rain-check, issued in the preface, has been honored in full.

12. This is my rendition of Nietzsche's notion of dreaming on knowing one is dreaming (#54, 116).

13. Fanon, *Les damnés de la terre*, 233.

14. For the quotation in full see note 39 in chapter two.

15. Chinua Achebe, *Anthills of the Savannah* (New York: Anchor Books, 1988), 114.

16. See endnote 11 above and endnote 10 in the preface to this study.

17. As noted in the introduction (endnote 13) this was the basic theme of the 1955 Bandung Conference.

18. Or as Nietzsche puts it; "*What does your conscience say?*—'You shall become the person you are'" (#270, 219).

19. Fanon, *Les damnés de la terre*, 233.

20. James Baldwin, "Faulkner and Desegregation," (1956), in *Nobody Knows My Name* (New York: Vintage Books, 1993), 126.

21. Aimé Césaire, "The Man of Culture and his Responsibilities," *Présence Africaine*, no. 24–25 (February–May, 1959), 127.

22. Fanon, *Les damnés de la terre*, 232–233.

23. Ibid. 141. "Each generation must out of a relative opacity discover its mission, fulfill or betray it."

24. Kathleen Freeman, *Ancilla to the Pre-Socratic Philosophers* (Cambridge, MA: Harvard University Press, 1983), 32.

Bibliography

Achebe, C. *Anthills of the Savannah*. New York: Anchor Books, 1989. Print.

———. *Home and Exile*. New York: Anchor Books, 2000. Print.

———. *Hopes and Impediments*. New York: Anchor Books, 1989. Print.

———. *The Trouble With Nigeria*. Enugu, Nigeria: Fourth Dimension, 1983. Print.

Afwerki, I. *President Isaias Afwerki's Address to the 66th Session of the United Nations General Assembly*. September 23, 2011. Web.

Ahmed, E. "The Postcolonial System of Power." *The Selected Writings of Eqbal Ahmed*. Ed. C. Bengelsdorf, M. Cerullo, and Y. Chandrani. New York: Columbia University Press, 2006. Print.

Ake, C. *Democracy and Development in Africa*. Washington, DC: The Brookings Institution, 1996. Print.

Allen, K. "South Africa Leaders Ignore Marikana Lessons at Their Peril." *BBC News*. September 7, 2012. Web.

Appiah, K. A. *In My Father's House*. New York: Oxford University Press, 1992. Print.

Aristotle. *Nicomachean Ethics*. Trans. J. Sachs. Newburyport, MA: Focus, 2002. Print.

Axelos, K. *Alienation, Praxis, & Techne in the Thought of Karl Marx*. Trans. R. Bruzina. Austin, TX: University of Texas Press, 1976. Print.

———. *Marx e Heidegger*. Naples, Italy: Guida Editori, 1977. Print.

Baker, A. J. *The Rape of Ethiopia*. New York: Ballantine Books, 1971. Print.

Baldwin, J. "Nationalism, Colonialism, and the United States: One Minute to Twelve—A Forum." *The Cross of Redemption*. Ed. R. Kenan. New York: Vintage Books, 2011. Print.

———. *Nobody Knows My Name*. New York: Vintage Books, 1993. Print.

Barrett, W. *Philosophy in the Twentieth Century*, vol. 3. New York: Random House, 1962. Print.

Berlin, I. *The Age of Enlightenment*. New York: Mentor Books, 1956. Print.

Bernasconi, R. "African Philosophy's Challenge to Continental Philosophy." *Postcolonial African Philosophy*. Ed. E. Eze. Cambridge, MA: The MIT Press, 1997. Print.

Bernasconi, R., and Mann, A. M. "The Contradictions of Racism: Locke, Slavery, and the Two Treatises." *Race and Racism in Modern Philosophy*, Ed. A. Valls. New York: Cornell University Press, 2005. Print.

Blaut, J. M. *The Colonizer's Model of the World*. New York: The Guilford Press, 1993. Print.

Blunt, E. "Corruption 'Costs Africa Billions.'" *BBC News*. September 18, 2002. Web.

Bohman, J., and Lutz-Bachmann, M., ed. *Perpetual Peace*. Cambridge, MA: The MIT Press, 1997. Print.

Bond, P. "From Racial to Class Apartheid." *Monthly Review* 55.10 (March, 2004): 45–59. Print.

Brun, E., and Hersch, J. "Faux Internationalism and Really Existing Imperialism." *Monthly Review* 63.11 (April, 2012): 36–48. Print.

Cabral, A. *Return to the Source*. New York: Monthly Review Press, 1973. Print.

———. *Revolution in Guinea*. New York: Monthly Review Press, 1969. Print.

Caplan, G. *The Betrayal of Africa*. Berkeley, CA: Groundwood Books, 2008. Print.

Carey, S. "Africa: What Aid Does to a Continent." *New Africa* 498 (September 2010). Print.

Castoriadis, C. "The Crisis of Western Society." *Telos* 53 (1982). Print.

———. *Crossroads in the Labyrinth*. Cambridge, MA: The MIT Press, 1984. Print.

———. "Intellectuals and History." *Philosophy, Politics, Autonomy*. Ed. D. A. Curtis. New York: Oxford University Press, 1991. Print.

———. "Reflections on 'Rationality' and 'Development.'" *Philosophy, Politics, Autonomy*. Ed. D. A. Curtis. New York: Oxford University Press, 1991. Print.

Césaire, A. *Discourse on Colonialism*. New York: Monthly Review Press, 1972. Print.

———. *Discours sur le Colonialisme*. Paris, France: Présence Africaine, 1955. Print.

———. *Lettre à Maurice Thorez*. Paris, France: Présence Africaine, 1956. Print.

———. "The Man of Culture and His Responsibilities." *Présence Africaine*. 24–25 (February-May, 1959). Print.

———. *A Season in the Congo*. New York: Grove Press, 1968. Print.

Chaliand, G. *Revolution in the Third World*. New York: The Viking Press, 1977. Print.

Clottey, P. "Eritrea Favors Investment Partnership Over Aid/" *Voice of America/* (June 10, 2012). Web.

Comte, A. *Introduction to Positive Philosophy*. Ed. And Trans. F. Ferré. Indianapolis, IN: Bobbs-Merrill, 1970. Print.

Dallmayr, F. *Alternative Visions*. Lanham, MD: Rowman & Littlefield, 1998. Print.

Danticat, E., and Dorfman, A. "The Torture Debate." *The Washington Post* (September 24, 2006). Print.

Davidson, B. *Africa in Modern History*. New York: Penguin Books, 1985. Print.

———. *Cross Roads in Africa*. Nottingham, England: Spokesman Press, Bertrand Russell House, 1980. Print.

de Beauvoir, S. *The Ethics of Ambiguity*. Secaucus, NJ: The Citadel Press, 1948. Print.

Derrida, J. *Learning to Live Finally*. Hoboken, NJ: Melville House, 2007. Print.

Descartes, R. *Discourse on Method and Meditations*. Ed. F. E. Sutcliffe. New York: Penguin Books, 1977. Print.

Diop, A. "Modern Culture and Our Destiny." *Présence Africaine* 8-9-10 (June-November, 1956). Print.

Dugger, C. W. "Charity Finds That U.S. Food Aid for Africa Hurts Instead of Helps." *The New York Times* (August 14, 2007). Web.

Dumont, R. "You Only Listen to Cassandra when Troy is on Fire." *New Africa* 500 (November, 2010). Print.

Einstein, A. *Essays in Humanism*. New York: Philosophical Library, 1950. Print.

Eisely, L. *Darwin's Century*. New York: Anchor Books, 1961. Print.

Emerson, R. W. "Self-Reliance." *Selected Essays*. Ed. L. Ziff. New York: Penguin Books, 1982. Print.

Eze, E., ed. *Postcolonial African Philosophy*. Cambridge, MA: Blackwell, 1997. Print.

Fanon, F. *Black Skin, White Masks*. Trans. C. L. Markmann. New York: Grove Press, 1967. Print.

———. *Les damnés de la terre*. Paris, France: Maspero, 1974. Print.

———. *Les damnés de la terre*. Paris, France: Éditions La Découverte & Syros, 2002. Print.

———. *Peau noire masques blancs*. Paris, France: Éditions du Seuil, 1952. Print.

———. *Pour la Revolution Africaine*. Paris, France: Maspero, 1964. Print.

———. *Towards the African Revolution*. New York: Grove Press, 1967. Print.

———. *The Wretched of the Earth*. Trans. Constance Farrington. New York: Grove Press, 1963. Print.

Fieldhouse, D. K. *The Colonial Empires*. New York: Delta Books, 1966. Print.

Ford, G. "Where Will the U.S. Strike Next in Africa?" *Democratic Underground* (Aug 8, 2012). Web.

Freeman, K. *Ancilla to the Pre-Socratic Philosophers*. Cambridge, MA: Harvard University Press, 1983. Print.

Fusaro, D., and Rebecchi, I. "Gianni Vattimo." *Filosofico.net*. Web.

Gadamer, H. G. *The Beginning of Knowledge*. Trans. R. Coltman. New York: Continuum, 2002. Print.

———. *A Century of Philosophy: Hans-Georg Gadamer in Conversation with Riccardo Dottori*. New York: Continuum, 2004. Print.

———. *Dialogue and Dialectic: Eight Hermeneutical Studies on Plato*. Trans. P. C. Smith. New Haven and London: Yale University Press, 1980. Print.

———. *The Enigma of Health*. Trans. J. Gaiger and N. Walker. Stanford, CA: Stanford University Press, 1996. Print.

———. *Gadamer in Conversation*. Ed. And Trans. R. E. Palmer. New Haven and London: Yale University Press, 2001. Print.

———. *Hegel's Dialectic*. Trans. P. C. Smith. New Haven, CT: Yale University Press, 1976. Print.

———. *Philosophical Hermeneutics*. Trans. and Ed. D. E. Linge. Berkeley: University of California Press, 1976. Print.

———. "The Problem of Historical Consciousness." *Interpretative Social Science, A Second Look*. Ed. P. Rabinow and W. M. Sullivan. Berkeley and Los Angeles: University of California Press, 1987. Print.

———. *Truth and Method*. Trans. W. Glen-Doepel. New York: Crossroad, 1982. Print.

———. *Verita e Metedo, traduzione e apparati di Vattimo*. Milan, Italy: Bompiani, 2005. Print.

———. *Wahrheit und Methode*. Tübingen: J.C.B. Mohr, 1965. Print.
Gasset, J. O. *History as a System*. New York: W.W. Norton and Company, 1961. Print.
Gibson, R. *African Liberation Movements*. New York: Oxford University Press, 1973. Print.
Gordon, L. *Disciplinary Decadence*. Boulder, CO: Paradigm, 2006. Print.
———. *An Introduction to Africana Philosophy*. Cambridge, UK: Cambridge University Press, 2008. Print.
Gramsci, A. "*Il nostro Marx*." *Scritti Giovanili*. Turin, Italy: Giulio Einaudi, 1972. Print.
———. "Oppressed and Oppressors." *History, Philosophy, and Culture in the Young Gramsci*. Saint Louis, MO: Telos Press, 1975. Print.
———. *Quaderni Del Carcere*, vol. 2. Turin, Italy: Giulio Einaudi, 1975. Print.
Guardini, R. *The End of the Modern World*. Chicago: Henry Regenery, 1968. Print.
Guignon, C. *The Good Life*. Indianapolis, IN: Hackett Publishing, 1999. Print.
Guterson, D. *Snow Falling on Cedars*. New York: Vintage Books, 1995. Print.
Gyekye, K. "Philosophy, Culture, and Technology in the Postcolonial." *Postcolonial African Philosophy*. Ed. E. Eze. Cambridge, MA: Blackwell, 1997. Print.
———. *Tradition and Modernity*. New York: Oxford University Press, 1997. Print.
Hailu, G. Aba. *The Conscript (1927)*. Trans. Ghirmai Negash. Athens: Ohio University Press, 2013. Print.
Hallen, B. A *Short History of African Philosophy*, 2nd ed. Bloomington: Indiana University Press, 2009. Print.
Hartung, W. D. "The New Imperialism." *The Nation* 276.6 (February 17, 2003). Print.
Hathaway, O. A. "Why We Need International Law." *The Nation* 285.16 (November 16, 2007). Print.
Hegel, G. W. F. *Hegel's Philosophy of Right*. Trans. T. M. Knox. New York: Oxford University Press, 1967. Print.
———. *Hegel's Science of Logic*. Trans. A. V. Miller. New York: Humanities Press, 1976. Print.
Heidegger, M. *Being and Time*. Trans. J. Macquarrie and E. Robinson. New York: Harper & Row, 1962. Print.
———. "Der Spiegel Interview with Heidegger (1966)." *Der Spiegel*, 1976, Web.
———. *Discourse on Thinking*. Trans. J. N. Anderson and E. H. Freund. New York: Harper & Row, 1966. Print.
———. *The Heidegger Reader*. Ed. F. Günter. Bloomington: Indiana University Press, 2009. Print.
———. *An Introduction to Metaphysics*. Trans. Ralph Manheim, New Haven and London: Yale University Press, 1977. Print.
———. *Martin Heidegger Basic Writings*. Ed. D. F. Krell. New York: Routledge, 1993. Print.
———. "Modern Natural Science and Technology." *Radical Phenomenology*. Ed. J. Sallis. Atlantic Highlands, NJ: Humanities Press, 1978. Print.
———. *Sein und Zeit*. Tübingen: Max Niemeyer Verlag, 1979. Print.

———. *What is Called Thinking?* Trans. J. G. Gray. New York: Harper & Row, 1968. Print.

———. *What is Philosophy?* Trans. W. Kluback and J. T. Wilde. New Haven, CT: College and University Press, 1956. Print.

Hiwet, A. *Ethiopia, From Autocracy to Revolution.* London, UK: Review of African Political Economy, 1975. Print.

Holcomb, B. K., and Ibssa, S. *The Invention of Ethiopia.* Trenton, NJ: Red Sea Press, 1990. Print.

Hountondji, P. *African Philosophy: Myth and Reality*, 2nd ed. Bloomington: Indiana University Press, 1996. Print.

———. "Daily Life in Black Africa: Elements of a Critique." *The Surreptitious Speech.* Ed. V. Y. Mudimbe. Chicago: The University of Chicago Press, 1992. Print.

———. "Reason and Tradition." *Philosophy and Culture.* Ed. O. H. Oruka and D. A. Masolo. Nairobi, Kenya: Bookwise, 1983. Print.

Hugon, A. *The Exploration of Africa.* New York: Henry N. Abrams, 1993. Print.

Hyland, Drew A. *The Origins of Philosophy.* Atlantic Highlands, NJ: Humanities Press, 1993. Print.

Ignatieff, M. "The Burden." *The New York Time Magazine* (January 5, 2003). Print.

International Jewish Anti-Zionist Network. "From Warsaw to Gaza: International Holocaust Remembrance Day 2009." 2009. Web.

Irigaray, L. *Between East and West.* Trans. Stephen Pluháček. New York: Columbia University Press, 2002. Print.

Jaspers, K. *The Future of Mankind.* Trans. E. B. Ashton. Chicago: The University of Chicago Press, 1961. Print.

Kafka, F. "A Report to an Academy." *Selected Stories.* New York: Random House, 1952. Print.

Kagan, R. "Europeans Are Sissies." *The New York Times Magazine.* (February 16, 2003). Print.

———. *Of Paradise and Power.* New York: Alfred A. Knopf, 2003. Print.

Kahin, G. M. *The Asian-African Conference.* New York: Kennikat Press, 1972. Print.

Kane, C. H. *L'aventure ambiguë.* Paris, France: Julliard, 1961. Print.

Kant, I. *Basic Writings of Kant.* Ed. A. W. Wood. New York: The Modern Library, 2001. Print.

———. *Critique of Pure Reason.* Trans. N. K. Smith. New York: St. Martin's Press, 1965. Print.

———. *Education.* Trans. A. Churton. Ann Arbor: University of Michigan Press, 1964. Print.

———. *Fundamental Principles of the Metaphysics of Morals.* Trans. T. K. Abbott. New York: The Liberal Arts Press, 1949. Print.

———. *Kant on History.* Ed. Lewis White Beck. Indianapolis, IN: Bobbs-Merrill, 1963. Print.

———. *Observations on the Feeling of the Beautiful and Sublime.* Trans. J. T. Goldthwait. Berkeley: University of California Press, 1960. Print.

———. *Perpetual Peace.* Ed. Lewis White Beck. Indianapolis, IN: Bobbs-Merrill, 1957. Print.

Karl Marx and Marxism. Dir. A. Horrox. Films for the Humanities, 2013. YouTube.

Kearney, R. "Dialogue with Emmanuel Levinas." *Face to Face with Levinas*. Ed. R. A. Cohen. New York: SUNY Press, 1986. Print.

Kimmerle, H. "The Intercultural Dimension in the Dialogue between African and Western Philosophy." *Perspectives in African Philosophy: An Anthology on Problematics of an African Philosophy: Twenty Years After (1976–1996)*. Ed. C. Sumner and S. W. Yohannes. Addis Ababa: Addis Ababa University Press, 2002. Print.

King, J. "Bush: Join 'Coalition of the Willing.'" *CNN.Com/World* (November 20, 2002). Web.

King, M. L. (Jr.). *I Have a Dream: Writings and Speeches that Changed the World*. Ed. J. M. Washington. New York: HarperCollins, 2003. Print.

Kinzer, S. *All the Shah's Men*. Hoboken, NJ: John Wiley & Sons, 2003. Print.

Kipling, R. "The White Man's Burden." *A Choice of Kipling's Verse Made by T. S. Eliot*. New York: Anchor Books, 1962. Print.

Kisiel, T. "Towards a Topology of Dasein." *Heidegger: The Man and the Thinker*. Ed. T. Sheehan. Chicago: Precedent, 1981. Print.

Klein, N. "Latin America's Shock Resistance." *The Nation* 285.17 (November 26, 2007). Print.

Kockelmans, J. J. "On the Problem of Truth in the Sciences." *Proceedings and Addresses of the American Philosophical Association* 6.1 (September, 1987). Print.

Kosik, K. *Dialectics of the Concrete*. Hingham, MA: D. Reidel, 1976. Print.

Kuhn, T. S. "Logic of Discovery or Psychology of Research." *Philosophy of Science*, 2nd ed. Ed. M. Curd, J. A. Cover, and C. Pincock. New York: W. W. Norton, 2013. Print.

———. "Scientists and Their World Views." *The Truth about The Truth*. Ed. W. T. Anderson. New York: Putnam, 1995. Print.

———. *The Structure of Scientific Revolutions*. Chicago: University of Chicago Press, 1970. Print.

Khayyám, O. *Rubáiyát of Omar Khayyám*. Trans. Edward Fitzgerald. New York: Random House, 1947. Print.

Latouche, S. *The Westernization of the World*. Cambridge, UK: Polity Press, 1996. Print.

Lauer, Q. *The Nature of Philosophical Inquiry*. Milwaukee, IL: Marquette University Press, 1989. Print.

Lefort, C. *Writing the Political Text*. Trans. and Ed. D. A. Curtis. Durham and London: Duke University Press, 2000. Print.

Levinas, E. *Alterity and Transcendence*. New York: Columbia University Press, 1999. Print.

———. *Entre Nous: Essais sur le penser-à-l'autre*. Paris, France: Editions Grasset & Fasquelle, 1991. Print.

———. *Entre Nous: Thinking of the Other*. New York: Columbia University Press, 1998. Print.

———. *Ethics and Infinity*. Pittsburgh, PA: Duquesne University Press, 1985. Print.

———. *The Levinas Reader*. Ed. S. Hand. Cambridge, MA: Blackwell, 1994. Print.

———. "Reflections on the Philosophy of Hitlerism." *Critical Inquiry* 17.1 (Autumn, 1990). Print.

———. *Totality and Infinity*. Pittsburgh, PA: Duquesne University Press, 1969. Print.

Levy, B-H. *Barbarism with a Human Face*. New York: Harper Colophon Books, 1980. Print.

Lévy-Bruhl, L. "How Natives Think." *African Philosophy: Selected Readings*. Ed. A. G. Mosley. Englewood Cliffs, NJ: Prentice Hall, 1995. Print.

Lowenfels, W., ed. *For Neruda, For Chile*. Boston, MA: Beacon Press, 1975. Print.

Lumumba, Patrice. *Lumumba Speaks: The Speeches and Writings of Patrice Lumumba (1958–1961)*. Ed. J. V. Lierde, Trans. H. R. Lane. Boston, MA: Little Brown & Co, 1963. Print.

Lyotard, J-F. *Peregrinations*. New York: Columbia University Press, 1988. Print.

———. *The Postmodern Explained*. Trans. D. Barry, B. Maher, J. Pefanis, and V. Sparte. Minneapolis: University of Minnesota Press, 1992. Print.

Machiavelli, N. *The Prince*. Ed. Q. Skinner and R. Price. New York: Cambridge University Press, 1990. Print.

Maldonado-Torres, N. "Decolonization and the New Identitarian Logics after September 11: Eurocentrism and Americanism against the New Barbarian Threats." *Radical Philosophy Review* 8.1 (2005). Print.

Malpas, J. "Hans-Georg Gadamer." *The Stanford Encyclopedia of Philosophy*. Ed. E. N. Zalta. Stanford, CA: Stanford University, 2009. Web.

Marcus, H. *The Life and Times of Menelik II: Ethiopia 1844–1913*. Trenton, NJ: Red Sea Press, 1995. Print.

Marcuse, H. "The Individual in the Great Society." *The Essential Marcuse*. Ed. A. Feenberg and L. William. Boston, MA: Beacon Press, 1965. Print.

———. *Studies in Critical Philosophy*. Boston, MA: Beacon Press, 1973. Print.

Mart, Ç. T. "British Colonial Education in Africa." *International Journal of English and Literature*. December, 2011. Web.

Marx, K. "Alienation and Social Classes." *The Marx-Engels Reader*, 2nd ed. Ed. R. C. Tucker. New York: W.W. Norton & Company, 1978. Print.

———. *Capital Vol. 1*. Ed. F. Engels. New York: International, 1967. Print.

———. *Early Writings*. Trans. Rodney Livingstone. New York: Vintage Books, 1975. Print.

———. *The Economic & Philosophic Manuscripts*. Ed. J. S. Struik. New York: International, 1972. Print.

Marx, K., and Engels, F. *On Colonialism: Articles from the New York Tribune and other Writings*. New York: International, 1972. Print.

Mbembe, A. *On the Postcolony*. Berkeley: University of California Press, 2001. Print.

McCarthy, T. *Race, Empire, and the Idea of Human Development*. New York: Cambridge University Press, 2009. Print.

Mckay, J. P. Bennett D. Hill, and John Buckler. *A History of Western Society*, 3rd ed., vol. 2. Boston, MA: Houghton Mifflin, 1987. Print.

McNeil, D. G. Jr. "Kamuzu Banda Dies: 'Big Man' Among Anticolonialists." *The New York Times*. November 27, 1997. Print.

Memmi, A. *The Colonizer and the Colonized*. Boston, MA: Beacon Press, 1967. Print.

———. *Dominated Man.* Boston, MA: Beacon Press, 1968. Print.

Micheli, G. "Faccetta Nera." *Wikipedia*. Web.

Missing. Dir. Costa-Gavras. Perf. Jack Lemmon, Sissy Spacek. MCA, 1982. Videocassette.

Moeller, R. "The Truth about Africom." *Foreign Policy*. July 21, 2010. Web.

Morales, E. "A Voice on the Left." *Time*, 167.23 June 5, 2006. Print.

Moran, D. *Introduction to Phenomenology*. New York: Routledge, 2000. Print.

Mortley, R. *French Philosophers in Conversation.* New York: Routledge, 1991. Print.

Mudimbe, V. Y. *The Invention of Africa.* Bloomington: Indiana University Press, 1988. Print.

Nemo, P. *What is the West?* Trans. K. Casler. Pittsburgh, PA: Duquesne University Press, 2006. Print.

"New General Assembly President Calls for Democratization of the United Nations." *UN News Centre*. 2008. Web.

"New U.S. Embassy in Iraq Cloaked in Mystery." *Associated Press*. April 14, 2006. Web.

Nietzsche, Friedrich. *The Gay Science*. Ed. And Trans. Walter Kaufmann. New York: Vintage Books, 1974. Print.

Nkrumah, K. *Class Struggle in Africa.* New York: International, 1975. Print.

Nyerere, J. K. "Africa: The Current Situation." *African Philosophy* 11.1(June, 1998). Print.

Obama, B. *The Audacity of Hope*. New York: Vintage Books, 2006. Print.

———. "Obama's Speech in Ghana." July 11, 2009. Web.

Ogot, B. A. "Rereading the History and Historiography of Epistemic Domination and Resistance in Africa." *African Studies Review* 52.1 (April, 2009). Print.

Okere, Theophilus. *African Philosophy: A Historico-Hermeneutical Investigation of the Conditions of its Possibility*. Lanham, MD: University Press of America, 1983. Print.

Okolo, Okanda. *Pour une Philosophie de la Culture et du Developpement*. Kinshasa, Zaire: Presses Universitiaires du Zaire, 1986. Print.

Ollman, B. *Alienation: Marx's Conception of Man in Capitalist Society*. New York: Cambridge University Press, 1973. Print.

Ouologuem, Y. *Bound to Violence*. London, UK: Heinemann Educational Books, 1968. Print.

Outlaw, L. "African Philosophy: Deconstructive and Reconstructive Challenges." *Contemporary Philosophy: A New Survey, vol. 5, African Philosophy*. Ed. G. Fløistad. Dordrecht, The Netherlands: Martinus Nijhoff, 1987. Print.

Oyono, F. *Houseboy*. Trans. J. Reed. Portsmouth, NH: Heinemann Educational Books, 1990. Print.

Palmer, R. E. *Hermeneutics*. Evanston, IL: Northwestern University Press, 1969. Print.

Parry, J. H. *The Age of Reconnaissance*. New York: A Mentor Book, 1963. Print.

Plato. *Plato Five Dialogues*. Trans. G. M. A. Grube. Indianapolis, IN: Hackett, 1981. Print.

———. *Plato's Republic*. Trans. G. M. A. Grube. Indianapolis, IN: Hackett, 1974. Print.

Plaut, M. "The UN's All-Pervasive Role in Africa." *BBC News*. July 18, 2007. Web.

Popkin, R. H. "Hume's Racism." *The Philosophical Forum* 9.2–3 (1977). Print.

Prashad, Vijay. *The Darker Nations*. New York: The New Press, 2007. Print.

Rodeny, W. *How Europe Underdeveloped Africa*. Washington, DC: Howard University Press, 1974. Print.

Rorty, R., and Vattimo, G. *The Future of Religion*. Ed. Santiago Zabala. New York: Colombia University Press, 2005. Print.

Roth, P. *The Human Stain*. New York: Vintage Books, 2001. Print.

Rötzer, F. *Conversations with French Philosophers*. Atlantic Highlands, NJ: Humanities Press, 1995. Print.

Rousseau, J-J. *The First and Second Discourses together with the Replies to Critics and Essay on the Origin of Languages*. Trans. and Ed. V. Gourevitch. New York: Harper & Row, 1986. Print.

———. *On the Social Contract Discourse on the Origin of Inequality Discourse on Political Economy*. Trans. D. A. Cress. Indianapolis, IN: Hackett, 1983. Print.

Rozoff, R. "The Pentagon's Last Frontier: Battle-Hardened Troops Headed for Africa." *Global Research*. June 13, 2012. Web.

Ryan, A. "Professor Hegel Goes to Washington." *The New York Review of Books* 39.6 (March 26, 1992). Print.

Said, E. W. *Culture and Imperialism*. New York: Vintage Books, 1994. Print.

———. "Never Just a Blind Supporter: Interview with Imad Musa." *Palestine Report* 24 (November, 1995). Print.

———. *Orientalism*. New York: Vintage Books, 1979. Print.

———. *The Pen and the Sword: Conversations with David Barsamian*. Monroe, ME: Common Courage Press, 1994. Print.

———. *Power, Politics, and Culture: Interviews with Edward Said*. New York: Pantheon Books, 2001. Print.

———. *Reflections on Exile and Other Essays*. Cambridge, MA: Harvard University Press, 2000. Print.

Salvador Allende. Dir. Patricio Guzman. Perf. Salvador Allende, Patricio Guzman. JBA, 2004. DVD.

Sartre, J-P. *Being and Nothingness*. Trans. H. E. Barnes. New York: Gramercy Books, 1956. Print.

———. *Search for a Method*. Trans. H. E. Barnes. New York: Random House, 1968. Print.

Schell, J. "The Case Against the War." *The Nation* 276.8 (March 3, 2003). Print.

Selassie, B. H. *Conflict and Intervention in the Horn of Africa*. New York: Monthly Review Press, 1980. Print.

Sembène, O. *Xala*. Trans. C. Wake. Chicago, IL: Lawrence Hill Books, 1976. Print.

Sénghor, L. S. *On African Socialism*. Trans. Mercer Cook. New York: Praeger, 1964. Print.

———. "The Spirit of Civilization or the Laws of African Negro Culture." *Présence Africaine* 8-9-10 (June–November, 1956). Print.

Serequeberhan, T. "Africa in a Changing World: An Inventory." *Monthly Review* 61.8 (January, 2010). Print.

———. *African Philosophy: The Essential Readings*. New York: Paragon House, 1991. Print.

———. "Africana Philosophy: Prospects and Possibilities." *The Oxford Handbook of World Philosophy*. Ed. J. L. Garfield and W. Edelglass. New York: Oxford University Press, 2011. Print.

———. "Africanity at the End of the 20th Century." *African Philosophy* 11.1 (June, 1998). Print.

———. "Contemporary African Philosophy: The Way Ahead." *Perspectives in African Philosophy*. Ed. C. Sumner and S. W. Yohannes. Addis Ababa: Addis Ababa University Press, 2002. Print.

———. *Contested Memory: The Icons of the Occidental Tradition*. Trenton, NJ: Africa World Press, 2007. Print.

———. "The Critique of Eurocentrism and the Practice of African Philosophy." *Postcolonial African Philosophy*. Ed. E. Eze. Cambridge, MA: Blackwell, 1997. Print.

———. "Decolonization and the Practice of Philosophy." *African Intellectuals and Decolonization*. Ed. N. Creary. Athens: Ohio University Press, 2012. Print.

———. "Eurocentrism in Philosophy: The Case of Immanuel Kant." *The Philosophical Forum* 27.4 (Summer, 1996). Print.

———. "Fanon and the Contemporary Discourse of African Philosophy." *Frantz Fanon: A Critical Reader*. Ed. L. R. Gordon. Cambridge, MA: Blackwell, 1996. Print.

———. "Heidegger and Gadamer: Thinking as 'Meditative' and as 'Effective-Historical Consciousness.'" *Man and World* 20.1 (1987). Print.

———. *The Hermeneutics of African Philosophy: Horizon and Discourse*. New York: Routledge, 1994. Print.

———. "The Idea of Colonialism in Hegel's *Philosophy of Right*." *International Philosophical Quarterly* 29.3 (September, 1989). Print.

———. "Karl Marx and African Emancipatory Thought: A Critique of Marx's Eurocentric Metaphysics." *Praxis International* 10.1, 10.2 (April & July, 1990). Print.

———. *Our Heritage*. Lanham, MD: Rowman & Littlefield, 2000. Print.

———. "Reflections on *In My Father's House*." *Research in African Literatures* 27.1 (Spring, 1996). Print.

Sheehan, T. "A Paradigm Shift in Heidegger Research." *Continental Philosophy Review* 34.2 (June, 2001). Print.

Sheridan, M. B., and Wilson S. "U.S. Actions in Libya May Speak Louder than Words." *The Washington Post*. March 19, 2011. Web.

Silverman, H. J., and Donn, W. "Introduction." *Postmodernism and Continental Philosophy*. New York: SUNY Press, 1988. Print.

Snow Falling on Cedars. Dir. S. Hicks. Perf. Ethan Hawke, Max von Sydow. Universal Studios, 2000. DVD.

Stella, G. C. "Anch'io Per La Tua Bandiera." *Africus, Periodico Dell'Associazione Onlus Italia Eritrea*. 2.6 (September, 2003). Print.

Sumner, C. *Classical Ethiopian Philosophy*. Addis Ababa, Ethiopia: Commercial Printing Press, 1985. Print.

Sweezy, P. M. "On Discovering Marxism." *New York: Monthly Review*. 24.10 (1973). Print.

Taiwo, O. "On the Misadventures of National Consciousness: A Retrospective on Frantz Fanon's Gift of Prophecy." *Fanon: A Critical Reader*. Ed. L. R. Gordon. Cambridge, MA: Blackwell, 1996. Print.

Taylor, C. "Understanding the Other: A Gadamerian View on Conceptual Schemes." *Gadamer's Century*. Ed. J. Malpas, U. Arnswald, and J. Kertscher. Cambridge, MA: The MIT Press, 2002. Print.

Tempels, P. *Bantu Philosophy*. Paris, France: Présence Africaine, 1945. Print.

Theophilus Okere. *African Philosophy, A Historico-Hermeneutical Investigation of the Conditions of its Possibility*. Lanham, MD: University Press of America, 1983. Print.

Towa, M. "Conditions for the Affirmation of a Modern African Philosophical Thought." *African Philosophy: The Essential Readings*. Ed. T. Serequeberhan. New York: Paragon House, 1991. Print.

———. "*Consciencisme*." *Présence Africaine* 85 (1973). Print.

———. *L'idee d'une philosophie négro-africaine*. Yaoundé, Cameroun: Editions Cle, 1979. Print.

———. *Marcien Towa's African Philosophy: Two Texts*. Trans. T. Serequeberhan. Asmara, Eritrea: Hdri, 2012. Print.

———. "Propositions sur l'identite culturelle." *Présence Africaine* 109 (1979). Print.

Tsotsi. Dir. G. Hood. Perf. Presley Chweneyagae. Miramax, 2005. DVD.

Ucuassapi, A. M. *Dalle Independenze Alle Libertà*. Milan, Italy: Mimesis Edizioni, 2013. Print.

Vattimo, G. "The Age of Interpretation." *The Future of Religion*. Ed. S. Zabala. New York: Columbia University Press, 2005. Print.

———. *Al di là del soggeto*. Milan, Italy: Idee/Feltrinelli, 1984. Print.

———. *Beyond Interpretation*. Trans. D. Webb. Stanford, CA: Stanford University Press, 1997. Print.

———. *Credere di Credere*, Milan, Italy: Garzanti, 1996. Print.

———. "Dialectics, Difference, and Weak Thought." *Graduate Faculty Philosophy Journal*. 10.1 (Spring, 1984). Print.

———. *L'Europa a Sud, Le speranze congiunte di Africa ed Europa*. Ed. M. A. Cedrini. Turin, Italy: Edizioni Trauben, 2003. Print.

———. "Gadamer and the Problem of Ontology." *Gadamer's Century*. Ed. J. Malpas, U. Arnswald, and J. Kertscher. Cambridge, MA: The MIT Press, 2002. Print.

———. *Nihilism and Emancipation*. Ed. S. Zabala, Trans. W. McCuaig. New York: Columbia University Press, 2004. Print.

———. "L'ontologia Ermeneutica Nella Filosofia Contemporanea." *Verità e Metodo*. Milan, Italy: Bompiani, 2005. Print.

———. *La società trasparente*. Milan, Italy: Garzanti, 1989. Print.

———. "Vattimo: Ermeneutica Parte 2 Gadamer." *YouTube*. 2012. Web.

———. *La vitta dell'altro*. Cosenza, Italy: Marco Editore, 2006. Print.

———. *Vocazione e responsabilità del filosofo*. Genoa, Italy: Melangolo, 2000. Print.

Vidall, G. "Introduction." *Tarzan of the Apes*. New York: A Signet Classic, 1990. Print.

Volman, D. "Africom and the Obama Administration." *African Security Research Project*. April, 2009. Web.

Walker, Portia. "Libyan Voters Prepare for New Political Freedom." *USA Today* (July 6, 2012) 4A. Print.

Wallerstein, I. *Africa and the Modern World.* Trenton, NJ: Africa World Press, 1986. Print.

———. *European Universalism.* New York: The New Press, 2006. Print.

Wa Thiong'o, N. *Homecoming.* Chicago: Lawrence Hill Books, 1983. Print.

Wilson, H. L. "Gadamer's Alleged Conservatism." *Phenomenology, Interpretation, and Community*. Ed. L. Langsdorf, S. H. Watson, and E. M. Bower. New York: SUNY Press, 1996. Print.

Wiredu, K. *Cultural Universals and Particulars*. Bloomington: Indiana University Press, 1996. Print.

———. "Democracy and Consensus in African Traditional Politics: A Plea for a Non-Party Polity." *Postcolonial African Philosophy*. Ed. E. Eze. Cambridge, MA: Blackwell, 1997. Print.

Wittgenstein, Ludwig. *Philosophical Investigations*, 3rd ed. Trans. G. E. M. Anscombe. New York: Macmillan, 1958. Print.

Wolin, R. *Heidegger's Children.* Princeton, NJ: Princeton University Press, 2001. Print.

Wood, A. W. *Basic Writings of Kant*. New York: The Modern Library, 2001. Print.

———. *Kant*. Malden, MA: Blackwell, 2005. Print.

Xala. Dir. O. Sembène. Doomireew Films,1974.

Zelizer, J. E. "It's Obama's White House, but it's Bush's world." *The Washington Post*. August 15, 2010. Web.

Zimmerman, M. E. "Karl Kosik's Heideggerian Marxism." *The Philosophical Forum* 15.3 (Spring, 1984). Print.

Zinn, H. A *People's History of the United States*. New York: HarperCollins, 2003.

Index